STO

Y0-BSM-454

# ORPHAN DRUGS

## Your Complete Guide to Effective, Tested Medications Outside the U.S. and Their Availability

by
Kenneth Anderson

Foreword by Stephen L. DeFelice, M.D.

A Stonesong Press Book
THE LINDEN PRESS
*New York*

The purpose of this book is to inform the reader about drugs that are available in other countries but are not currently obtainable in the United States because they lack FDA approval, cannot be patented, or lack a sponsoring manufacturer. The author, editors, and publisher do not advocate the use of any of the pharmaceutical products listed, and their inclusion in this book should not be interpreted as an endorsement. The reader should always consult his or her own physician about the use of any medication or other therapy. Any drug, by definition, is a substance capable of altering one or more bodily functions and therefore should be taken with caution.


Published by The Linden Press/Simon & Schuster
A Division of Simon & Schuster, Inc.
Simon & Schuster Building
Rockefeller Center
1230 Avenue of the Americas
New York, New York 10020
THE LINDEN PRESS/SIMON & SCHUSTER and colophon are trademarks
of Simon & Schuster, Inc.
Designed by Irving Perkins Associates
Manufactured in the United States of America

10 9 8 7 6 5 4 3 2 1

A Stonesong Press Book
Library of Congress Cataloging in Publication Data

Anderson, Kenneth.
Orphan drugs: Your complete guide to effective,
tested medications outside the U.S. and their
availablility.

"A Stonesong Press book."
Bibliography: p.
Includes indexes.
1. Chemotherapy. 2. Drugs. 3. Drug trade—Dictionaries. I.Title. [DNLM: 1.Drugs—Handbooks. 2.Drugs —Directories. QV 55 A547o]
RM263.A53 1983 615'.1 83-16216
ISBN 0-671-47172-4
0-671-49521-6 pbk

# CONTENTS

# Foreword

## To the Patient and Physician

Many valuable new drugs available in other countries are prohibited from use in the United States because our government regulations require that these drugs first undergo redundant and exhaustive animal and clinical testing. Ironically, it is far easier for a patient or a physician to buy marijuana, cocaine, or heroin than to take advantage of many of the legitimate new therapies developed abroad. The majority of physicians and patients are not aware of a substantial number of tested medicines available only in foreign countries. Many Americans afflicted by a wide variety of diseases have suffered or died needlessly.

This book represents a major step forward in pharmaceutical information for the public. It lists and describes certain drugs that exist in foreign markets but are not yet available in the United States. *Orphan Drugs* provides patients and physicians with an information resource that is long overdue.

What are the causes that have created this rather unfortunate situation? They are in large part related to "bad consumerism," which has resulted in misguided government policies.

Bad consumerists almost always appear benevolent, claiming to protect the patient. Their reasoning is a combination of well-meaning paternalism and xenophobic arrogance. They claim, in effect, to know better than patients and physicians what is good for them. They also lack faith in foreign studies on new drugs, even though the drugs have been approved by government regulatory authorities there.

Our rebuttal is simple. Many of the government-approved drugs U.S. physicians now prescribe were available in international markets long before they reached our shores. To cite just two examples: beta blockers for the treatment of various cardiovascular disorders, and sodium valproate for the treatment of epilepsy.

The list of FDA-approved drugs which were once available only outside the United States is long and impressive.

The reasoning that something foreign is inferior simply will not hold up to reality. American business has learned the hard way that foreign companies are quite capable of developing competitive products. Witness the invasion and acceptability of foreign computers and television sets. And drugs are no exception. An increasing number of new drugs approved by the Food and Drug Administration (FDA) were discovered in foreign research laboratories. The pharmaceutical research in Western Europe and Japan is among the best in the world.

Nifedipine, a very effective drug for the treatment of angina pectoris, was developed in German laboratories. Sucralfate, an effective antiulcer substance, is of Japanese origin.

Misguided government regulation of medical therapies developed abroad reflects an attitude whose time has passed. Many of us prefer to make our own decisions when they involve our body and mind. A new ethic of enlightened self-help that stresses individual initiative has arisen in many areas of life, including health care. Patients should form partnerships with their physicians so that the two may work together with mutual respect to make decisions regarding the choice of appropriate therapy. It is not only unnecessary but inappropriate for the government to interfere with this almost sacred social contract. Why should U.S. cancer patients be allowed to die without recourse to potentially helpful drugs just because they haven't been tested in the United States?

The question is especially pressing in a life-threatening situation. Law or no law, patients with little hope of survival have, understandably, flocked to illegal sources to buy laetrile without the supervision of their physicians. Wouldn't it be better for them to obtain it but from their own physician, legally? Surely all reasonable people agree that a U.S. citizen has such a right.

Where does this leave the patient? Fortunately, the federal government has become aware that valuable therapies do exist in other countries and that U.S. patients have a right to these therapies. There is, therefore, cause for hope. The FDA has recently proposed that U.S. citizens be permitted to buy drugs in other countries that are not yet available in the United States, stipulating that they must be bought in reasonable quantities and for personal use. By the time this book reaches you, this proposal may be written into our regulations.

An immediate first step is for the FDA to press forward with its new proposal. If it passed, I would strongly recommend that you include your physician in your decision to take advantage of these therapies, for minor or major conditions.

With or without the passage of the proposal, *Orphan Drugs* provides an overview that summarizes the usage, precautions, dosage and sources for drugs, and Mr. Anderson does so in a manner that does not offer miracles.

And finally, no single expert, myself included, can judge the value of all the drugs listed in *Orphan Drugs*. A detailed analysis of the individual therapeutic agents desired should be made by the physician.

STEPHEN L. DEFELICE, M.D.
CHAIRMAN, THE FOUNDATION FOR INNOVATION IN MEDICINE

# ORPHAN DRUGS

# Introduction

## Background of Orphan Drugs

Calorie-conscious Canadians sweeten their coffee with cyclamate. In the United States the usual packet of artificial sweetener contains, not cyclamate, but saccharin. The U.S. Food and Drug Administration has banned the use of cyclamate sweeteners because of reports that cyclamate may be a cause of cancer. The FDA's Canadian counterpart, meanwhile, contends that cyclamate sweeteners are safe but evidence indicates that saccharin is a cancer-causing agent.

This controversy over which artificial sweetener is carcinogenic began in the 1960s. After two decades, one might expect that medical scientists who share the same language and published data might agree that either (a) saccharin causes cancer, (b) cyclamate causes cancer, (c) saccharin does not cause cancer, (d) cyclamate does not cause cancer, (e) both sweeteners cause cancer, or (f) neither of the synthetic sweeteners is a cause of cancer.

One possibly simple way to resolve the controversy might be to examine the mortality statistics of the two countries. After numerous years of cyclamate use north of the border and saccharin use south of the border, one finds that average lifespans in both countries remain approximately equal—around 69 years for men and 77 years for women. Canada actually has a somewhat lower death rate of 7.1 per 1,000 population as compared with 8.9 in the United States, but the difference has not yet been linked to the cyclamate-saccharin decisions.

## Why Travel May Be Healthful

Canada and the United States have also made differing decisions regarding the safety and effectiveness of a number of pharmaceutical products. Until 1982, U.S. citizens traveled north to Canada for treatment of sciatic pain associated with a herniated intervertebral disk of the spine because the therapy, injection of a papaya enzyme, was not available in the United States. U.S. residents still travel north of the border, south of the border, and across the oceans to obtain health care products that are not currently available in their own country, primarily because of well-meaning but complex and conflicting laws and regulations.

United States citizens who travel beyond their own country's boundaries for pleasure or business quickly become aware that in addition to currency and perhaps language differences, people in other parts of the world have remedies for head colds, headaches, stomachaches, asthma, arthritis, and skin disorders that are unheard of in the United States. Drugstores and doctors in other lands offer a pill for hemorrhoids, a tablet for impotency or frigidity, and an arsenal of other "wonder drugs" for infections, heart disease, mental disorders, cancer, and aging. The foreign medications have been used by millions of patients for many years and are considered to be as safe and effective by foreign physicians and health agencies as drugs approved by the FDA for use by Americans. This is not to suggest that American doctors and FDA officials are less knowledgeable or less competent. They simply go about the business of approving and prescribing medications in a different manner. The difference is due in part to events involving the U.S. Congress and the pharmaceutical industry in the early 1960s.

The basic law covering the manufacture and distribution of medications in the United States is the Federal Food, Drug, and Cosmetic Act, which began as a simple seven-page document in 1906. The original law remained essentially unchanged until 1930, when it was amended to require canned-food labels to include information about the quantity and quality of the contents. But as new food additives and drugs began to proliferate, so did changes in the law. Antibiotics did not exist, even in the imagination of medical scientists, when the original law was passed, so Congress had to amend the act to cover antibiotics. More amendments, new laws, and hundreds of pages of regulations quickly accumulated. Eventually from Washington's legal morass arose law firms that specialized in the interpretation of FDA regulations.

## The Thalidomide Story

The greatest overhaul of U.S. laws governing the manufacture and use of drugs followed an unfortunate incident involving a promising new tranquilizer introduced in Europe in the 1950s. The tranquilizer was called thalidomide, a word derived from one of its chemical sources, phthalyglutamic acid. Thalidomide was regarded by some authorities as perhaps the best tranquilizer ever developed. It was considered to be virtually nontoxic. The drug was tested in mice, rats, rabbits, guinea pigs, cats, and dogs and was found to be safe. It failed to cause any animal deaths even when fed in massive doses. When the drug was ready for human use in Europe in 1956, thalidomide had been tested as rigorously for safety and effectiveness as any pharmaceutical product that had been developed to that time.

Unfortunately, the scientists who discovered and tested thalidomide overlooked one aspect of drug action. They forgot to determine whether thalidomide crossed the placental barrier between a pregnant female and the developing embryo. Five years of use elapsed before a British doctor noted that three of his female patients had delivered deformed babies, and the only factor they had in common was the use of thalidomide during the first trimester of pregnancy. By the time medical scientists had confirmed the association between thalidomide use during pregnancy and the birth of babies with abnormally short arms and legs, thousands of deformed babies had been born in nearly 50 countries where thalidomide was prescribed as a tranquilizer.

News of the thalidomide tragedy reached the United States just as the FDA was considering an application for its introduction. Thalidomide did not receive FDA approval, but the impact of the European reports on members of Congress, already involved in investigations of alleged improprieties by the drug industry, was enough to tip the scales in favor of a drastic overhaul of the Federal Food, Drug, and Cosmetic Act.

The 1962 revision of the law spelled out strict new procedures for drug clearance, recording and reporting experiences with new drugs, drug labeling, factory inspection, drug manufacturing controls, drug patents, and control of information and drug advertising to physicians. New regulations required relatively long and exhaustive animal testing and human testing with more difficult approval procedures. The backlash effect, as measured in dollars required to discover and develop a new drug for use in the United States, was an increase from an average of $6,500,000 in 1961 to more than $70,000,000 in 1981. To advance a new drug from investigational status to consideration for approval by the FDA could require ten years. As a result, the United States began to lose its postwar leadership in the development of innovative drugs. It has been noted that in the first ten years following the 1962 revision of FDA regulations, the U.S. pharmaceutical industry failed to introduce any new drugs for the treatment of heart disease, high blood pressure, or chronic lung diseases—three of the major causes of death and disability.

With our hindsight advantage, we can now see that perhaps Congress overreacted in 1962. Thalidomide has regained some respectability as a drug that is helpful in relieving the painful symptoms of leprosy; physicians simply do not give the drug to women who are pregnant or who may become pregnant. And despite the implementation of strict new rules for drug safety in the United States, tragedies involving FDA-approved drugs are frequent occurrences. Examples of the 1980s include the deaths of 852 patients injected with a heart drug, epinephrine; the discovery that ordinary aspirin may be a cause of Reye's syndrome, which affects about 1,000 American children each year; the deaths of patients using the pain-reliever zomepirac sodium (Zomax); and the deaths of more than 100 patients around the world due to the use of the FDA-approved antiarthritis remedy benoxaprofen (Oraflex). A prime example of misdirected federal health protection efforts of the previous decade was the 1976 campaign to inoculate millions of Americans against a "swine flu" epidemic that did not occur with a serum that produced death and the paralysis of Guillain-Barre syndrome in some of the people receiving injections.

It appears in retrospect that the FDA system designed to protect the public against adverse effects of drugs failed to provide the expected safety barrier. Meanwhile, the system denied U.S. citizens access to new drugs that had become available in other countries until many years after they had been tested and approved overseas. In studies published by Dr. William Wardell of the University of Rochester (N.Y.) Medical Center, the United States was found to lag behind Great Britain by as much as 85 months in the introduction of new drugs for heart disease, peptic ulcer, depression, epilepsy, migraine, and high blood pressure.

## What Is an Orphan Drug?

Some pharmaceutical products that are commercially available in other countries but not in the United States are called "orphan drugs." They are "orphans" because they have not been "adopted" by any of the U.S. pharmaceutical companies. In some cases an orphan drug may lack a home because it is needed to treat a rare or obscure disease, in which case the medical problem is labeled an "orphan disease." The number of patients requiring the drug is so small that a drug manufacturer cannot make a profit by developing and marketing the drug. Many existing drugs have annual sales totals of less than $1,000,000. It is understandable that a pharmaceutical company would be reluctant to spend $70,000,000 to develop, test, and fight for FDA approval of a product that might earn less than $1,000,000 per year of income.

An example of an orphan disease is amyotrophic lateral sclerosis, also known as ALS and "Lou Gehrig's disease." Gehrig was a New York Yankees baseball star and was dubbed the "iron man of baseball" because of his stamina; his career was ended by ALS, the degenerative nerve disease that progresses rapidly toward death within a few years after the onset of symptoms. The U.S. Department of Health and Human Services has estimated that 9,000 Americans are afflicted with ALS. Medical researchers are experimenting with drugs to treat the disease, but many of the patients are unlikely to survive until a new product has been approved by the FDA.

Pimozide (p.196) and penfluridol (p. 189) are drugs that were developed in overseas markets for the treatment of a neurological disorder called Gilles de la Tourette syndrome, or Tourette's syndrome. The disorder is characterized by jerking body movements, involuntary outbursts of foul language, and echolalia (a form of speech that consists of echoing of words heard by the patient). An estimated 100,000 persons in the United States are affected by the syndrome, which usually begins in childhood, and therefore not nearly enough to justify U.S. research and manufacture. The drugs for treatment of Tourette's syndrome have been available in Canada and Europe since 1971. But they are not currently obtainable in the United States.

An orphan drug also may be a common natural substance, and a natural substance cannot be strongly patented in the U.S. This rule makes some sense when one considers the alternative of permitting an enterprising individual to obtain patent rights for the control of human blood or oxygen. On the other hand, if a natural substance is found to have previously unknown health benefits—and it can be weakly patented—most pharmaceutical companies still will not adopt the product. A product that cannot be strongly patented also cannot be protected against exploitation by competing drug companies after a pioneering firm has invested millions of dollars in the necessary research and development of the medication. Such an orphan drug is carnitine (p. 70).

Carnitine is obtained from meat extracts and is normally present in skeletal and heart muscle tissue. The role of carnitine in human health is that of helping the heart and other body tissues to burn fat as a fuel. A healthy person usually produces enough carnitine to maintain normal heart function. But a deficiency of carnitine can lead to symptoms of heart disease. Carnitine has been used in the treatment of angina pectoris, cardiac depression, congestive heart failure, heart arrhythmias, and a disorder called endocardial fibroelastosis (a congenital defect that is a leading cause of heart disease deaths in infants and small children). Europeans have consumed carnitine health tonics for years. But because of U.S. patent laws, more than 30 pharmaceutical companies have refused to manufacture and distribute it.

## The Orphan Drug Act

At the urging of 21 "orphan disease" groups, such as the National Myoclonus Foundation and the Wilson's Disease Association, the 97th Congress took action to encourage the development and introduction of orphan drug products in the United States. The Orphan Drug Act, sponsored by Representative Henry Waxman of California and others, became law in 1983, making federal financial assistance available to pharmaceutical companies, individual researchers, and nonprofit organizations for the development and marketing of some drugs previously unavailable in the United States. In addition to federal grant money and tax incentives, the act includes proposals for accepting clinical research data from foreign countries, so drug studies do not have to be repeated in the United States, and the elimination of routine case report forms on each patient used in tests of an investigational drug. The routine case report forms required 100,000 pages of paperwork for each new drug application.

In a parallel action, the FDA has proposed a change in policy that would permit an individual entering the United States—either a foreign visitor or a returning American citizen—to bring in a reasonable quantity of an orphan drug from another country for personal use. The rule is intended only for individuals carrying medicines obtained abroad for their personal use, and it does not apply to manufacturers or distributors of drugs who could profit financially from the unlawful importation of overseas drugs that do not have FDA approval. The rule also does not apply to "controlled substances," a term that is generally applied to narcotics or other potential drugs of abuse.

## How to Use This Book

This book contains basic information about tried and tested remedies for most common and many uncommon diseases that afflict millions of Americans which, for various reasons, are not currently obtainable in the United States. In most cases, these drugs, both prescription and nonprescription, can be obtained from foreign sources for personal use during travel outside the United States, by following special regulations for the import of nonregulated, or narcotic-free, substances in limited quantities for personal use, and in concert with your physician. (For more information, see "How to Use the Sources in This Book.")

The pharmaceutical products listed in this book are among those without FDA approval at the time of compilation. The drugs are identified both by generic names and by brand names in the index beginning on page 259. The diseases, disorders, or other conditions for which the drugs are used in other countries are listed in a separate index beginning on page 275.

The main body of the book is divided into a series of short descriptive entries which identify the pharmaceutical products by their generic and brand names and explain their actions and uses, potential adverse effects, the dosages usually used or recommended by their manufacturers, and the names and addresses of manufacturers or distributors overseas. The inclusion of a drug in this book should not be interpreted as an endorsement of the product by the author, editors, or publisher. Readers who lack a medical background are advised to consult a physician before using any of the products.

A physician with access to the reader's medical records can usually advise whether an individual is likely to benefit from or be sensitive to the effects of a particular drug. A person who is familiar with his own physical condition and drug sensitivities, if any, obviously is in a better position to discuss such matters with a physician and to understand the doctor's advice. One should discuss quite frankly with a physician, domestic or foreign, any pertinent aspects of one's physical health, known drug sensitivities, the history of any chronic complaint, such as arthritis or asthma, and the effects of whatever medications were previously taken for the problem.

## Organization of the Book

The orphan drugs on the following pages are arranged in alphabetical order of the generic names of the products. The generic name is a generally accepted official drug name agreed upon by pharmaceutical manufacturers and health agencies as a word that identifies a particular kind of medicine, such as aspirin or penicillin. The first name at the beginning of each entry, in boldface, is its most commonly used generic name. A second generic name, or synonym, may follow the primary generic name.

Following the generic name are the brand names or product names used by different manufacturers or distributors of drugs containing the same generic substance. There may be a single brand name or many brand names for each generic drug name. A single manufacturer may own several brand names, each representing a different formulation, strength, or method of administration. In the United States alone, penicillin is sold under 50 different brand names, and acetaminophen, a popular aspirin substitute, is sold under 85 different brand names.

Frequently, a brand-name pharmaceutical product will contain, in addition to the generic drug, varying amounts of other drugs plus substances added to help the medicine go down. When a brand-name drug contains additional active substances, the effects can be expected to differ from those in the simple generic form. In selecting a brand-name drug, one should determine whether the additional active ingredients may be the cause of allergies or other reactions.

Even a basic generic product usually contains additional materials called "excipients," a term used to identify inert or generally harmless substances mixed with a drug to give it a desired consistency or to hasten or retard the rate at which a tablet or capsule will disintegrate to release the active ingredient. Glycerin, casein, sugar, and starch are commonly used excipients. Coloring agents also may be added to help identify a product. Some people are allergic to the chemicals in coloring agents or other additives used in drug manufacture and should be watchful for them. Some drug manufacturers identify the excipients in their products. Some European manufacturers label their products to identify artificial coloring agents, such as FD&C Red No. 2, that may be a part of the drug product.

## Drug Actions and Uses

The "Actions and Uses" section of each entry describes the medical conditions for which the drug is used and how the agent interacts with living-tissue systems. Pharmaceutical products and human organs function according to the basic laws of chemistry and physics. The phenomenon of a tablet relieving a headache or a capsule calming an anxious elderly patient may be due, in the final analysis, to differences in electrical energy charges on the drug molecule and the molecules of the body's tissue cells. Even an antibiotic may produce its curative effect by forming an electrochemical bond with a vital part of the disease microorganism so the infectious agent is rendered harmless.

It is not unusual for one drug to produce a wide range of effects, some of which may appear to be contradictory—as when a drug may act both as a tranquilizer and as an antidepressant. Although drugs usually are chosen for a specific action, many medications have more than one specific use, and a few may be useful in treating a dozen different diseases or conditions. The reasons are complicated and require a deep understanding of the biochemistry of living systems. Occasionally, new uses for old drugs are discovered by serendipity. The antidepressant drug iproniazid, for example, was originally used to treat tuberculosis but was found to produce a side effect of euphoria. The heart disease benefits of carnitine were discovered when a patient with angina pectoris was given the drug during a study of its effects on thyroid disease.

## When Is a Drug Safe?

A drug is often defined as a substance that, when taken into the body, may modify one or more of the body's functions. Thus, the purpose of taking a drug usually is to produce a change in the body that may restore its functions to a normal healthy state. But there is always a risk that in correcting an unhealthy condition, the drug may also produce one or more undesirable or adverse effects. In the "Precautions" sections an effort has been made to list as many as possible of the adverse effects that have been observed in or reported by patients using the particular drug. Generally, only a small percentage of patients have experienced one of the reported side effects, and a still smaller proportion have reported two or more of the adverse effects. Only a very few drugs, usually natural substances, are relatively free of side effects.

A frequent cause of adverse effects is the dose size, or the amount of the drug administered within a certain amount of time. The same rule applies to the use of alcoholic beverages. The old saying that too much of a good thing can be harmful can explain many of the adverse effects reported. Most drugs require a certain minimum-size dose to reach what is called the "threshold," or the level needed to trigger a desired effect. For certain medications, the difference between a threshold dose and an overdose can be very small. And the size of the difference can vary among different patients.

Because of the accumulation of many generations of assorted genes in any individual, it is likely that the person has inherited an allergy or hypersensitivity to one or more substances in the environment. Some people have more allergies or hypersensitivities than others and are often the people who are most susceptible to certain adverse effects of drugs. A drug allergy is quite similar to hay fever, a reaction to a bee sting, or a tissue transplant rejection. The body's immune system, which protects it from bacteria, viruses, and other foreign invaders, may regard the drug molecule as a "nonself" substance and attempt to reject it. The rejection is experienced as a "drug reaction." A physician who is thoroughly familiar with a patient's medical history can often reduce such risks by advising against the use of a drug that is likely to cause a hypersensitivity reaction.

## The Drug Industry's Role

Most drug manufacturers are quite frank about potential side effects associated with their products. For both humanitarian and financial reasons, responsible members of the drug industry never encourage the use of a product by any patient who may experience a severe reaction. Most foreign governments today follow a procedure similar to that of the FDA in maintaining "alert" systems whereby any serious adverse reaction observed in a patient using a new drug is reported immediately to a central office where the information can be evaluated and relayed quickly to all physicians. Drug manufacturers are particularly cautious about the effects of their products in pregnancy and generally urge that women who are at all capable of becoming pregnant avoid the use of drugs unless the physician believes the potential benefits outweigh the risk of birth defects.

Drug manufacturers also tend to report any patient complaint, even though the reported adverse effect may have been coincidental to the use of the product. As a result, it is easily possible that many of the minor side effects listed, such as nausea, vomiting, headache, or diarrhea, may not have been caused by the drug itself. The side effects associated with the use of a medication often are the same symptoms experienced by other persons who have not taken any drugs. In a study of this aspect of drug testing published in *The New England Journal of Medicine*, a group of more than 400 university students and hospital staff members who had not taken any medication during the previous 72 hours were asked to report any symptoms of ill health. More than 80 percent of the interview subjects reported feeling nausea, headache, diarrhea, skin rash, muscle or joint pain, nasal congestion, or other symptoms commonly identified as side effects of drug use.

Those findings were reinforced by a Canadian study in which half of a group of patients were given a sample dose of a new drug and the other half were given a placebo, or harmless sugar pill. The patients did not know whether they had received the real pill or the dud. Afterward, 8.1 percent of the patients receiving the real medication complained of nausea, vomiting, diarrhea, headache, dizziness, and other side effects. However, 7.7 percent of the patients who received the sugar pill also reported experiencing those side effects. Nevertheless, most drug manufacturers will advise the physician and the patient of any and all side effects reported, even though there may be reason to doubt a causal relationship between the drug and the reported effect. The entries in this book also list, as a precaution, all or nearly all the reported side effects.

## Individual Drug Effects

Mention was made earlier of genetic factors that often determine how a particular drug may affect a certain individual. This concept has been well tested in twins. Because identical twins have the same genetic factors inherited from their parents, one might assume that both of the twins would react in the same manner to a drug. And that is exactly what happens. But when the same drug is tested on fraternal twins—born at the same time of the same parents, but without the identical sets of genes—the reactions usually show a significant variation. One member of the pair may have inherited a gene for an enzyme that helps metabolize a drug molecule, but the other member may lack that gene and be unable to handle the drug as well. Because of genetic variations, some individuals are resistant to coumarin anticoagulant drugs and require doses as much as 20 times larger than doses given other patients. They also may be 20 times more sensitive to vitamin K. Even within the range of what is considered "normal" there may be great individual variations in body functions. For example, two individuals may produce a "normal" amount of stomach acid even though one person's output is 1,000 percent that of the other's.

Other factors that can influence drug reactions include body weight, physical fitness, blood group, sex, amount of body fat, and age. Children and elderly persons have a much greater risk of adverse drug reactions than young adults. The same factors can influence the dosage and administration of medications.

Individual responses to drugs can vary from one day to the next and at different hours of the same day. Experiments with various medications have shown that rates of metabolism of a number of drugs can vary in one person from 3 to 50 percent between 8 A.M. and 8 P.M. or between noon and midnight. Also the rates may vary among different individuals and with different drugs in the same individual. All of these factors make it difficult to establish a "standard" dosage of a drug that is correct for all patients. An effective individual dosage often is established in the same way that one makes an individual adjustment to the amount of coffee or tea consumed during the day—by the trial-and-error technique, sometimes called titration. Most people learn to estimate through experience how much of the drug caffeine is too little or too much and adjust their daily caffeine beverage intake accordingly. The same system works for many medications.

## Drug Dose Measurements

The dosages of drugs listed in the entries are based on recommendations of the manufacturers. Recommended dosages may be based on the smallest amount of a medication that is effective in 50 percent of the patients tested. It usually includes a safety margin to reduce the risk of overdosage in most patients. Many drugs also have a ceiling effect, or a point beyond which increasing the size of the dose fails to benefit the patient and usually results in adverse effects.

Dose sizes are expressed as "mg" for milligram and "mcg" for microgram. A milligram is approximately 1/30,000 ounce, and a microgram is 1/1,000 milligram. The abbreviation "ml" stands for milliliter, which is roughly equivalent to 1/1,000 quart. A standard teaspoon holds about 5 ml, and there are 20 average drops to 1 ml. Drugs supplied for injection may be measured in mg/ml, which is equivalent to a ratio of one part per thousand. In converting body weight from pounds to kilograms, 1 kg is equal to 2.2 pounds. Some drug dosages are based on square meters of body surface because two patients with the same body weight can actually vary considerably in body area.

When a drug is supplied in tablets, it means the dried powdered medication has been mixed with excipients and compressed in a mold to the shape of a small disk. A tablet may be scored with engraved lines indicating where it should be broken to make half or quarter doses. The excipients usually are starch and casein, chosen because they expand in fluid and help the tablet disintegrate. Tablets that are not intended to disintegrate rapidly have a coating that resists the erosion of stomach acid.

The term "pill" usually refers to a tablet that is candy-coated. In Europe and Latin America, candy-coated tablets are sometimes identified as *grageas* or *dragees*.

Capsules are small oval gelatin containers of powdered or liquefied medications. They are usually sealed, particularly if they contain liquids. Some capsules, like tablets, may be coated with substances that delay disintegration as they travel through the gastrointestinal tract.

Ampules are small glass vials that have been heat-sealed to keep the contents sterile until the drug is to be administered, usually by intravenous or intramuscular injection.

Some drugs are supplied as powders or granules. They are equivalent to tablets that have not been compressed into disks. Powders and granules usually are intended to be dissolved in water or a flavored liquid before being ingested.

A suppository is a medication that has been mixed with a waxy substance that melts at body temperature. It has been molded into a solid body that can be inserted into the rectum, vagina, or urethra. Rectal suppositories often provide an alternative route of administration for drugs that the patient cannot take by mouth.

Children's doses are sometimes supplied in a syrup. The drug is mixed in a watery solution with a high concentration of sugar, flavoring, and coloring. An elixir is similar to a syrup but it contains alcohol in addition to the sugared and flavored water. A drug dissolved in water that has a high concentration of alcohol is sometimes identified as a tincture. An emulsion is a water solution to which gum has been added to hold the drug mixture in suspension.

Drugs for external use are supplied as powders, lotions, ointments, or pastes. Lotions are watery solutions of drugs, whereas ointments are prepared by mixing the powdered drug in a base of oil, fat, or wax, depending upon the consistency desired. A paste is an ointment that also contains a material such as gelatin to give the medication firmness.

This book should be a valuable source of information for the millions of Americans who until now have been unaware of the hundreds of alternative therapies available in countries outside the United States for the many disabling and life-threatening health problems that sooner or later may affect ourselves, our families, and our friends. In order to ensure improvements in the health and longevity of all citizens, it is important that an informed and intelligent public remain alerted to the medical progress being accomplished in all countries throughout the world.

# How to Use the Sources in This Book

The "Sources" of drugs listed at the end of each entry are the names and addresses of some of the suppliers of the drug. Where possible, an effort has been made to offer several alternative sources for a drug. In many instances, a single manufacturer is the ultimate source of a drug that may be available in many countries outside the United States. The source data serve two purposes: they indicate the country or countries in which the drug is approved for use, and they can be used by your physician to locate a supply of a drug that could be imported with FDA authorization for treatment of your own health problem.

Although the Food and Drug Administration does not approve of patients making "mail-order" purchases of pharmaceutical products from other countries, there is a relatively simple and legitimate procedure that can be used to obtain medications that are used in most other countries although they have not yet been given the FDA seal of approval. Here is how it works: Suppose you have a type of arthritis that does not improve when treated with drugs currently available in the United States. However, you have learned from this book that a drug that has been tested and approved for use in Canada, England, or Switzerland might be effective in the treatment of your condition. Take the information to your doctor and discuss the various risks and benefits involved in using the new drug. If your doctor needs further data about the product, he can write to the supplier listed under "sources." The doctor also can order a review of the medical literature about the drug from various medical journals or computer data bases.

If the doctor feels that you might benefit from use of the orphan drug, the doctor can contact the Food and Drug Administration and request an "IND," an abbreviation for the investigational drug use authorization. Once your doctor has received the IND authorization, the drug can be ordered from the overseas supplier for your personal use. The doctor, in effect, becomes a medical researcher and you become a test subject. The doctor may be expected by the FDA to report eventually on the effectiveness of the new arthritis drug obtained for your use.

Your personal physician also can obtain information about orphan drug study projects in which the FDA may be currently involved by contacting the agency at 5600 Fishers Lane, Rockville, Maryland 20852. If a formal clinical study of an overseas drug is planned in the United States, your physician may be able to learn the name and address of the individual or group sponsoring the study. If the purpose of the study is to test, for example, a new arthritis drug, your physician can request permission to participate or to include you as a test subject. One advantage of becoming a subject in a large sponsored study is that the cost of the drug and related tests usually is paid for by the drug manufacturer, a federal grant, or some other source than the patient's own checkbook.

Hundreds of millions of dollars are contributed annually by government agencies and private organizations such as the American Cancer Society or the American Heart Association to sponsor studies of new therapies. One source of information regarding current medical projects funded by the U.S. government is an annual publication of the National Institutes of Health. The *Research Grants* directory of the NIH lists all federally funded studies according to the location of the project by state and city, the name of the university or other institution involved, the name of the doctor or scientist directing the project, the subject of the study (such as "treatment of Wilson's disease with zinc"), and the amount of money allocated for the research. By scanning the directory, your doctor can quickly learn the names, addresses, and other information about researchers who are testing new therapies for arthritis.

Even when a new drug study has already started, the medical personnel conducting the research often can be a source of information for your doctor about similar studies being planned in the near future by the same investigators or their colleagues. The NIH *Research Grants* directory is published by the Department of Health and Human Services,

Public Health Service, National Institutes of Health, 900 Rockville Pike, Bethesda, Maryland 20014.

Still another way your doctor can learn about proposed and ongoing research projects involving arthritis therapies or other new drug studies is by contacting the Smithsonian Science Information Exchange, at 1730 M Street N.W., Washington, D.C. 20036. The Smithsonian Science Information Exchange provides a detailed file of research grants from 1,300 institutions. The file is updated every month. Each research report provides, in addition to the names and addresses of the doctors conducting a research project, a one-page summary describing the background and purpose of the research, the amount and source of funding, and the time period during which the study will be conducted.

An advantage of using the Smithsonian Science Information Exchange is the accessibility of the information by computer. If your doctor would like to "investigate the investigators" anonymously while seeking an appropriate study group for your own health problem, a rather detailed background report on any of the research projects can be obtained through either the Orbit or Dialog computer search services. Smithsonian Science Information Exchange reports can be obtained either online or offline through Orbit's SSIE file or Dialog's File 65. The Smithsonian Science Information Exchange files cover most medical research projects in the United States but also include some overseas studies that are funded by the U.S. government or private agencies in the United States.

## Finding a Doctor Overseas

You may also obtain an orphan drug by, of course, traveling to a country where the medication is marketed. Your own doctor can again be helpful in suggesting names and addresses of physicians in foreign lands.

Regardless of your reason for traveling outside your own country, it's wise to have the name of a physician you can contact in a foreign country in the event of a sudden illness or injury. Your personal doctor usually can provide a few names through his own professional contacts overseas.

Because of the large number of foreign medical graduates who now practice in North America, opening channels of communication to doctors overseas can be fairly simple. Some foreign medical school graduates have even formed their own "medical associations" in the United States; an example is "Graduates of Italian Medical Schools," which claims 500 members.

Several medical directories, such as *Medical and Health Information Directory* (Gale Research Company, Penobscot Building, Detroit, Michigan 48226), are sources of such information. The *Directory of Medical Specialists* (Marquis–Who's Who, Inc., 200 East Ohio St., Chicago, Illinois 60611) contains biographical information about physicians practicing in the United States, including the names of medical schools attended and hospitals where the doctors interned. In many entries, overseas background of the doctors is detailed. The *American Medical Directory* (American Medical Association, 535 North Dearborn, Chicago, Illinois 60610) lists every physician in the United States and, like the *Directory of Medical Specialists*, identifies the medical school attended by the doctor, whether in Afghanistan or Zambia, as well as U.S. and Canadian medical schools. The AMA source is more difficult to use because the information is contained in code numbers, but each of the several volumes of the directory contains an explanation of how to translate the code. The *American Medical Directory* and the *Directory of Medical Specialists* can be found in doctors' offices, clinics, hospitals, and some larger public libraries. They are used by doctors to help patients find physicians in other localities or specialists in nearby communities.

Names and addresses of overseas physicians can be found in the country visited by contacting American embassies or consulates, cultural or trade missions, Red Cross offices, and travel agencies. Other overseas sources include local medical associations, hospitals, clinics, police, and churches or religious groups. In countries where the United States has military establishments, the base medics often can recommend a good local physician. Even the local American Express office can be a source of information about area physicians.

And there is always the basic approach of asking members of the hotel staff or other local residents. Every Berlitz or other foreign-language phrase guide contains the appropriate words for communicating with doctors or pharmacists in their native tongue. Once communication has been established, obtaining a drug with or without a prescription is essentially the same as it would be in a doctor's office or drugstore in your home neighborhood. The reader should not feel reluctant about approaching medical personnel in a foreign country.

# Orphan Drugs Directory

## Acebutolol Hydrochloride—Neptall, Prent, Rhodiasectral, Secadrex, Sectral

**ACTIONS AND USES**—Acebutolol hydrochloride is a beta-blocking drug used in the treatment of hypertension, angina pectoris, and heart arrhythmias. It is similar to propranolol, another beta nerve blocker that produces its action by suppressing the autonomic nerve impulses along the beta receptor pathways that drive the heart contractions. The result is a reduced work load on the heart and a reduced oxygen requirement. Acebutolol is considered to be more cardioselective than some other beta-blocking drugs in that its effects are directed primarily at heart action, with minimal influence on beta nerve pathways of other organ systems. Acebutolol also has been used in the management of certain types of schizophrenic patients, although the pharmacological activity in such cases is not well understood.

**PRECAUTIONS**—Acebutolol hydrochloride should not be given to patients being treated for asthma, uncompensated heart failure, abnormally slow heartbeat, abnormally low blood pressure, cardiogenic shock, or heart block. Acebutolol should not be administered to patients also taking monoamine oxidase inhibitors, verapamil antiarrhythmic drugs, or to patients who may receive cardiac-depressant anesthetics. Side effects of acebutolol are similar to those reported for other beta-blocking drugs and include dry eyes, skin rashes, low blood pressure, slow heartbeat, gastrointestinal disturbances, and depression. Serious complaints of side effects have been eliminated by withdrawing the medication. Caution should be exercised in the administration of acebutolol to insulin-dependent patients, because beta-blocking drugs may enhance the hypoglycemic effect of insulin. Caution also should be used in giving acebutolol with reserpine-type drugs, including clonidine, which may have a depressing effect on the central nervous system. Acebutolol should not be given to women during the first trimester of pregnancy unless the doctor determines that the benefits outweigh the risks.

**DOSAGE AND ADMINISTRATION**—Acebutolol is supplied in 100 and 200 mg capsules, 200 and 400 mg tablets, and 5 ml injection ampules containing 5 mg per ml. The usual initial dose for hypertension is 400 mg daily, as a single morning dose or as 200 mg twice a day, with increases of up to a maximum of 1,200 mg per day in divided doses of 800 and 400 mg if needed to achieve a satisfactory response. The usual dose for angina pectoris is 400 mg daily in two divided doses and up to 900 mg in three divided doses per day if required. The usual dose for heart arrhythmias is 200 to 600 mg per day in two or three divided doses as needed. Emergency treatment of heart arrhythmias is by slow intravenous injection of one ampule, or 25 mg, with repeated injections to a maximum of 100 mg if necessary. Effects of an intravenous injection may not be observed for at least 10 minutes; oral doses may require 3 hours to show a full effect. The drug is not recommended for children.

**SOURCES**—May & Baker Limited, Dagenham, Essex RM10 7XS, England; Specia, 16, rue Clisson, 75646 Paris Cedex 13, France.

## Acefylline Piperazine (Acepifylline)—Etafillina, Etaphylate, Etaphylline, Minophylline

**ACTIONS AND USES**—Acefylline piperazine is a smooth muscle relaxant, diuretic, antispasmodic, and blood vessel dilator used for a wide range of respiratory and circulatory disorders. The drug has been used for the relief of bronchospasms in bronchitis and asthma, for emergency relief of status asthmaticus, and for cor pulmonale marked by enlargement or failure of the right ventricle of the heart due to respiratory disorders. Acefylline piperazine also has been used to increase the rate and force of heart contractions, to relieve respiratory effects of failure of the left ventricle of the heart, and to reduce the work load on the heart. Acefylline piperazine is related chemically to theophylline and aminophylline, which produce similar effects on the circulatory and respiratory systems; but acefylline piperazine reportedly causes fewer side effects, particularly less gastric distress and nausea, and is better tolerated by intramuscular injection.

**PRECAUTIONS**—Caution is advised in administering acefylline piperazine to patients with heart disease, liver impairment, or patients being treated for epilepsy. Care also should be exercised in giving the drug to elderly patients or nursing mothers. The agent may interact with other drugs. Side effects, which may include nausea, vomiting, falling blood pressure, rapid heartbeat, or collapse, may be due to overdosage or to administration of the drug at an excessively rapid rate. Intravenous injection of a dose should be given slowly over a period of one minute.

**DOSAGE AND ADMINISTRATION**—Acefylline piperazine is supplied as 250 and 500 mg tablets, a syrup providing 125 mg per 5 ml and a syrup forte providing 500 mg per 5 ml, 250 and 500 mg suppositories, and 250 and 500 mg ampules for intravenous or intramuscular injection. Tablets, syrup, and suppositories are available in pediatric formulations for children under 13 years of age. The usual recommended adult dosage is 500 mg to 1 g by tablet three times daily, preferably after meals, 500 mg to 1.5 g by suppository daily in divided doses, or one or two spoonfuls of the syrup forte three times daily. The syrup forte should not be given to children. For children under 13 years of age, the recommended oral dose is calculated at 62.5 mg for infants, 125 mg for children 1 to 5 years of age, and 250 mg for children 5 to 12 years old, three to four times daily. A suppository dose for children 1 to 5 years of age is recommended at 200 mg daily and for children between 5 and 12, 300 mg daily.

**SOURCES**—Delandale Laboratories Limited, Delandale House, 37 Old Dover Road, Canterbury, Kent CT1 3JB, England; Difrex (Aust.) Laboratories, 13–19 Glebe Street, Glebe, N.S.W. 2037, Australia.

## Acenocoumarol (Acenocoumarin, Nicoumalone)—Sinthrome, Sintrom

**ACTIONS AND USES**—Acenocoumarol is an oral anticoagulant used in the prevention or treatment of deep vein thrombosis, transient brain ischemic attacks or mild strokes, clot formation associated with artificial heart valves, pulmonary embolism, thrombophlebitis, coronary thrombosis, and myocardial infarction. It also has been used to prevent blood-clotting complications in rheumatic heart disease and atrial fibrillation marked by extremely rapid twitching of the heart's muscle fibrils. Acenocoumarol produces its effects by interfering with the formation of prothrombin and at least 2 of the 12 steps in the natural process of blood-clot formation. The drug is fast-acting, is easily controlled, is excreted unchanged, and allows prothrombin time to return to normal about 48 hours after administration of the last dose.

**PRECAUTIONS**—Acenocoumarol should not be administered to patients prior to surgery, to patients with severe hypertension, capillary lesions, peptic ulcers, blood diseases such as leukemia or hemophilia, impaired liver or kidney function, or in pregnancy. Caution should be exercised in administering acenocoumarol concurrently with drugs that may increase or decrease prothrombin time. Factors that increase prothrombin time include analgesics, antibiotics, sulfa drugs, monoamine oxidase inhibitors, thyroid and antithyroid drugs, B vitamins, alcohol, radiation therapy, and hot weather. Factors that can decrease prothrombin time include vitamin K, barbiturates, antihistamines, diuretics, and corticosteroid drugs. Overdosage may lead to hemorrhage. Individual hypersensitivity to acenocoumarol is unusual, and side effects, such as local skin necrosis, are rare. However, it is advised that care be exercised with subcutaneous, intravenous, and intramuscular injections during anticoagulant therapy because of the risk of hematomas, marked by bleeding beneath the skin.

**DOSAGE AND ADMINISTRATION**—Acenocoumarol is supplied as 1 and 4 mg tablets. The dosage varies according to the prothrombin index of the individual patient, determined by laboratory tests of the clotting time of the patient's blood. For prothrombin times within the normal range, the initial dose may be 8 to 12 mg the first day and 4 to 8 mg the second day, followed by a maintenance dose to be determined by the daily check of the patient's prothrombin index.

**SOURCES**—Ciba-Geigy Australia Ltd., P.O. Box 76, Lane Cove, N.S.W. 2006, Australia; Geigy Pharmaceuticals, Horsham, West Sussex RH12 4AB, England; Ciba-Geigy, S.A. de C.V., Calzada de Tlalpan No. 1779, Mexico 21, D.F. Mexico.

## Acetyldigitoxin—Acetil Digitoxina, Acylanid, Acylanide

**ACTIONS AND USES**—Acetyldigitoxin is a form of the widely used heart tonic, digitalis, used for centuries to increase the work performed by the heart in order to prevent heart failure. Digitoxin is the main active ingredient of digitalis drugs, which are obtained from leaves of foxglove and other plants. Acetyldigitoxin has a somewhat longer half-life than ordinary digitoxin, thereby extending its heart-strengthening effects for the patient. Although each of the several digitalis-derived drugs has different effects in toxicity, half-life, areas of the heart affected, and other factors, they have in common an effect of increasing the force of the heart muscle contractions, thereby increasing the efficiency of the heart. The heart moves a greater amount of blood per contraction and in less time, giving it longer rest periods between contractions and reducing the dilation of the heart caused by blood accumulation in the ventricles. Meanwhile, peripheral blood circulation and kidney function are improved, and edema is reduced because excess fluid from tissues can be excreted faster. By improving the efficiency of the heart per contraction, fewer contractions per minute are required. Thus, acetyldigitoxin also relieves the symptom of tachycardia, or abnormally rapid heartbeat.

**PRECAUTIONS**—Acetyldigitoxin should not be given to patients with heart block or an excessively slow heartbeat, particularly patients with the Stokes-Adams syndrome, in which any temporary interference with heart output can interrupt blood flow to the brain. Caution should be used in giving the drug to patients with impaired kidney or liver function or mineral imbalance. Caution also should be observed in the intake of calcium by the patients because of an interaction with digitalis drugs, resulting in arrhythmias or fibrillation due to effects of calcium on heart muscle contractions. Side effects of the use of acetyldigitoxin include gastrointestinal complaints such as loss of appetite, nausea, and vomiting, and skin allergies such as pruritis, urticaria, and rashes. Older patients, particularly those with arteriosclerosis, may experience nervous system aberrations such as confusion, disorientation, aphasia, and visual difficulties, including abnormal color vision.

**DOSAGE AND ADMINISTRATION**—Acetyldigitoxin is supplied in 200 mcg tablets. The usual oral dose is 100 to 200 mcg per day for maintenance therapy after initial doses of 600 mcg to 1 mg per day. Effects of acetyldigitoxin may not be observed until several hours after the initial dose.

**SOURCES**—Sandoz De Mexico, S.A. de C.V., Amores No. 1322,

Mexico 12, D.F., Mexico; Laboratoires Sandoz S.A.R.L., 14, bvd Richelieu, 92500 Rueil-Malmaison, France.

**Adenosine Triphosphate (Adenosine Triphosphoric Acid, ATP)**—Adenotriphos, Adephos, Adetol, Adynol, Atepodin, Atriphos, Estriadin, Glucobasin, Myotriphos, Nucleocardyl, Striadyne, Striadyne Forte, Triadenyl ATP, Triadesin A, Trinosin, Triphosaden, Triphosphodine

**ACTIONS AND USES**—Adenosine triphosphate is a natural component of animal cells that is used therapeutically to increase muscle power, heart activity, and blood circulation near the body surface and in the arms and legs. The function of the agent in animal cells is that of storing and releasing energy as needed for cellular activities such as muscle contractions. Adenosine triphosphate is administered to elderly patients to give increased strength and range of motion when skeletal muscles have become weaker and the movements slower and more difficult. The product has been used experimentally in the treatment of muscular dystrophies with varied results. The drug has been used with greater reported success in overcoming the pain and stiffness of patients afflicted with rheumatic or arthritic disorders, also increasing the range of motion of their limbs. Adenosine triphosphate increases the blood flow to the heart while improving the strength of heart contractions and improving the blood flow to the outer areas of the body. The drug has been used in the treatment of coronary insufficiency and some cases of abnormal heart rhythms. Some evidence of protection against radiation has been reported as a result of administration of adenosine triphosphate to medical workers chronically exposed to x-rays. The rate of chromosome damage in the tissues of the radiologists decreased after treatment with the drug.

**PRECAUTIONS**—No adverse side effects from the administration of adenosine triphosphate have been reported as of this writing.

**DOSAGE AND ADMINISTRATION**—Adenosine triphosphate is supplied in tablets providing 3 mg of a sodium salt of adenosine triphosphate and in 2 ml ampules containing 20 mg of the drug for injection. The usual recommended dose for oral administration is two tablets three times daily, for a total of 18 mg per day, for one week, followed by a maintenance dose of four to eight tablets daily. By intramuscular injection, the initial dose is 20 to 40 mg daily for two to four days, followed by the same or half dosage every other day to a total of 200 to 400 mg.

**SOURCES**—Rona Laboratories Ltd., Cadwell Lane, Hitchin, Herts SG4 OSF, England; Riker Laboratories Australia Pty Ltd., 9 Chilvers Road, Thornleigh, N.S.W. 2120, Australia.

## **Alfacalcidol**—Delakmin, Einsalpha, Etalpha, One-Alpha, Un-Alpha

**ACTIONS AND USES**—Alfacalcidol is a metabolic product of vitamin D needed to regulate the body's use of calcium and other vital minerals. It is used as a medication in the treatment of hypoparathyroidism, vitamin D–resistant rickets, malabsorption rickets, nutritional rickets, osteomalacia, osteoporosis, and renal osteodystrophy, all of which involve skeletal disorders due to a failure in the body's normal bone-building chemistry. Hypoparathyroidism, a deficiency of parathyroid hormone, results in failure to maintain normal levels of calcium in the blood and other tissues. Rickets is characterized by soft, pliable bones in childhood due to lack of vitamin D, calcium, and phosphorus. Osteomalacia is an adult form of rickets. Osteoporosis is marked by a thinning of the skeletal bones to a level that may not support the weight of the body. Renal osteodystrophy is a mixture of osteomalacia, osteoporosis, and other bone disorders due to a kidney defect. Alfacalcidol is converted by the liver into a form of vitamin D that improves the body's use of calcium and phosphorus, and a normal kidney converts vitamin D into a factor that prevents rickets. Alfacalcidol also is used as a preoperative medication for patients about to undergo surgical removal of the parathyroid glands and in the management of calcium levels of kidney patients receiving dialysis treatment.

**PRECAUTIONS**—In the administration of alfacalcidol caution should be exercised to prevent hypercalcemia (excessive levels of calcium in the body). Symptoms of hypercalcemia include confusion, loss of appetite, muscle pain and weakness, abdominal pain, and in severe cases shock and kidney failure. Alfacalcidol should be used by pregnant women and nursing mothers only if it is considered necessary by the physician. Blood plasma levels of calcium should be checked at weekly or monthly intervals and the dosage adjusted to prevent hypercalcemia. Patients using barbiturates or anticonvulsant drugs may require larger than usual doses of alfacalcidol. Alfacalcidol also may result in excessive levels of phosphorus in the patient's tissues, which may be treated with phosphate-binding agents.

**DOSAGE AND ADMINISTRATION**—Alfacalcidol is supplied in capsules containing 0.25 mcg (250 nanograms) or 1.0 mcg and drops containing 5 mcg per ml, or 250 nanograms per drop. The usual initial dosage for adults and children weighing more than 20 kg is 1 mcg daily, with usual maintenance doses between 0.25 and 1.0 mcg daily. Some patients may require up to 3 mcg daily. For children weighing less than 20 kg, the daily dosage is calculated at 0.05 mcg (50 nanograms) per kg of body weight.

**SOURCES**—Løvens kemiske Fabrik, Industriparken 55, DK-2750 Ballerup, Sweden; Pennwalt of Canada Ltd., Pharmaceutical Division, 393 Midwest Road, Scarborough, Ontario M1P 3A6, Canada; Leo Laboratories Limited, Longwick Road, Princes Risborough, Aylesbury, Bucks. HP17 9RR, England.

## **Alphadolone-Alphaxalone**—Alfatesin, Alfatesine, Alphadione, Alfathesin, Althesin

**ACTIONS AND USES**—Alphadolone-alphaxalone is an injectable steroid anesthetic with a rapid onset and short duration of action. The product is a combination of two substances, alphadolone acetate, a nearly white odorless crystalline powder that is practically insoluble in water, and alphaxalone, a similar-appearing white crystalline powder that is also nearly insoluble in water. But when combined, alphadolone increases the solubility of alphaxalone. Both chemicals have anesthetic properties, but alphadolone is only about half as potent as alphaxalone. The combination of alphadolone and alphaxalone can induce anesthesia in little more than 30 seconds when administered intravenously. However, the product does not possess analgesic properties, so it is necessary to administer an appropriate pain-killer when the anesthetic is used. Muscle relaxant drugs also may be required, particularly if small doses of alphadolone-alphaxalone are used. Alphadolone-alphaxalone may be used to initiate anesthesia for major surgical procedures or be used alone for outpatient surgery or similar short-term procedures. Alphadolone-alphaxalone is more potent than other injectable general anesthetics. Unconsciousness may last only 5 to 10 minutes with a single dose, but the effect may be prolonged with repeated doses or by intravenous slow infusion. The precise manner in which alphadolone-alphaxalone produces its anesthetic effect has not been determined. Clinical studies indicate recovery is more rapid in outpatient procedures than with some alternative types of injectable anesthetics. In neurosurgery, alphadolone-alphaxalone is reported to be superior to gas anesthetics because intracranial pressure is reduced by as much as 50 percent when using the injectable product. The component chemicals are rapidly metabolized and excreted, which makes it easier for medical personnel to differentiate between aftereffects that may be due to the anesthetic and those related to the surgical problem being treated. Alphadolone-alphaxalone is compatible with most muscle relaxants, inhalation anesthetics, and drugs administered before surgery.

**PRECAUTIONS**—Alphadolone-alphaxalone should not be administered in cases of pregnancy or in obstetrical procedures, including cesarean section. It also should not be given to patients who may be hypersensitive to the chemicals used in the anesthetic, to patients with impaired liver or kidney function, or in cases of cardiac insufficiency or reduced cardiac reserve. Hyoscine is not recommended as a surgical premedicant with alphadolone-alphaxalone because the scopolamine product appears to increase the incidence of excitatory effects and involuntary muscle movements. Alphadolone-alphaxalone should be used only when full resuscitative equipment is readily available under the supervision of a qualified anesthetist. Severe hypersensitivity reactions may include bronchospasm, which may be accompanied by flushing of the skin over the chest and falling blood pressure, leading to cardiovascular collapse. Administration of alphadolone-alphaxalone to the same patient in subsequent procedures may increase the risk of histaminoid reactions, including anaphylactic shock.

**DOSAGE AND ADMINISTRATION**—Alphadolone-alphaxalone is supplied in 5 and 10 ml ampules containing 12 mg of the combined drugs per ml. The average adult dose is 0.075 ml per kg of body weight, with a dose range of 0.05 to 0.1 ml per kg. The induction dose is administered slowly, over a period of 15 to 30 seconds. The pediatric dose is 0.07 to 0.12 ml per kg of body weight. For infusion, the usual dosage is 20 mcl per kg of body weight per minute to 50 mcl per kg per minute. For longer procedures, the products are diluted in a ratio of 25 ml of anesthetic to 250 ml of sodium chloride or dextrose intravenous solution. The pediatric infusion dosage is the same as for adults.

**SOURCES**—Glaxo Laboratories, 1025 The Queensway, Toronto, Ontario M8Z 5S6, Canada; Glaxo Laboratories, Ltd., Greenford, Middx, UB6 OHE, England; Laboratoires Glaxo, 43, rue Vineuse, 75764 Paris Cedex 16, France; Glaxo de Mexico, S.A. de C.V., Centeno No. 132, Col. Granjas Esmeraldo, Mexico D.F., Mexico.

## **Alprenolol Hydrochloride**—Apllobal, Aptin, Aptine, Aptol, Betacard, Gubernal, Regletin, Sinalol, Vasoton

**ACTIONS AND USES**—Alprenolol hydrochloride is a beta-blocker used in the treatment of hypertension and angina pectoris. It has pharmacological activity similar to that of propranolol, a widely used heart drug that reduces the oxygen requirements of heart muscle during periods of stress or exercise by blocking nerve impulses along beta autonomic nervous system pathways. By inhibiting normal responses to physical and psychological stress, beta-blocking drugs such as alprenolol and propranolol moderate heart activity so that the pain-producing effect of oxygen deprivation in the heart muscle is not experienced. Like other beta-blockers, alprenolol also reduces blood pressure. In addition to its therapeutic uses in angina pectoris and hypertension, alprenolol has been employed in the treatment of anxiety, tachycardia (abnormally rapid heartbeat) and other heart arrhythmias, and in reducing the incidence of second heart attacks in patients recovering from myocardial infarction.

**PRECAUTIONS**—Alprenolol hydrochloride should not be given to patients with diabetes mellitus, abnormally slow heartbeat, bronchial asthma, symptoms of heart failure, some forms of heart block, or metabolic acidosis characterized by an increase in acids in the body. The drug also should not be used in surgery or other procedures when ether or chloroform anesthesia or narcotic agents that depress heart activity also are used. Alprenolol is not recommended for use in pregnancy or in patients subject to spontaneous attacks of hypoglycemia, or low blood sugar. Beta-blocking drugs can suppress some of the early signs of hypoglycemia; but under conditions such as fasting or following surgery, beta-blockers can deplete energy reserves and trigger severe attacks of hypoglycemia. Side effects include headache, nasal congestion, mild depression, sedation, dizziness, nausea, dry mouth, diarrhea, decreased libido, and under certain conditions precipitation of angina symptoms.

**DOSAGE AND ADMINISTRATION**—Alprenolol hydrochloride is supplied in 50 and 100 mg tablets and in injection ampules containing 1 mg per ml. For treatment of angina pectoris and other heart disorders, the recommended dosage is 200 to 400 mg daily divided into four equal doses. For hypertension, the recommended initial dosage is 200 mg daily, in two to four equal doses, with gradual weekly increments as needed up to a maximum of 800 mg per day. When used in combination with other antihypertensive drugs, the maximum daily dose may be reduced to 400 mg. Intravenous administration is intended for emergency use in hospital settings where heart and blood pressure can be monitored during therapy.

**SOURCES**—Department Geigy, Laboratoires Ciba-Geigy, 2–2, rue Lionel-Terray, 92506 Rueil-Malmaison, France; Pharmaceutical Div., Beecham (Australia) Pty Ltd., 212 Chesterville Rd., Moorabbin, Vic. 3189, Australia; Astra Chemicals, S.A., Division Astra Farmaceutica, Av. Urbina No. 15, Parque Industrial, Naucalpan de Juarez, Edo. de Mexico.

## Alverine Citrate (Dipropyline Citrate, Phenpropamine Citrate)—Antispasmin, Calmabel, Gamatran, Normacol Antispasmodic, Prefnine, Profenil, Prophelan, Proverine, Sestron, Spacolin, Spasmaverine, Spasmonal

**ACTIONS AND USES**—Alverine citrate is an oral drug used in the treatment of spasmodic diseases of the gastrointestinal and genitourinary tracts. The product has been used in therapy for irritable colon syndrome, spastic and hypertonic constipation, and other smooth muscle disorders of the digestive tract. Alverine has a direct effect on smooth muscle but does not exert the parasympathetic nervous system blocking effect that results in reduced stomach motility and secretions.

**PRECAUTIONS**—Adverse effects may include lowered blood pressure, dizziness, drowsiness, headache, and a feeling of weakness and dry mouth. The drug should not be administered to patients suffering from an intestinal obstruction.

**DOSAGE AND ADMINISTRATION**—Alverine citrate is supplied as 60 mg tablets, suppository doses of 80 mg, as 0.5 percent granules, and in injection doses equivalent to 40 mg of alverine. The usual recommended dosage for tablets is one or two tablets from one to three times daily. The granules are taken as one or two heaping teaspoonfuls once or twice daily, preferably after meals or at bedtime. The suppository and intramuscular injection doses are given at the usual adult rate of 60 to 120 mg once or twice daily. Children's dosages are one-half the adult level.

**SOURCE**—Norgine Ltd., 59–62 High Holborn, London WC1V 6EB, England.

## Amiodarone Hydrochloride (Aminodarone)—Atlansil, Cordarone, Cordarone X, Coronovo, Trangorex

**ACTIONS AND USES**—Amiodarone is used in the treatment of heart rhythm abnormalities. It also is used in the management of angina pectoris, a suffocative chest pain due to a lack of oxygen reaching the heart muscle. Amiodarone is particularly beneficial in the treatment of the Wolff-Parkinson-White syndrome, which is marked by excessively rapid heartbeats, or atrial fibrillation, atrial flutter, and ventricular tachycardia or fibrillation (excessively rapid contractions of the ventricles of the heart). Amiodarone was originally developed in the 1960s as a drug to control the symptoms of angina pectoris and only recently was found to have value as an antiarrhythmic heart agent that could be used in cases where other drugs could not be administered. It is similar to propranolol in the way it acts on heart muscle.

**PRECAUTIONS**—Amiodarone should not be used for patients with sinus bradycardia, heart block, thyroid disorders, or in elderly patients taking digitalis. The product also should not be administered to pregnant patients. A common side effect is the appearance of yellowish-brown microdeposits in the cornea, which gradually disappear when the medication is discontinued. Amiodarone contains iodine, which may be released to disturb thyroid function. Other side effects may include photosensitivity, occasional skin discoloration, nausea, vomiting, headaches, dizziness, and nervous system disorders. The product should be used with caution in patients with heart failure.

**DOSAGE AND ADMINISTRATION**—Amiodarone may be administered intravenously or by tablets. Tablets are scored and contain 200 mg of amiodarone hydrochloride each. The usual recommended dosage is one 200 mg tablet three times a day for at least one week, after which a maintenance dose of one 200 mg tablet daily will maintain a therapeutic effect in most patients.

**SOURCE**—Labaz Sanofi UK Ltd, Regent House, Heaton Lane, Stockport SK4 1AG, England.

## Ancrod—Arvin

**ACTIONS AND USES**—Ancrod is an anticoagulant prepared from the venom of the Malayan pit viper, *Agkistrodon rhodostoma*. It is used in the treatment of priapism; thrombosis of deep, branch, or central retinal veins; hypertension due to embolism; and embolisms caused by insertion of artificial heart valves. Ancrod also is used to prevent thrombosis of the deep veins after surgical repair of leg fractures, to prevent the reformation of a thrombus after thrombolytic therapy or surgical procedures on blood vessels, and in patients recovering from myocardial infarction. The product was found to be less effective in the treatment of sickle-cell disease and in hemodialysis. Ancrod acts by reducing the blood concentration of fibrinogen and by breaking up particles of fibrin involved in the formation of blood clots. Ancrod reduces the viscosity (thickness) of blood. However, it appears to have no effect on blood clots, or thrombi, already formed.

**PRECAUTIONS**—Hemorrhage may occur from the use of ancrod, particularly from recent wounds or surgical incisions, but the effect can be controlled by withdrawal of ancrod and injection of an antiserum. The product should not be administered in pregnancy, nor to patients with coronary thrombosis, severe infections, or blood disorders. It should be used with caution in patients with certain heart and kidney disorders. Ancrod appears to have a half-life of between three and five hours, and studies indicate that 10 percent remains after four days. Care should be exercised in giving ancrod to patients with peptic ulcers, ulcerative colitis, or other gastrointestinal disorders with lesions likely to bleed. And patients using drugs likely to cause gastrointestinal bleeding should not be given ancrod. Less serious side effects may include edema, redness and swelling at the site of injection, skin rash, and headache.

**DOSAGE AND ADMINISTRATION**—Ancrod is supplied in ampules containing 70 units per ml. Dosage is calculated at 2 to 3 units per kg of body weight in 50 to 500 ml sodium chloride solution administered by continuous intravenous drip, slowly over a period of 4 to 12 hours. The maintenance dose is 2 units per kg of body weight in 10 to 50 ml of sodium chloride solution by intravenous injections at 12-hour intervals, given slowly over a period of 5 minutes. The length of treatment may last from 7 to 28 days, depending upon the individual case. For prevention of deep vein thrombosis after surgery for a fractured head of the femur in the leg, the recommended dosage is 4 ampules as a single subcutaneous injection immediately after surgery, followed by 1 ampule daily for the next 4 days.

**SOURCE**—Berk Pharmaceuticals Limited, St. Leonards House, St. Leonards Road, Eastbourne, East Sussex BN21 3UU, England.

## Anetholtrithion (Anethole Trithione, Trithioanethol, Trithioparamethoxyphenypropene)—Colerene Antispastico, Farmades, Felviten, Heporal, Liverin, Mucinol, Noristan, Sialor, Sulfarlem, Sulfogal, Sulfralem, Tiotrifar, Trithio

**ACTIONS AND USES**—Anetholtrithion is a drug used both as a stimulator of saliva flow and as a stimulus for bile production by the liver. As a stimulator of saliva flow, the drug is used to treat the severe mouth dryness that results from taking tranquilizers, antidepressants, monoamine oxidase inhibitors, antiparkinsonism medications, and other nervous system drugs. The lack of normal saliva flow also can result from radiation therapy of the mouth and throat region. Studies indicate that anetholtrithion acts directly on the secretory cells of the salivary glands. As a bile stimulator, anetholtrithion is used in the treatment of nausea, flatulence, belching or eructation, distention of the gastrointestinal tract, and sluggish digestion. Anetholtrithion also has been used to stimulate the flow of tears in patients afflicted with a dry eye condition due to an impairment of the lacrimal glands.

**PRECAUTIONS**—Anetholtrithion should not be administered to patients with certain liver or gallbladder disorders, particularly cirrhosis of the liver, obstruction of the liver canals, biliary tract, or common bile duct, or jaundice. The safety of anetholtrithion in pregnant women or nursing mothers has not been established, and the product therefore should not be given to patients in these categories. In certain individuals, the use of anetholtrithion can result in a softening of the stools or diarrhea, an effect that usually can be controlled by reducing the dosage of the drug. Clinical studies have failed to demonstrate any pattern of adverse effects that could be related to the pharmacological activity of the drug when used at recommended dosages. The drug can add a yellow coloration to urine. The physician should be aware of interactions between anetholtrithion and drugs prescribed for psychiatric treatments, which usually can be managed by adjusting the dosage of the psychotropic drugs.

**DOSAGE AND ADMINISTRATION**—Anetholtrithion is supplied in 12.5 and 25 mg tablets and as 12.5 mg doses in granule form. The usual recommended dosage for treatment of hyposialosis (lack of saliva) is 75 mg per day in three divided doses, taken before each meal. The treatment may be continuous or intermittent, with five drug-free days each month, concurrently with the psychotropic or antiparkinsonian drugs that are the cause of dryness of the mouth. When dryness of the mouth is due to radiation therapy, administration of anetholtrithion should be continued indefinitely. Peak concentrations in the patient's tissues are not reached until about five days after starting the use of the drug, so the therapeutic effects usually develop gradually. When used to treat bile-deficiency disorders, anetholtrithion generally is administered at a rate of 50 mg per day, in divided doses before meals. Therapy for bile-flow deficiency also can be intermittent, with 10 to 15 drug-free days per month. The usual recommended dosage of anetholtrithion for children is 12.5 to 25 mg per day in divided doses.

**SOURCES**—Herdt & Charton (1971) Inc., 9393 Louis-H. Lafontaine, Montreal, Quebec H1J 1Y8, Canada; Laboratoires de Therapeutique Moderne Latema, 42, rue Rouget-de-Lisle, B.P. 22, 92151 Suresnes Cedex, France; Perkins Chemical Co., s.a.s., Via Passo Buole 166, 10135 Torino, Italy.

## Anti-Human Lymphocyte Globulin (Equine)—ALS, Immossar, Pressimmun, Pressimmune

**ACTIONS AND USES**—Antilymphocyte immunoglobulin is used to suppress the thymus and bone marrow lymphocytes involved in the immune response in humans. For immunosuppression, antilymphocyte immunoglobulin is needed to prevent or control rejection by the patient's body of organ transplants, particularly kidney transplants. Antilymphocyte immunoglobulin also may be used in combination with other immunosuppressive agents to permit the reduction of dosages of azathioprine or steroids in the treatment of autoimmune disorders. There are several theories to explain the mechanism of immunosuppression by antilymphocyte immunoglobulin. It is believed the action prevents sensitivity of the recipient patient to foreign transplant tissue by cell destruction, attack by the body's defense system, or other means. It also has been proposed that the antilymphocyte immunoglobulin masks the transplant and protects it from attack by the cellular defenses of the patient. Anti-human lymphocyte globulin (equine) is a purified preparation of horse immunoglobulins containing antibodies to human lymphocytes. It is prepared by injecting viable lymphoid cells into the animal and collecting the sera.

**PRECAUTIONS**—Patients should be tested for hypersensitivity to normal horse serum. Anti-human lymphocyte globulin should not be given to patients with a history of serum (including antitetanus serum) allergies or other known allergies. The recipient should be watched carefully during infusion for possible adverse effects, which may include fever, chills, nausea, tachycardia, and hypotension. The desired lymphocytopenia may be accompanied by thrombocytopenia and leukopenia. Anaphylactic reactions, serum sickness with serum nephritis, urticaria, and pruritis are among other possible side effects.

**DOSAGE AND ADMINISTRATION**—Anti-human lymphocyte globulin is supplied in 5 to 10 ml vials, which may be administered intramuscularly or intravenously. When given intravenously, the globulin is diluted in 250 to 500 ml of physiological saline or a 2.5 percent dextrose solution containing 0.45 percent sodium chloride. The recommended initial dose is 20 to 30 mg globulin/kg body weight. The exact procedure varies according to whether the product is administered prior to or after transplantation, the patient response, and the use of other immunosuppresive agents.

**SOURCES**—Hoechst Pharmaceuticals, Canadian Hoechst Limited, 4045 Côte Vertu Blvd., Montreal, Quebec H4R 1R6, Canada; Hoechst UK Ltd., Pharmaceutical Division, Hoechst House, Salisbury Rd., Hounslow, Middx TW4 6JH, England.

## **Aprotinin**—Antagosan, Antikrein, Gordox, Iniprol, Kir, Midran, Onquinin, Repulson, Trasylol, Trazinin, Tzalol, Zymofren

**ACTIONS AND USES**—Aprotinin is a substance obtained from the lungs of cows that is used to block the activity of proteolytic enzymes, or enzymes that break down protein molecules. Aprotinin has been used in the treatment of pancreatitis, certain types of hemorrhage, and in support of insulin therapy for diabetes. The product also has been used with some success in the treatment of osteoarthritis and chronic urticaria. In pancreatitis, enzymes that digest proteins become overly active and begin digesting pancreatic tissue, meanwhile producing excessive amounts of the same or similar protein-digesting enzymes. Aprotinin inactivates the protein-digesting enzymes, which otherwise continue destroying tissues including blood vessels, leading to circulatory collapse. Plasmin, a substance in the blood that dissolves clots and may cause bleeding, is inhibited by aprotinin. Aprotinin may be administered before surgery to patients with a known propensity to excessive plasmin activity. In the treatment of diabetes, aprotinin blocks the activity of protein-digesting enzymes that would break down the molecules of insulin, which is a protein hormone. Aprotinin potency is measured in terms of the number of units of the enzyme trypsin that can be inactivated by a given number of units of aprotinin.

**PRECAUTIONS**—Aprotinin occurs as a chain of amino acids with the potential risk of producing allergic reactions. Allergic reactions that have been observed include bronchospasm and skin disorders. Allergic reactions usually occur at the start of treatment and can be stopped by discontinuing treatment. Other side effects have included nausea, vomiting, diarrhea, muscle pain, breathing difficulty, palpitations, and blood pressure changes. Because aprotinin blocks the breakdown of blood clots, there is a possibility that excessive coagulation could occur. However, no evidence of this effect has been reported in the medical literature.

**DOSAGE AND ADMINISTRATION**—Aprotinin is supplied in ampules of 100,000 units each. It is administered intravenously, by either injection or slow infusion, or both. For hemorrhage, the initial dose consists of 200,000 units by injection and up to 300,000 additional units by slow IV infusion. As much as 1,000,000 units per day may be required to control the bleeding. For pancreatitis, the initial dose is 100,000 to 200,000 units, followed by 100,000 units every six hours for up to five days. Aprotinin administration is intended to be in addition to the usual therapeutic measures prescribed for the treatment of pancreatitis. When children have been treated with aprotinin, the usual dose was 50 percent of the recommended adult dose.

**SOURCE**—Bayer UK Ltd., Pharmaceutical Division, Haywards Heath, West Sussex RH16 1 TP, England; Miles Pharmaceuticals, Division of Miles Laboratories Ltd., 77 Belfield Road, Rexdale, Ontario M9W 1G6, Canada.

## Azapropazone (Apazone)—Cinnamin, Pentasol, Prolix, Prolixan, Prolixana, Rheumox

**ACTIONS AND USES**—Azapropazone is a nonsteroidal antiinflammatory drug with analgesic and antipyretic properties used in the treatment of rheumatoid arthritis, osteoarthritis, ankylosing spondylitis, and other rheumatic or musculoskeletal disorders. The product also is used in the treatment of acute gout. Azapropazone is related chemically to phenylbutazone, but it reportedly produces fewer blood disorders.

**PRECAUTIONS**—Azapropazone should be used with caution by patients with peptic ulcers or other serious gastrointestinal disorders or impaired kidney function. The drug should not be given to individuals with a history of sensitivity to phenylbutazone or similar antiinflammatory drugs. The drug is not recommended for children or pregnant patients. Azapropazone can interact with anticoagulant drugs, sulfonamides, antiepileptic medications, and oral diabetic drugs. Side effects may include gastrointestinal disturbances, skin rashes, edema, dizziness, kidney disorders, and allergies.

**DOSAGE AND ADMINISTRATION**—Azapropazone is supplied in 300 mg capsules and 600 mg scored tablets. The usual recommended dose is 1,200 mg daily, taken as 300 mg four times daily or 600 mg twice daily. The drug should be taken after meals, if feasible. A lower maintenance dose may be established. For acute gout, the usual recommended dose is an initial intake of 2,400 mg daily in divided doses, gradually reducing the intake to 1,200 mg in divided doses daily.

**SOURCE**—A. H. Robins Co., Ltd., Redkiln Way, Horsham, West Sussex RH13 5QP, England.

## Azidocillin—Astracillina, Globacillin, Nalpen, Syncillin

**ACTIONS AND USES**—Azidocillin is an antibiotic used primarily in the treatment of whooping cough, bronchitis, and other respiratory tract infections. It is related to benzylpenicillin in many pharmacological actions and uses, exerting an effect against multiplying bacteria by suppressing an enzyme they require for building their cell walls. Azidocillin has been used in the treatment of a variety of bacterial infections, including sinusitis, conjunctivitis, influenzal meningitis, otitis media, epiglottitis, pharyngitis, bacterial endocarditis, and some types of pneumonia.

**PRECAUTIONS**—Azidocillin should not be given to patients who are allergic to antibiotics, particularly penicillin and cephalosporin and related products. Side effects reported include skin rashes and gastrointestinal disorders, particularly diarrhea.

**DOSAGE AND ADMINISTRATION**—Azidocillin is supplied in 750 mg tablets. The recommended dosage for adults and children over 12 years of age is 750 mg taken twice daily, once in the morning and again in the evening. For smaller children, the recommended dosage is 375 mg, or one-half tablet, twice daily.

**SOURCES**—Wulfing International Gmbh, Stresemannalle 6, PF. 25, 4040 Neuss, West Germany; Astra Farmasøytiske A/S, Skårersletta 50, Bostboks 1, 1473 Skårer, Norway.

## Benproperine—Blascorid, Cofrel, Pirexil, Pirexyl, Tussafug

**ACTIONS AND USES**—Benproperine is an antitussive drug used to suppress coughing by blocking the sensory nerve impulses traveling from the lungs and pleural tissues to the so-called cough-control center in the brain. It is employed in the relief of symptoms of whooping cough, nonproductive coughing, pharyngitis, laryngitis, tracheitis, and tracheobronchitis.

**PRECAUTIONS**—Caution should be observed in administering benproperine to women of childbearing potential. Caution also should be observed in giving the drug to nursing mothers because of a lack of information about the transmittal of benproperine through breast milk. A common side effect is a dry mouth.

**DOSAGE AND ADMINISTRATION**—Benproperine is supplied in 25 mg tablets and in suspensions providing 3 mg per ml. The recommended adult dosage is 50 to 200 mg per day. For children, the recommended dosage is 25 to 50 mg per day for those over 7 years of age. Suspension dosages are 2.5 ml two to four times a day for children between the ages of 1 and 3, 5 ml two to four times a day for children between 3 and 7 years of age, and 5 to 10 ml two to four times a day for children 7 to 15 years of age.

**SOURCES**—Norsk Pharmacia A/S, Postboks 2005 Grunerløkka, Oslo 5, Norway; Laboratorio Guidotti & C. s.p.a., Via Trieste 40, 56100 Pisa, Italy.

**Benzarone**—Benzaran, Benzaron, Fragivil, Fragivix, Venagil

**ACTIONS AND USES**—Benzarone is a drug used in the treatment of a variety of circulatory disorders. Described as an angiotrophic (blood vessel nutrition) product, benzarone acts on the inner, endothelial layer of blood vessels, reinforcing the structure and normalizing the function. Benzarone also has fibrinolytic properties, enabling it to dissolve blood clots as they occur. The product is used in the treatment of varicose veins, phlebitis, fragile capillary disorders, poor circulation in the lower extremities, and various eye disorders caused by circulatory diseases, including angioretinopathies associated with diabetes, hypertension, senile arteriosclerosis, exudation, hemorrhage, or thrombosis.

**PRECAUTIONS**—Benzarone should not be administered to any patient who is sensitive to the product. Side effects include hyperacidity and gastrointestinal distress.

**ADMINISTRATION AND DOSAGE**—Although benzarone has been applied topically, the usual route of administration is by mouth. The product is supplied in 200 mg tablets. The usual recommended dosage is three tablets daily, after meals, for three weeks.

**SOURCE**—Bracco de Mexico, S.A. de C.V., Calzada de las Armas No. 110, Tlalnepantla, Edo. de Mexico.

**Benzyl Benzoate Application (Linimentum Benzyli Benzoatis)**—Antiscabiosum, Ascabiol, Benzemul, Scabanca

**ACTIONS AND USES**—Benzyl benzoate is an insect repellent that is used in the treatment of scabies (itch mite) and pediculosis (lice infestation). The product also has been used alone or in combination with other substances, such as dibutyl phthalate, as a repellent for chiggers, fleas, mosquitoes, and ticks. Benzyl benzoate solutions are used to treat clothing so that the garments have insect repellent properties. However, the use of insecticides on synthetic fabrics is not recommended.

**PRECAUTIONS**—Benzyl benzoate should not be allowed to contact the eyes or mucous membranes. The product may irritate the skin, and occasional cases of dermatitis have been reported among hypersensitive individuals. If accidentally ingested, benzyl benzoate should be regarded as a poison to be treated by inducing emesis or gastric lavage. Symptoms of benzyl benzoate poisoning include central nervous system disorders, particularly convulsions, which require the administration of anticonvulsants.

**DOSAGE AND ADMINISTRATION**—Benzyl benzoate application is supplied as an emulsion containing 25 percent benzyl benzoate. The product is applied over the entire body, from the neck down, after the patient has been well scrubbed with soap in a hot bath, to open the infested skin burrows, and dried. The procedure is repeated the following day, or three applications may be made over a period of 36 hours. In different cases of scabies, the application procedure should be repeated after an interval of five days.

**SOURCE**—Rivopharm Pharmaceutical Laboratories, Rivopharm SA, 6911 Manno, Lugano, Switzerland.

## Bephenium Hydroxynaphthoate (Naphthammonium)—Alcopar, Alcopara

**ACTIONS AND USES**—Bephenium hydroxynaphthoate is an antihelmintic drug that is effective against various species of hookworms, roundworms, and other intestinal parasites. The product is reported to have a cure rate of 80 to 98 percent in administration of a single oral dose. Bephenium has been used against species of *Ancylostoma duodenale*, the common European or Old World hookworm; *Necator americanus*, or American hookworm; *Ascaris lumbriocoides*, or common intestinal roundworm; and species of *Trichostrongylus* nematode worms that infest humans. The drug has been less successful in treating infestations of *Trichuris trichiura*, or whipworm. In tropical areas, bephenium has been used against *Ternidens diminutus*, a nematode worm commonly found in monkeys but which also can be transmitted to humans. The drug acts by paralyzing the parasites so they are unable to maintain their attachment to the wall of the intestine and they are excreted in feces.

**PRECAUTIONS**—Few adverse effects have been reported except for nausea, vomiting, headache, diarrhea, and dizziness. It is recommended that conditions of diarrhea, dehydration, or mineral imbalance be corrected, whenever possible, before the drug is given to the patient. Because of a lack of information about effects of bephenium on the fetus, the drug should not be given to women who may be pregnant unless the potential benefits outweigh the risks. Bephenium hydroxynaphthoate also should not be given to nursing mothers.

**DOSAGE AND ADMINISTRATION**—Bephenium hydroxynaphthoate is supplied in packets of granules containing approximately 2.5 g of the drug. The contents of a packet are mixed in water or a flavored drink to mask the bitter taste and swallowed. The dosage for children over the age of 2 years is the same. Although a single dose may clear an infection of some intestinal parasites, it may be necessary to repeat the medication after three days. For eradication of an infestation of *Necator americanus* hookworms, it is recommended that the patient take two doses daily for three successive days. The medication should be taken on an empty stomach at least one hour before eating a meal.

**SOURCES**—Rivopharm Pharmaceutical Laboratories, Rivopharm SA, 6911 Manno, Lugano, Switzerland; Wellcome Medical Division, The Wellcome Foundation Ltd., Crewe Hall, Crewe, Cheshire CW1 1 UB, England; Laboratoires Wellcome S.A., 159, rue Nationale, 75640 Paris Cedex 13, France.

## Betahistine—Aequamen, Betaserc, Deanosart, Extovyl, Hainimeru, Medan, Meginalisk, Meniace, Menitazine, Meotels, Merislon, Microser, Pyritylulon, Remark, Riptonin, Serc, Sinmenier, Suzotolon, Tenyl-D, Urutal, Vasomotal

**ACTIONS AND USES**—Betahistine is used to treat a variety of disorders involving the functions of the inner ear, including vertigo, loss of hearing, Meniere's disease, and tinnitus (ringing in the ears). Betahistine also has been used to treat headache, bedsores, and certain forms of organic brain disease marked by dementia. Betahistine is a close chemical relative of histamine, a natural body substance that stimulates certain glands and muscles and also dilates arteries. Betahistine is a dilator of arteries with activity that is directed primarily to the capillaries, or microcirculation of the body. The disorders of the labyrinthine areas of the inner ear are believed to be caused by an accumulation of lymphatic fluid which in turn produces increasing pressure on the organs associated with hearing and the sense of balance. By causing a dilation of the capillaries, the pressure and symptoms are relieved.

**PRECAUTIONS**—Betahistine should not be used with antihistamine drugs, which produce an antagonistic effect toward betahistine. The drug should not be administered to patients with a type of adrenal tumor called pheochromocytoma. Betahistine also should not be given to children, and care should be exercised in administering betahistine to pregnant patients or patients with bronchial asthma, peptic ulcers, or a history of peptic ulcers. Adverse effects reported include nausea and other forms of gastric distress, headache, and skin rash.

**DOSAGE AND ADMINISTRATION**—Betahistine is available in both a hydrochloride and a mesylate form and generally in tablets containing 4 or 8 mg of the drug. A granule form containing 12 mg per dose also is available. The usual recommended dosage is 8 mg taken three times a day, preferably with meals. The maximum daily dosage is 48 mg.

**SOURCES**—Laboratoires Duphar & Cie, B.P. 6020, 60, rue de Verdun, 69604 Villeurbanne Cedex, France; Duphar Laboratories Limited, Gaters Hill, West End, Southampton SO3 3JD, England; Unimed Canada Inc., 626 Meloche, Dorval, Quebec H9P 2S4, Canada; Prodotti Formenti s.r.l., Via Correggio 43, 20149 Milano, Italy.

## Betamethasone Disodium Phosphate (Betamethasone Sodium Phosphate)—Bentelan, Betnesol, Emilan

**ACTIONS AND USES**—Betamethasone disodium phosphate is an oral form of betamethasone, a corticosteroid drug used in short-term therapy of a variety of allergy-related diseases. They include acute asthma, hay fever that fails to respond to other therapies, severe eczema, and other inflammatory skin diseases, including urticaria, or hives. Betamethasone disodium phosphate also is employed as long-term therapy for rheumatoid arthritis, severe ulcerative colitis, Crohn's disease, certain kidney disorders, collagen diseases, steroid-responsive leukemias, thrombocytopenias, the hemolytic anemias. The disodium phosphate form of betamethasone is water-soluble and formulated as an effervescent tablet which is dissolved in water before administration, so the drug becomes dispersed in a clear solution, with a minimum of inconsistency of absorption and minimal risk of solid steroid reaching the stomach to produce a gastric intolerance reaction. Betamethasone disodium phosphate also is produced as a sterile injectable solution and as drops for noninfective inflammatory disorders of the eye, ear, and nose. A retention enema product also is available. Betamethasone is about eight to ten times as potent as prednisolone, a commonly used corticosteroid drug, which is important when high dosages are required, as in immunosuppresive therapy. Other corticosteroids are not easily soluble and are therefore more likely to produce gastric irritation when taken orally. Betamethasone medications also are less likely than other corticosteroid drugs to cause water and sodium retention, thereby reducing the risk of edema and hypertension.

**PRECAUTIONS**—Because corticosteroid drugs may cause hyperacidity in the digestive tract and increase the risk of peptic ulcers, x-ray studies are recommended when patients receive long-term therapy or there are signs of gastric distress. The safety of corticosteroids in human pregnancy has not been established, and special care is required in the administration of the drugs to pregnant patients, particularly during the early months of pregnancy. Because corticosteroids can be transmitted through breast milk, caution also should be observed in giving the drug to nursing mothers. When patients on corticosteroid therapy are subjected to unusual stress, the physician should consider increasing the dosage of rapidly acting corticosteroid medications before, during, and after the period of stress. The use of corticosteroids may impair the ability of the patient to resist and counteract infections. Therefore, the patient should be monitored for signs or symptoms of infection that may be suppressed by the drug. Betamethasone products also may cause suppression of natural production of adrenocortical hormones, so treatment should be tapered off gradually when the course of therapy is ended. Betamethasone products should not be given to patients with osteoporosis, marked emotional instability, peptic ulcers, herpes simplex of the eye, or chickenpox or similar diseases characterized by a skin rash or eruption. Prolonged treatment or high doses of corticosteroid drugs can exacerbate symptoms of diabetes mellitus and hypertension and may result in glaucoma or cataracts. In children, prolonged therapy may result in growth retardation.

**DOSAGE AND ADMINISTRATION**—Betamethasone disodium phosphate is supplied in 500 mcg and 5 mg tablets, which may be scored with dividing marks so they can be broken into uniform smaller doses. The drug also is available in sterile drops and ointments and in intravenous injection ampules to be used with either sodium chloride or dextrose solutions. The tablets are effervescent and dissolve quickly in water for oral administration. The usual initial dose for short-term therapy is 2 to 3 mg per day for several days, after which the daily dosage is gradually reduced by 250 to 500 mcg every two to five days. For rheumatoid arthritis, the recommended dosage is 500 mcg to 2 mg daily, using the minimum effective dose. For most other conditions, the initial dose is 1.5 to 5.0 mg daily for one to three weeks, followed by reducing the daily dosage to the minimum effective level. For children, the suggested dosage is 25 percent of the adult dosage for those between 1 and 7 years, 50 percent between 7 and 12, and 75 percent for children 12 years and older.

**SOURCES**—Glaxo Laboratories, 1025 The Queensway, Toronto, Ontario M8Z 5S6, Canada; Glaxo Laboratories, Ltd., Greenford, Middx UB6 OHE, England; Perkins Chemical Co. s.a.s., Via Passa Nuole 166, 10135 Torino, Italy.

## Bietamiverine Hydrochloride (Dietamiverine Dihydrochloride)—Fine-Dol, Novosparol, Spasmaparid, Spasmisolvina, Spasmo-Paparid

**ACTIONS AND USES**—Bietamiverine hydrochloride is an antispasmodic drug used in the treatment of smooth muscle disorders of the gastrointestinal and urinary tracts. The product also has been used in the relief of symptoms of dysmenorrhea, postpartum spasms of the uterus, complications of duodenal and stomach ulcers, kidney stones, esophageal spasms, spastic colon, biliary spasms, and other digestive diseases.

**PRECAUTIONS**—Adverse effects of bietamiverine hydrochloride have not been reported in the available medical literature.

**DOSAGE AND ADMINISTRATION**—Bietamiverine hydrochloride is supplied in 50 mg tablets, 100 mg suppositories, and injection vials of 25 mg per 2 ml. The usual dosage is two or three tablets, or 100 to 150 mg, or one or two suppositories, or 100 to 200 mg, per day.

**SOURCES**—Isola Ibi, Instituto Bioterapico Internazionale, Viale Pio VII 50, 16148 Genova Quarto, Italy; Prophin s.p.a., Via A. Binda 21, 20143 Milano, Italy; Instituto Biologico Dessy, s.p.a., Via S. Domenico 107–109, 50133 Firenze, Italy.

## Bromazepam—Compendium, Lectopam, Lexatin, Lexomil, Lexotan, Lexotanil

**ACTIONS AND USES**—Bromazepam is an antianxiety drug, or minor tranquilizer, used in the relief of anxiety and tension states and anxiety associated with organic illness. It has been used in the treatment of depression, hypertension, insomnia, psychosomatic disorders, irritable colon, nervous diarrhea, and various psychogenic problems of the respiratory and circulatory system, such as rapid heartbeat and hyperventilation. Bromazepam has pharmacological activity similar to diazepam and chlordiazepoxide, two of the most commonly prescribed tranquilizers. Bromazepam is more effective than barbiturates in reducing anxiety, produces little change in a patient's sleeping pattern, has a long duration of action, and is not easily used for suicide. Because of its muscle relaxant property, bromazepam has been recommended for treatment of neurogenic bladder, gastrointestinal disorders, and heart and lung complaints that appear to be psychosomatic in nature. Clinical studies have found that the relief of psychosomatic symptoms by bromazepam is superior to the effects of placebos.

**PRECAUTIONS**—Bromazepam is not recommended for use by women of childbearing potential or nursing mothers; animal studies indicate the drug is more than 25 times as toxic to newborn offspring as to adult animals. The drug also should not be given to myasthenia gravis patients or to persons sensitive to either bromazepam or the artificial coloring tartrazine, used in the formulation of the drug. Paradoxical reactions have been reported, appearing as rage, excitement, or stimulation. In animal studies, low doses were found to increase the effects of cocaine and amphetamine. A small percentage of patients have experienced amnesia extending to the period before the start of bromazepam administration. Dosage for elderly or debilitated patients should be limited to the lowest amount that is effective. Patients should be advised that mental and physical abilities may be impaired and that operating motor vehicles or machinery can be hazardous, and in some patients being a pedestrian could be dangerous. The drug should not be given to psychotic patients, and persons on long-term therapy should be monitored for liver and kidney functions. Bromazepam may interact with alcohol and other drugs. It is not recommended for use in children. Side effects include drowsiness, dizziness, muscle incoordination, behavioral disorders, confusion, headache, and gastrointestinal distress.

**DOSAGE AND ADMINISTRATION**—Bromazepam is supplied in 1.5, 3, 6, and 12 mg capsules and tablets and in suspensions providing 2.5 mg per ml of fluid. The dosage of bromazepam is individualized but usually is started at 6 to 18 mg per day in equally divided doses, depending upon the severity of the disorder and the patient response. The dosage may be adjusted in small increments every two or three days up to a maximum of 60 mg per day. Most patients respond to doses within the range of 6 to 30 mg per day. For elderly and debilitated patients, the recommended initial dosage is not more than 3 mg per day in divided doses. It is recommended that bromazepam be taken on an empty stomach due to a lack of information about the effect of food on absorption of the drug.

**SOURCES**—Polifarma s.p.a., Via Tor Sapienza 138, 00155 Roma, Italy; Hoffman-LaRoche Ltd., 1000 boulevard Roche, Vandreuil, Quebec J7V 6B3, Canada; Roche Products Pty Ltd., Box 255, P.O. Dee Why, N.S.W. 2099, Australia; Produits Roche S.A., 52, bvd. du Parc, 92521 Neuilly-Sur-Seine Cedex, France.

## **Bufexamac (Bufexamic Acid)**—Droxarol, Droxaryl, Flogocid, Flogocid N Plastigel, Mofenar, Norfemac, Paraderm, Parfenac, Parfenal

**ACTIONS AND USES**—Bufexamac is a nonsteroidal drug with antiinflammatory, analgesic, antipyretic, and antiexudative properties. It is used as a topical dressing for a wide variety of skin disorders, including eczema, atopic dermatitis, periphlebitis, pruritus, diaper rash, contact dermatitis, folliculitis, and complications of acne and psoriasis. The product also has been used in treating vulvitis and other inflammatory conditions of the genitalia, for acute hemorrhoids and other anorectal disorders, osteoarthritis, rheumatoid arthritis, periarthritis, mild burns, and insect bites. Studies indicate that bufexamac has a stabilizing effect on enzyme substances normally released when tissue cells are damaged.

**PRECAUTIONS**—The safety of bufexamac in pregnancy has not been established. Side effects reported after the application of the medication to body surfaces include burning and stinging sensations, some mild skin irritation, and allergies.

**DOSAGE AND ADMINISTRATION**—Bufexamac is supplied as creams or ointments in water-soluble or lanolin petrolatum base in tubes and jars. The medication is applied sparingly two or three times daily. When applied to skin surfaces, the product is massaged gently to enhance dermal penetration.

**SOURCES**—Continental Pharma S.A., ave. Louise 135, 1050 Brussels, Belgium; Lederle Laboratories, Division of Cyanamid of Great Britain Ltd., Fareham Rd., Gosport, Hants PO13 OAS, England; Nordic Laboratories, Inc., 2775 Bovet Street, Laval, Quebec H7S 2A4, Canada.

## Buformin Hydrochloride—Azucar, Diabrin, Silubin, Sindiatil

**ACTIONS AND USES**—Buformin hydrochloride is an oral hypoglycemic drug for the treatment of maturity-onset diabetes that can be controlled without insulin injections. Buformin is a type of oral diabetic medication which is believed to act by extending the availability of the insulin produced by the patient's own pancreas rather than stimulating insulin production, the alternative method of controlling maturity-onset diabetes. Buformin is similar in action to phenformin, another biguanide-type oral diabetic drug, but buformin reportedly causes fewer episodes of lactic acidosis than phenformin. Buformin is prescribed for patients whose adult diabetes mellitus fails to respond adequately to other kinds of oral hypoglycemic drugs.

**PRECAUTIONS**—Buformin hydrochloride should not be given to patients with impaired kidney or liver function, patients with heart disorders including congestive heart failure or myocardial infarction, or patients whose diabetes is complicated by acidosis. The drug also should not be given to patients with infections or gangrene, during pregnancy, or while undergoing surgery. Patients using buformin should be advised to avoid the use of alcoholic beverages. Adverse effects may include lactic acidosis, (characterized by abdominal pain, vomiting, hyperventilation, and clouding of consciousness), loss of appetite, loss of weight, diarrhea, weakness, skin rash, and a metallic taste. Lactic acidosis is a serious complication that often requires emergency care.

**DOSAGE AND ADMINISTRATION**—Buformin hydrochloride is supplied in 100 mg tablets. The usual dosage is 100 to 300 mg per day, beginning with an initial daily dose of 100 mg and gradually increasing the dose if necessary to achieve a satisfactory response.

**SOURCES**—Schering s.p.a., Via Cassanese, 20090 Segrate (M1), Italy; Bayer Italia s.p.a., Viale Certosa 126, 20156 Milano, Italy.

## **Bumetanide**—Aquazone, Bumedyl, Burinex, Burinex K, Butinat, Cambiex, Diurama, Fontego, Fordiuran, Lixil-Leo, Lunetoron, Miccil, Segurex

**ACTIONS AND USES**—Bumetanide is a diuretic used in the treatment of edema, or fluid collection in the tissues, due to congestive heart failure, cirrhosis of the liver, or kidney disease. The drug also has been used for pulmonary edema, arterial hypertension, toxemia of pregnancy, and edema associated with premenstrual tension. Bumetanide is a potent, fast-acting diuretic that produces its effects 30 minutes after ingestion of an oral dose and within a few minutes after intravenous injection. The diuretic effect is complete within two to three hours. Bumetanide is similar in action to furosemide, although the two substances are not related. Bumetanide is much more potent than furosemide, a commonly prescribed diuretic; 1 mg of bumetanide produces a diuretic action equivalent to about 50 mg of furosemide. Bumetanide inhibits the reabsorption of sodium and chloride ions, causing increased excretion of water as blood is filtered through the tubules of the kidney. The drug has been used by injection to initiate rapid diuretic action in cases of salicylate or barbiturate poisoning.

**PRECAUTIONS**—Bumetanide should not be given to patients who show signs of mineral imbalance, such as potassium depletion, severe liver impairment, or kidney failure or complete inability to urinate. Because of the ability of bumetanide to draw large quantities of fluid from body tissues for rapid excretion, some patients, particularly elderly individuals, may experience abrupt changes in blood pressure leading to circulatory collapse. Patients on low-sodium diets should be monitored closely to avoid excessive losses of fluids and minerals. The drug should not be administered to patients also receiving medications containing lithium salts, because diuretics tend to increase blood levels of lithium. Bumetanide also may cause an increase in blood uric acid. Caution should be used in giving bumetanide with antihypertensive medications; the dosage of the antihypertensive drug should be adjusted when bumetanide is administered as part of hypertensive therapy. Because diuretics can alter blood and urine levels of glucose, patients receiving bumetanide should be observed for signs of latent diabetes. The use of bumetanide should be avoided during the first trimester of pregnancy. Side effects may include skin rashes; abdominal discomfort, changes in blood platelet count; muscle cramps, particularly in the legs, and gynecomastia (breast enlargement in male patients). Musculoskeletal pain, sometimes associated with muscle cramps, can occur in patients given high doses of bumetanide. It is believed the pain is due to effects of the diuretic on mineral balance in the muscle tissues.

**DOSAGE AND ADMINISTRATION**—Bumetanide is supplied in 1 and 5 mg tablets for oral administration and in injection ampules containing 250 or 500 mcg per ml. Usually recommended is 1 mg orally given as a single dose in either the morning or early evening. If needed, a second 1 mg dose may be given six to eight hours later. In severe cases, up to 20 mg per day has been administered after gradually increasing the initial daily dosage upward to achieve a satisfactory response while carefully monitoring the patient's blood and urine samples. The initial intravenous dose is 1 to 2 mg, repeated 20 minutes later, if necessary. When used in cases of salicylate or barbiturate poisoning, the recommended dose is 2 mg intravenously, followed by 1 mg every 4 hours to a maximum of 7 mg per 24 hours. The recommended initial dose for intramuscular injection is 1 mg, followed by upward increments as needed to achieve a diuretic response.

**SOURCES**—Laboratoire Leo, 38, avenue Hoche, 75008 Paris, France; Sensian, S.A., Laboratorios, Lago Silverio No. 177, Mexico 17, D.F., Mexico; Leo Laboratories Limited, Longwick Road, Princes Risborough, Aylesbury, Bucks. HP17 9RR, England; Løvens kemiske Fabrik, Industriparken 55, DK-2750 Ballerup, Sweden.

## Butethal (Butobarbitone)—Etoval, Neonal, Sonabarb, Sonalgin, Sonergan, Soneryl

**ACTIONS AND USES**—Butethal is a barbiturate used in the treatment of insomnia and other conditions that may respond to sedation. Butethal is sometimes combined with analgesics, but it possesses some analgesic action of its own, particularly in cases of insomnia due to pain. Butethal induces sleep within 30 to 40 minutes after oral dosage, and the sleep lasts from 6 to 10 hours. In addition to its use in cases of mild and intractable insomnia, butethal is employed as a hypnotic and sedative in the treatment of mental disorders and feverish cases. In therapeutic doses, butethal produces a minimal respiratory depression and in general it does not result in headache or other hangover symptoms the next day.

**PRECAUTIONS**—The use of butethal by pregnant women or nursing mothers is not recommended unless the benefits outweigh the potential risks. Caution should be exercised in administering the drug to elderly or enfeebled patients or persons suffering from kidney or liver failure. It should not be given to persons consuming alcohol because the combination of alcohol and barbiturates can result in death. Butethal should not be given to persons known to be afflicted with the inherited metabolic disorder acute intermittent porphyria, who are hypersensitive to barbiturates and certain other drugs. Side effects may include urticaria, itching, or skin redness, which may warrant discontinuing the use of the product. Some breakthrough bleeding and loss of effectiveness of oral contraceptives has been reported among women who use oral hormones and barbiturates concomitantly. Patients should be advised that barbiturates can impair their mental and physical abilities for operating motor vehicles or machinery.

**DOSAGE AND ADMINISTRATION**—Butethal is supplied in 100 mg tablets. The usual recommended adult dose is one or two tablets, 100 to 200 mg, at bedtime. The maximum daily dose is 600 mg. The product is not recommended for children.

**SOURCES**—May & Baker Limited, Dagenham, Essex RM10 7XS, England; Protea Pharmaceuticals, 13–19 Glebe Street, Glebe, N.S.W. 2037, Australia.

## Calcium Carbimide (Calcium Cyanamide)—Abstem, Dipsan, Temposil

**ACTIONS AND USES**—Calcium carbimide is used as an alcohol challenge reaction drug in the treatment of alcoholism. Its action is similar to that of disulfiram, sometimes sold under the proprietary name of Antabuse, in that administration of the product causes a very unpleasant reaction in the patient who has ingested an alcoholic beverage. The antialcohol drugs block the normal oxidation of acetaldehyde, a metabolic product of alcohol, so that excessive levels of acetaldehyde accumulate in the blood. The patient who consumes even a small amount of alcohol within 12 to 24 hours after a dose of calcium carbimide will experience flushing, headache, breathing difficulty, heart palpitations, tremor, dizziness, drowsiness, nausea, vomiting, increased pulse rate, and blood pressure changes. The effects may begin within minutes after ingesting alcohol and last for 30 minutes to an hour or more. The drug is not a cure for alcoholism and is intended to be used as a part of a long-term therapy program that may include psychiatric consultation.

**PRECAUTIONS**—Calcium carbimide medication requires the willing cooperation of the patient. It should never be administered without the patient's knowledge and consent. It should never be given when the patient is in a state of intoxication and not sooner than 36 hours after the patient's last drink. The product should not be given to patients whose physical condition might be endangered by the effects of the alcohol challenge. Persons with asthma or heart disease are particularly vulnerable to serious adverse effects. In addition to the symptoms of the alcohol challenge, side effects have included giddiness, fatigue, psychological depression, impotence, increased urinary frequency, and a ringing in the ears. The white blood count of patients may increase when calcium carbimide is taken, but the blood count returns to normal after the medication is discontinued. A severe reaction in most cases can be controlled by administration of 100 percent oxygen or the intravenous injection of antihistamines.

**DOSAGE AND ADMINISTRATION**—Calcium carbimide is supplied in 50 mg doses in tablets that may contain a mixture of the drug and citric acid. The recommended dosage is 50 or 100 mg every 12 hours.

**SOURCE**—Lederle Products Dept., Cyanamid Canada Inc., 2255 Sheppard Ave. East, Willowdale, Ontario M2J 4Y5, Canada; Lederle Laboratories, Division of Cyanamid of Great Britain Ltd., Fareham Rd., Gosport, Hants PO13 OAS, England.

## Carbenoxolone Sodium—Biogastrone, Bioral, Duogastrone, Gastrausil, Neogel, Pyrogastrone, Sanodin, Sustac, Terulcon, Ulcus-Tablinen

**ACTIONS AND USES**—Carbenoxolone is a drug used in the treatment of gastric ulcers and related types of erosion of the lining of the digestive tract. The drug has been used in the healing of stomach ulcers, duodenal ulcers, lesions of the mouth and surrounding area, and inflammation, erosion, or ulcers of the esophagus due to hiatus hernia in which there is a reflux of gastric juices into the lower esophagus. The drug also has been used to treat flatulence and symptoms of heartburn. Studies indicate that carbenoxolone, which is derived from licorice ingredients, acts directly on the cells lining the digestive tract, stimulating the production of a protective layer of mucus to prolong cell life and also stimulating a proliferation of new tissue cells. The product reportedly has been found to be most effective in younger, otherwise healthy patients and least effective in older persons with health problems.

**PRECAUTIONS**—Carbenoxolone interacts with a number of other drugs and should be used with extreme caution in patients receiving digitalis therapy. Interactions with antihypertensive drugs results in a reduced effect of such drugs. Carbenoxolone may have an antagonistic effect on diuretics, resulting in sodium and fluid retention while producing a loss of potassium from the body tissues. An increased potassium loss also can be caused by interactions between carbenoxolone and corticosteroid drugs. On the other hand, certain diuretic drugs such as spironolactone tend to diminish the therapeutic action of carbenoxolone. Because of the tendency of carbenoxolone to increase potassium loss while enhancing an accumulation of salt and body fluids, it should be avoided or used with extreme caution in patients with impaired kidney or liver function. It also is recommended that patients receiving carbenoxolone follow a no-salt diet while increasing their consumption of such potassium-rich foods as bananas, oranges, and tomato juice. Patients in poor general physical condition or who are malnourished are susceptible to serious potassium loss, in the absence of drugs that tend to interact with carbenoxolone. The patient should be monitored closely for signs of edema, weight gain, or hypertension, which may require discontinuing use of carbenoxolone, reducing the dose, or administering a diuretic of the thiazide category, which can correct fluid and salt retention without inhibiting the peptic ulcer therapy of carbenoxolone.

**DOSAGE AND ADMINISTRATION**—Carbenoxolone is supplied in 50 mg tablets and capsules, in fruit-flavored chewable tablets containing 20 mg of carbenoxolone, in a 2 percent oral paste, and in 5 mg pellets. The paste and pellet forms are designed for use on ulcers or lesions of the inner surfaces of the mouth or cheeks. The usual recommended dosage is one pellet or application of paste after each meal and at bedtime. The capsules are designed to deliver the dose to the duodenum, the capsule rupturing at the time it passes through the pyloric valve between the stomach and the first segment of the small intestine. The recommended dosage is one capsule swallowed whole and unbroken four times daily, 15 to 30 minutes before meals, for a period of at least 6 to 12 weeks. The 50 mg tablets are intended for stomach ulcers and are taken at a rate of two tablets, or 100 mg, three times daily, after meals, for the first week, followed by one tablet three times daily for the next 4 to 12 weeks. The chewable tablets are designed for relief of symptoms of esophagitis, heartburn, flatulence, and complications of hiatus hernia. The recommended dosage for chewable tablets is one to be chewed immediately after each meal and two to be chewed at bedtime.

**SOURCE**—Winthrop Laboratories, Sterling-Winthrop House, Surbiton-upon-Thames, Surrey KT6 4PH, England.

## Carnitine (L-Carnitine)—Carnetina

**ACTIONS AND USES**—L-Carnitine acts as a carrier of fatty acid molecules into the mitochondria of heart and skeletal muscle tissue, where the fatty acid can be utilized by the tissue cells as a source of energy. L-Carnitine is a natural substance, present in heart and skeletal muscle tissue; it is produced in the liver from the amino acid lysine. A carnitine deficiency can occur if the liver fails to synthesize the substance or the carnitine is not transported from the liver to the heart or skeletal muscle. A carnitine deficiency may be characterized by abnormal functioning of the muscle tissue; the body also tends to accumulate fat that cannot be carried into the muscle cells to be burned as an energy source. By supplying carnitine to correct a natural deficiency, the heart rate and force of contractions are increased. Carnitine has been used to relieve the symptoms of angina pectoris, the congenital disorder endocardial fibroelastosis, and other heart disorders. It is also used for the treatment of patients on renal dialysis. Studies are currently under way to evaluate its utility in other disease states.

**PRECAUTIONS**—Large doses of carnitine have been associated with gastrointestinal symptoms, including diarrhea. L-Carnitine is a natural substance. There are potentially dangerous impure forms of carnitine available in various countries known as D,L-carnitine. Little is known about the safety of this substance, and at this point it is not recommended for human use.

**DOSAGE AND ADMINISTRATION**—Carnitine usually is administered orally or by intravenous infusion. Dosages used for treating deficiency conditions have ranged from 1 to 4 g daily in three divided doses.

**SOURCES**—Sigma Tau s.p.a., Vina Pontina Km. 30.400, 00040 Pomezia, Italy.

## Carticaine Hydrochloride (Carticain Hydrochloride)—Ultracain, Ultracain D-S, Ultracaine DS, Ultracaine DS Forte

**ACTIONS AND USES**—Carticaine hydrochloride is a local anesthetic used primarily in dentistry. It also has been used for infiltration anesthesia and nerve block in minor surgical procedures. In laboratory tests with animals, carticaine hydrochloride was found to be superior to prilocaine and procaine as a topical anesthetic but inferior to lidocaine and tetracaine. Carticaine hydrochloride is one of the more recently developed local anesthetics which are regarded as more stable and less likely to produce adverse effects than the older types, such as cocaine and procaine. Carticaine hydrochloride produces its effect by entering the nerve fiber to block conduction of the nerve impulse that would be perceived as pain. The anesthetic alters the normal electrochemical activity within the nerve cell and the electrical charge necessary to trigger release of the nerve impulse. The changes produced by the anesthetic include an increase in the threshold of stimulation needed to fire the pain impulse, a reduction in the rate of propagation of the impulse, and eventually a complete blockade of pain impulse conduction. When used as an infiltration anesthetic, carticaine hydrochloride directly blocks the nerve endings in the tissue area infiltrated by the drug. As a nerve block, carticaine hydrochloride infiltrates a main nerve trunk or a nerve plexus (network of nerves). In order to block conduction, a concentration of anesthetic that is many times the level that would theoretically be toxic must be built up around the nerve to be affected. The potent concentration around the nerve is necessary to ensure that an adequate amount of anesthetic passes through the nerve membrane. However, the higher the concentration, the greater the risk of side effects. The newer local anesthetics generally are more potent and require a smaller concentration to block nerve conduction.

**PRECAUTIONS**—Carticaine hydrochloride should not be administered to patients with a known hypersensitivity to local anesthetics of the amide group, which includes carticaine and some of the other newer anesthetics. It also should not be used in patients with severe shock or in patients with any degree of heart block, neurological disease, or severe hypertension. A local anesthetic should not be used when there are signs of infections near the proposed injection site. When carticaine is used with epinephrine, or adrenaline, caution is recommended because of effects of epinephrine on the patient's heart and blood pressure. Like other local anesthetics, carticaine hydrochloride is capable of producing methemoglobinemia, a condition in which hemoglobin molecules in the red blood cells are converted to a form that does not carry oxygen. This effect reportedly has occurred when carticaine hydrochloride has been used as an intravenous anesthetic but not when used in general dental procedures. Clinical signs of methemoglobinemia, such as cyanosis or bluish coloration of the lips and nail beds, can be reversed by intravenous administration of methylene blue. Resuscitative equipment and drugs should be readily available when any local anesthetic is used. Solutions containing epinephrine should be used with caution, if at all, in patients taking monoamine oxidase inhibitors or tricyclic antidepressants. The safety of carticaine hydrochloride in pregnancy has not been established, although animal studies have failed to demonstrate a birth defect risk.

**DOSAGE AND ADMINISTRATION**—Carticaine hydrochloride, including preparations with epinephrine, is supplied in injection cartridges. The dose used depends upon the area to be anesthetized, the blood vessel beds in the area, the number of nerve segments to be blocked, technique of anesthesia, and tolerance of the patient to the drug. The lowest dose needed to achieve effective anesthesia is recommended. The usual dose is calculated at 500 mcg to 2.5 mg per kg of body weight for infiltration anesthesia in adults. For nerve block, the usual recommended dose is 500 mcg to 3.6 mg per kg of body weight. For dental work, including oral surgery, the usual dose is 1.0 to 5.4 mg per kg of body weight. The maximum recommended dose for adults is 7 mg per kg of body weight, and for children the maximum is 5 mg per kg of body weight. The drug is not recommended for children under 4 years of age.

**SOURCES**—Hoechst Canada, Inc., 4045 Côte Vertu Blvd., Montreal, Quebec H4R 1R6, Canada; Hoechst Aktiengesellschaft, Bruningstrasse 45, Postfach 800320, 6230 Frankfurt (Main) 80, West Germany.

## **Cefuroxime Sodium**—Curoxim, Curoxime, Itorex, Kesint, Ultroxim, Zinacef

**ACTIONS AND USES**—Cefuroxime sodium is a cephalosporin-type antibiotic that is considered particularly useful in combating infections of gonorrhea and a species of bacteria, *Hemophilus influenzae*, that is the cause of influenzal meningitis, septicemia, conjunctivitis, and respiratory infections. (*H. influenzae* was so named when medical scientists believed it was the cause of influenza, a disease now known to be caused by a specific type of virus.) Cefuroxime also is highly active against other strains of bacteria that have developed resistance to penicillin. Cefuroxime is used to treat acute and chronic bronchitis, infected bronchiectasis, bacterial pneumonia, lung abscesses, pharyngitis, sinusitis, tonsillitis, cellulitis, erysipelas, peritonitis, cystitis, pyelonephritis, bacteriuria, osteomyelitis, and septic arthritis. The antibiotic also is used as a preventive measure in surgical procedures where there is a risk of infection and as a treatment for postoperative infections. Because cefuroxime is active against a wide range of bacteria, it often is administered in the treatment of infections before the infectious agent has been identified. Laboratory studies show cerfuroxime acts by penetrating the cell walls of bacteria, then interfering with the enzymes required to build new cell walls.

**PRECAUTIONS**—Cefuroxime sodium should not be administered to patients who have shown a sensitivity to cephalosporin antibiotics, and extreme caution should be used in giving cefuroxime to patients with a sensitivity or allergy to any drugs, particularly any antibiotic. The safety of cefuroxime in pregnant women, nursing mothers, and infants or children has not been established and use by patients in these categories should be avoided, or the drug should be administered with extreme caution. Caution also should be exercised in giving the product to patients with impaired kidney or liver function, or those using certain diuretics, such as furosemide. Prolonged use of cefuroxime may result in an overgrowth of infectious organisms that are not susceptible to the action of the antibiotic. Side effects include drowsiness, loose stools, faintness, palpitations, sweating, and skin rashes. Changes in blood chemistry have been observed, and local reactions at the site of injection, such as stiffness and inflammation, have been reported by patients.

**DOSAGE AND ADMINISTRATION**—Cefuroxime sodium is supplied in vials containing 250, 500, 750, and 1,500 mg of the drug for intramuscular or intravenous injection. The recommended dosage for treatment of gonorrhea is a single intramuscular injection of 1,500 mg. The usual dosage for mild to moderate infections is 750 mg every eight hours; for severe infections, the dosage may be increased to 1,500 mg every six hours. For short intravenous infusion of up to 30 minutes, a 1,500 mg dose of cefuroxime sodium can be dissolved in 50 ml of water.

Otherwise, the recommended proportions are 1 ml of water per 250 mg of the drug for intramuscular injection and at least 2 ml of water per 250 mg of cefuroxime sodium for intravenous injection. When administered to children, the recommended dosage is 30 to 100 mg per kg of body weight per day in three or four divided doses.

**SOURCES**—Laboratoires Glaxo, 43, rue Vineuse, 75764 Paris Cedex 16, France; Glaxo Laboratories Limited, Greenford, Middlesex UB6 OHE, England; Proter s.p.a., Via Lambro 38, 20090 Opera (Milano), Italy; Duncan Farmaceutici s.p.a., Via Fleming 2, 37100 Verona, Italy.

## Cephacetrile Sodium—Celospor

**ACTIONS AND USES**—Cephacetrile sodium is a semisynthetic antibiotic with a broad range of activity against various strains of bacteria. Its bactericidal effect is due to its ability to prevent bacteria from building their cell walls. Cephacetrile sodium is most effective against *Staphylococcus*, *Streptococcus*, and *Pneumococcus* and moderately active against a number of other strains of infectious agents. The drug is used in the treatment of infections of the respiratory tract, urogenital tract, skin and soft tissues, bones, and joints. The product also is used in treatment of bacterial endocarditis, an infection of the membrane lining the heart, and septicemia, an infection marked by the multiplication of disease microorganisms in the bloodstream. The drug is not active against certain strains of respiratory bacteria that produce influenzalike symptoms and affect mainly children.

**PRECAUTIONS**—The safety of cephacetrile sodium in pregnancy has not been established, although there have been no clinical reports of birth defects at this writing. The safety of the drug for use in infants also has not been established. Prolonged use of the drug may result in an overgrowth of infectious agents that are immune to its bactericidal effects. The drug should be used with caution in patients known to be sensitive to penicillin and other antibiotics and in patients with impaired liver or kidney function. Intramuscular injection of cephacetrile sodium can be painful, and intravenous injection may result in phlebitis (vein inflammation) or thrombosis (clot formation). Otherwise, the drug reportedly is well tolerated. Side effects have included headache, skin rashes, drug fever, dizziness, blurred vision, and blood changes. The drug should not be used in the treatment of meningeal infections because it does not penetrate the cerebrospinal fluid in concentrations great enough to be effective.

**DOSAGE AND ADMINISTRATION**—Cephacetrile is supplied in 15 and 50 mg vials of powder, containing 1 and 4 g respectively of the product for use in intravenous injection. For intramuscular injection, cephacetrile sodium is supplied as the powder with a 2 percent solution of lignocaine hydrochloride; the concentrations are 32 mg/1.5 ml and 53 mg/1.5 ml. The total daily dosage should be divided into two to six doses. For adults, the recommended dosage is 500 mg to 1 g every four to six hours for mild infections and 1.5 to 2 g every four hours for severe infections, with a maximum of 12 g daily. For children, the dosage is calculated at 50 to 75 mg/kg of body weight daily for mild to moderate infections and 75 to 100 mg/kg of body weight for severe infections. For children under 6 years of age, the intramuscular dose should not be used with lignocaine hydrochloride. And the total daily dose should never exceed the amount administered to an adult suffering from an infection of similar severity.

**SOURCES**—Ciba/Geigy Australia Ltd., 14 Orion Road, Lane Cove, N.S.W. 2066, Australia; Ciba-Geigy AG, Schwartzwaldallee 215, 4058 Basel, Switzerland.

## Cetrimide—Ceanel Concentrate, Cetavlex, Cetavlon, Cetridal, Dermanatal, Morpan CHSA, Savloclens, Savlodil, Savlon, Silquat C100, Solufen, Travasept 100, Vesagex

**ACTIONS AND USES**—Cetrimide is a type of disinfectant that breaks down in water to produce emulsifying, detergent, and bactericidal actions. The product is employed in cleansing and descaling skin surfaces in cases of seborrheic capitis and dermatitis (dandruff) or psoriasis, for cleansing and disinfecting burns and wounds, and for cleansing the skin before procedures such as taking of blood samples. Cetrimide has greater bactericidal activity against gram-positive organisms than gram-negative organisms and is relatively ineffective against viruses, fungi, acid-fast bacteria, and bacterial spores. Cetrimide is not compatible with chemicals in ordinary soaps, and the skin should be free of soap residues before cetrimide is applied. The effectiveness of cetrimide also is reduced by the presence of iodine, alkali hydroxides, and certain soaps and detergents on the skin.

**PRECAUTIONS**—Cetrimide should not be allowed to contact the eyes and should not be allowed to enter any of the body cavities. Skin irritation may develop in hypersensitive individuals or as a result of prolonged use of the product. Necrosis of the skin surfaces can result from the use of occlusive dressings over cetrimide applications. Accidental ingestion of cetrimide results in nausea and vomiting, and strong solutions of the product can cause permanent tissue damage, depression of the central nervous system, and paralysis of the respiratory muscles. Emergency procedures for accidental ingestion include treatment of shock and difficult breathing, control of convulsions, and administration of milk, egg white, or other appropriate substances. At concentrations usually recommended for administration to skin surfaces, reactions to external use are relatively unusual, although hypersensitivity can result from repeated applications.

**DOSAGE AND ADMINISTRATION**—Cetrimide is supplied as creams, ointments, paints, solutions, and waxes. Concentrations vary from a 0.1 percent solution for burns and wounds to 3.0 percent or more for dandruff shampoos and treatment of psoriasis or other skin disorders.

**SOURCES**—Rivopharm SA, Rivopharm Building, 6911 Manno, Lugano, Switzerland; Imperial Chemical Industries Ltd., Pharmaceuticals Division, Alderley Park, Macclesfield, Cheshire SK10 4TG, England.

## Chenodiol (Chenic Acid, Chenodeoxycholic Acid, CDC)—Carbicolina, Chelobil, Chemicolina, Chendal, Chendol, Chenix, Cheno-Caps, Chenodecil, Chenodex, Chenofalk, Chenolith, Chenomas, Chenossil, Cholanorm, Fluibil, Hekbilin, Hepanem, Kebilis, Quenobilan, Ulmenid

**ACTIONS AND USES**—Chenodiol is a naturally occurring bile acid that is used to dissolve cholesterol gallstones in patients with a functioning gallbladder. Because of the minute amounts available from natural animal sources, the drug is manufactured synthetically from the more abundant cholic acid, also present in animal bile. Chenodiol is not effective against gallstones in which a main component is calcium or other noncholesterol substances. And it is not effective in patients who lack a functioning gallbladder. The product also has been used in the treatment of hyperlipidemia (excess fats in the blood), rheumatoid arthritis, and migraine headaches.

**PRECAUTIONS**—Chenodiol should not be used in cases in which gallstones are calcified, pigmented, or otherwise appear opaque on x-ray film. The product is not recommended for women of childbearing age and should not be administered to pregnant women because of the risk of causing liver damage in the offspring. The physician should carefully monitor the use of chenodiol in women taking hormonal contraceptives, which may retard the dissolution of gallstones. The product should not be given to patients with chronic liver disease, inflammatory diseases of the intestinal tract, or an inflamed or nonfunctioning gallbladder. It is not recommended for nursing mothers unless the expected benefits outweigh the possible risk that the drug will be transmitted in breast milk. The product should be used with caution in patients with peptic ulcers or those who may be allergic to the color additive tartrazine used in some chenodiol capsules. Adverse effects are generally limited to diarrhea, which usually can be controlled by reducing the dosage for a few days, and pruritus.

**DOSAGE AND ADMINISTRATION**—Chenodiol is supplied in 125 and 250 mg capsules. Dosage usually is calculated at about 15 mg per day per kg of body weight, although individual dosages may range from 10 to 20 mg per kg of body weight. Obese patients may not respond to the normal adult dosage. It is recommended that the medication be taken in three to four divided doses, and taken with meals. The duration of the treatment is related to the size of the gallstone, or stones, but may range from six months to two years. Some authorities recommend continuing the chenodiol treatment for three months after the stones have been dissolved.

**SOURCES**—Weddel Pharmaceuticals Limited, Weddel House, 14 West Smithfield, London EC1A 9HY, England; Armour Pharmaceutical Company Limited, Hampden Park, Eastbourne, East Sussex BN22 9AG, England.

**Choline Bitartrate (Choline Acid Tartrate)**—Colyne, Sulfarlem-Choline

**ACTIONS AND USES**—Choline bitartrate is a form of the essential nutritional factor choline and is used to prevent fatty infiltration of the liver and as a preventive and therapeutic agent for cirrhosis of the liver and other kinds of hepatic degeneration. Choline compounds, chemically related to the neurotransmitter acetylcholine, have also been used, with varying results, in the treatment of a number of disorders associated with cholinergic activity of the nervous system, such as ataxia, tardive dyskinesia, Alzheimer's disease, and Huntington's chorea.

**PRECAUTIONS**—Most side effects have involved gastrointestinal complaints and have included softening of the stools, incontinence or exacerbation of incontinence, nausea, vomiting, and diarrhea. Some cases of depression or increased depression have been reported among patients using choline bitartrate. In many instances, adverse side effects followed intakes of larger than recommended doses of the product.

**DOSAGE AND ADMINISTRATION**—Choline bitartrate is supplied in 300 mg tablets. The usual recommended adult dose is two to four tablets taken orally before each meal.

**SOURCE**—Herdt & Charton (1971) Inc., 9393 Louis-H. Lafontaine, Montreal, Quebec H1J 1Y8, Canada.

**Citicoline (Cytidine Diphosphate Choline)**—Brassel, Cereb, Cidifos, Cidilin, Colite, Corenalin, Cyscholin, Difosfocin, Ensign, Neucolis, Nicholin, Recognan, Rexort, Sinkron, Suncholin

**ACTIONS AND USES**—Citicoline is a brain circulation stimulator used to treat disturbances of consciousness that may follow brain surgery or a brain injury. Citicoline also is used to correct mental disturbances and motor nerve dysfunction caused by acute or chronic stages of cerebrovascular diseases and is used with levodopa or other drugs to treat parkinsonism. Citicoline is derived from choline, a constituent of lecithin, and cytidine, a component of ribonucleic acid (RNA) which is involved in the synthesis of proteins in all living cells. It is believed to increase blood flow and oxygen use in brain tissues. Citicoline has been identified by some authorities as a coenzyme. It has been used in the treatment of depression, particularly involutional melancholia, and senile dementia.

**PRECAUTIONS**—Caution should be used in administering citicoline in cases of acute or severe disturbances of consciousness, such as coma or intracranial hemorrhage. Brain-pressure-reducing agents or antihemorrhagic medications should be given concomitantly and the body temperature maintained at a low level. Side effects may include a skin rash, indicating hypersensitivity to the product; insomnia; headache; dizziness; agitation; and muscle spasms. Other possible adverse effects include nausea; loss of appetite; a feeling of warmth, lassitude, and temporary fluctuations in blood pressure. Hypotension may be associated with rapid intravenous administration of the drug.

**DOSAGE AND ADMINISTRATION**—Citicoline is supplied in 2 ml injection ampules containing either 100 or 250 mg of citicoline. The recommended dosage for disturbances of consciousness after brain injury or brain surgery is 500 mg given once or twice a day by intravenous drip or intravenous or intramuscular injection. For Parkinson's disease, the usual procedure is the administration of a single 500 mg dose intravenously or intramuscularly together with drugs that block nerve impulses of the parasympathetic system. The usual dosage for mental disorders and motor nerve disturbances associated with cerebrovascular diseases is 500 mg given once or twice daily by intravenous or intramuscular injection.

**SOURCES**—Laboratoires Cassenne-Takeda, 3, square Desaix, 75015 Paris, France; Takeda Chemical Industries, Ltd., 27, Doshomachi 2-chome, Higashi-ku, Osaka, Japan; Laboratorio Magis Farmaceutici, Viale Europa 36, 25100 Bescia, Italy; Laboratorios Takeda de Mexico, S.A. de C.V., Calz. de Tlalpan No. 1924, Mexico 21, D.F., Mexico.

## Clobetasol Propionate—Butavat, Clobesol, Dermadex, Dermatovate, Dermoval, Dermovat, Dermovate, Dermoxin, Dermoxinal, Psorex

**ACTIONS AND USES**—Clobetasol propionate is a very potent corticosteroid used in the treatment of inflammatory skin disorders that fail to respond to less potent medications. It is employed in the treatment of severe eczema, contact dermatitis, lichen simplex and lichen planus eruptions, psoriasis, discoid lupus erythematosus, and hyperkeratosis. Clobetasol is a white to cream-colored crystalline powder that is prepared as a cream, ointment, or lotion for application to the skin or scalp. Clobetasol is a class I topical corticosteroid, which ranks it as the most potent of the corticosteroid drugs available for use on body surfaces. Like other topical corticosteroids, clobetasol propionate acts by suppressing the manifestations of the disease.

**PRECAUTIONS**—Class I corticosteroids require more caution than preparations that are less potent because they are more likely to be a source of adverse effects. The use of clobetasol propionate products should be limited to a total of 50 g or 50 ml or less per week. Clinical studies have indicated that application of more than 50 g of clobetasol propionate per week can result in signs of adrenal hormone suppression; patients who have used over 100 g per week showed profound suppression signs and withdrawal symptoms of adrenocortical insufficiency when use of the drug was discontinued. Physicians should be advised of any previous use of corticosteroids by the patient. Animal experiments have shown that topical corticosteroids can result in birth defects. While the significance of the studies in human terms has not been established, caution should be exercised in the use of clobetasol propionate during pregnancy; and its use, when deemed necessary, should be limited in amounts and length of therapy. Long-term use of clobetasol propionate in infants and children should be avoided and the therapy reviewed weekly. The product should not be used in the eye, and applications to lesions near the eye should be handled with extreme care. Clobetasol propionate should not be used in the presence of skin lesions caused by infection with viruses (such as herpes simplex or chickenpox), bacteria (such as impetigo), or fungal or tuberculous agents, if appropriate antimicrobial therapy, such as antibiotics, has not been used. Because the drug may be absorbed through the skin and be transmitted to breast milk, clobetasol propionate should not be used by nursing mothers. Prolonged treatment with potent corticosteroid medications for skin disorders can result in skin atrophy, marked by streaks; thinning of the skin; dilation of blood vessels beneath the skin; and other irreversible effects. The atrophic changes are most likely to occur in the facial skin.

The product should not be applied to skin areas in which there are lesions of acne, rosacea, or perioral (around the mouth) dermatitis. Adverse reactions may include local burning, irritation, itching, skin pigmentation changes, secondary infections, abnormal hair growth, and suppression of adrenal gland functions. Occlusive dressings that fit tightly over the treated area so as to prevent air from reaching the medicated skin can increase the effect of the corticosteroid. However, such dressings should be limited to highly resistant lesions and used for short time periods, such as overnight. Occlusive dressings increase the risk of side effects and also encourage the development of bacterial infections. In treating infants, it should be noted that a baby's diaper has the effect of an occlusive dressing.

**DOSAGE AND ADMINISTRATION**—Clobetasol propionate creams and ointments are supplied in 15, 25, 50, and 100 g tubes and jars. A scalp lotion is supplied in 20, 25, 60, and 100 ml bottles. The products are applied thinly to cover the affected area and rubbed gently into the skin two to three times daily. If continuous treatment is needed, the patient should change to a less potent corticosteroid preparation.

**SOURCES**—Glaxo Laboratories, 1025 The Queensway, Toronto, Ontario M8Z 5S6, Canada; Glaxo Laboratories, Ltd., Greenford, Middx UB6 OHE, England; Laboratoires Glaxo, 43, rue Vineuse, 75764 Paris Cedex, France.

## Clobetasone Butyrate—Emovat, Emovate, Eumovate, Molivate, Trimovate

**ACTIONS AND USES**—Clobetasone butyrate is a synthetic corticosteroid applied as a cream or an ointment in the treatment of various skin diseases. It is used in the treatment of eczema, seborrheic dermatitis, and the milder forms of steroid-responsive skin disorders, such as sunburn. Clobetasone butyrate is a class II topical corticosteroid, being moderately potent and many times more active than hydrocortisone, one of the early corticosteroid drugs still in use as a mild medication for certain skin disorders. However, clobetasone butyrate is less active than betamethasone and less likely than the more potent corticosteroids to produce adverse effects. Clinical studies indicate that clobetasone butyrate use results in less risk of skin atrophy than the more active corticosteroids. Clobetasone is recommended by some authorities as a maintenance drug to be used as therapy between courses of one of the more active topical steroids. Clobetasone butyrate acts by suppressing the manifestations of inflammatory skin conditions. Clobetasone also has a vasoconstrictive action (an ability to constrict blood vessels), although it is less vasoconstrictive than betamethasone.

**PRECAUTIONS**—The safety of topical corticosteroids during pregnancy and lactation has not been established. Therefore, they should not be used during those periods. Clobetasone butyrate also should not be used when there are infected skin lesions if an antiinfective medication is not used simultaneously. In addition to bacterial infections, clobetasone butyrate should not be applied in the presence of tuberculous skin lesions; infections caused by fungi, such as candidiasis or moniliasis; or viral infections, including herpes simplex, vaccinia or cowpox, or chickenpox. Clobetasone butyrate should not be used in the eyes and should be applied with extreme caution to lesions near the eyes. Although clobetasone butyrate is a mild topical corticosteroid, such drugs can be absorbed through the skin to cause impaired carbohydrate metabolism and suppression of normal corticosteroid production by the body's hormonal system. Abrupt withdrawal of corticosteroid medications after extensive use can result in acute adrenal insufficiency, and full recovery of the body's hypothalamic-pituitary-adrenal hormone system can require several months. Prolonged use of corticosteroids also may cause atrophy of the skin and subcutaneous tissues, particularly on the face and surfaces around joints. If skin does atrophy—characterized by thinning of the skin, appearance of streaks and purplish discoloration—use of the product should be discontinued. Patients should advise physicians of any prior use of corticosteroid medications and of any hypersensitivity to such drugs. Clobetasone should be used with caution in patients with stasis dermatitis or other skin diseases associated with impaired circulation. Local burning, itching, irritation, secondary infections, dryness of the skin, and changes in pigmentation are among the more common side effects of topical corticosteroid use. Extreme caution should be exercised in using occlusive dressings, such as plastic sheeting, which prevent air circulation around the lesions being treated. Although the dressing may enhance the activity of the corticosteroid in suppressing inflammation, it also increases the risk of side effects, including suppression of adrenal hormone production. If symptomatic response is not noted within a few days to a week, local applications of corticosteroids should be discontinued.

**DOSAGE AND ADMINISTRATION**—Clobetasone creams and ointments are supplied in 15, 25, 30, and 100 g tubes. A special preparation of drops for use in treating inflammations of the external eye surfaces also is available in 5 and 10 ml bottles. The creams and ointments are spread thinly over the affected area and rubbed gently into the skin two or three times daily. Care should be exercised in applying the product around areas of raw or broken skin, where absorption into the deep body tissues may be enhanced. The maximum adult dosage recommended is 100 g of cream or ointment per week.

**SOURCES**—Glaxo Laboratories, 1025 The Queensway, Toronto, Ontario M8Z 5S6, Canada; Glaxo Laboratories, Ltd., Greenford, Middx, UB6 OHE, England.

## Clofazimine—Lampren, Lamprene

**ACTIONS AND USES**—Clofazimine is used in the treatment of leprosy, particularly in patients infected with strains of the organism *Mycobacterium leprae* that are resistant to therapy with sulfone medications. Clofazimine also is used to treat lepra (reversal) reactions that occur in most forms of leprosy when a patient's immune system suddenly reacts against the infection and may change the leprotic lesion into dead tissue or an ulceration. Clofazimine is used in Australia, Africa, and Mexico for the treatment of Buruli ulcers, which are skin infections caused by the microorganism *Mycobacterium ulcerans*. Clofazimine usually is administered in association with other antileprosy drugs. The product has been used in the treatment of American leishmaniasis (a parasitic disorder caused by sand flies), psoriasis, vitiligo, discoid lupus erythematosus, a tropical yeast infection of the skin called keloidal blastomycosis, and a skin ulcer condition known as pyoderma gangrenosum. The drug was found to be less effective in the treatment of an atypical form of pulmonary tuberculosis. Like the antileprosy drug dapsone, clofazimine damages or destroys the leprosy bacterium, but clofazimine is less likely than dapsone to cause inflammatory reactions.

**PRECAUTIONS**—The active ingredient of clofazimine crosses the placental barrier, and the drug therefore should not be used during pregnancy unless the potential benefits outweigh the risks. When clofazimine is administered during pregnancy, newborn infants may show some discoloration. Clofazimine may also cause discoloration of breast milk and cause red to brown discoloration of skin areas exposed to sunlight, particularly in light-skinned patients. A deeper discoloration usually occurs in areas of leprotic lesions. Discoloration also may appear in the patient's urine and in the corneas of the eyes. The discoloration is due to a dye effect of the drug and gradually disappears after the drug has been discontinued. Other side effects include abdominal pain, diarrhea, dry and scaling skin, nausea, and loss of appetite. The drug should be used with caution in patients with impaired kidney or liver function, and periodic tests of function are recommended for such patients. Daily doses of 300 mg or more should not be administered in treatment courses of more than three months.

**DOSAGE AND ADMINISTRATION**—Clofazimine is supplied in 100 mg capsules. Dosages should be adjusted to the patient's body weight and the severity of the leprotic infection. For the prevention of resistance to sulfone drugs, such as dapsone, the usual dosage is 50 to 100 mg of clofazimine daily or three times weekly during the first four to six months of long-term therapy with sulfones. For cases resistant to sulfones, the usual dosage of clofazimine is 100 mg daily for two to three months, combined with rifampicin, an antibiotic used primarily in the treatment of tuberculosis. For lepra reactions, clofazimine is administered in doses of up to 300 mg daily for up to three months, but the dosage is lowered gradually when the reaction subsides. It is recommended that clofazimine capsules be taken with meals or with milk.

**SOURCES**—Geigy Pharmaceuticals, Wimblehurst Road, Horsham, West Sussex RH12 4AB, England; Ciba-Geigy Australia Ltd., P.O. Box 76, Lane Cove, N.S.W. 2066, Australia.

**Clomethiazole (Chlormethiazole Edisylate, S.C.T.Z.)**—Distraneurin, Distraneurine, Hemineurin, Hemineurine, Heminevrin

**ACTIONS AND USES**—Clomethiazole is a drug used as a sedative, a tranquilizer, and an anticonvulsant. It has been used as a hypnotic for elderly patients and in the treatment of insomnia, agitation, and acute alcohol withdrawal. As an anticonvulsant, clomethiazole has been found effective in the treatment of status epilepticus, preeclamptic toxemia of pregnancy, and the delirium tremens of alcoholism. Other uses include the control of involuntary muscular movements in hemiballismus, as an anesthestic, in the treatment of withdrawal from narcotics, in the treatment of the manic phase of manic-depressive psychosis, to reduce sleep disturbances in the elderly, and to treat geriatric psychosis symptoms of restlessness and confusion. The action of clomethiazole is similar to that of nitrazepam, a commonly used sedative and hypnotic, but clomethiazole reportedly has fewer and milder side effects, the doses are lower, and there are fewer patient categories of special risk.

**PRECAUTIONS**—Clomethiazole can interact with other depressant drugs, including alcohol, to produce an increased effect of intoxication. When used in an intravenous infusion, the patient should be monitored closely to prevent accidental overdosage, resulting in deep unconsciousness with the risk of respiratory depression and circulatory collapse, or mechanical airway obstruction during deep sleep. Side effects from oral doses have included gastrointestinal complaints. Some patients have experienced headaches, tingling in the nose and sneezing, irritation of the conjunctival membranes about the eye, and increased salivation after taking clomethiazole. Intravenous injections of the drug at a rapid rate can produce a sudden drop in blood pressure. Caution should be exercised in administering clomethiazole to alcoholic patients, who may have impaired liver function. Some caution also should be used in giving the drug to patients who may be addiction-prone, particularly outpatients. All patients should be advised that driving motor vehicles or operating machinery can be dangerous while using the product.

**DOSAGE AND ADMINISTRATION**—Clomethiazole is supplied in capsules, a syrup, and intravenous infusion vials. The capsules contain 192 mg of clomethiazole and the syrup 50 mg of the product per ml. One capsule is equivalent to 5 ml of syrup in terms of therapeutic effect. The recommended dosage for nighttime sedation is 2 capsules or 10 ml of syrup at night; for daytime sedation, 1 capsule or 5 ml of syrup three times daily. The recommended dosage for alcohol or drug withdrawal is 3 capsules or 15 ml of syrup every 6 hours for the first 2 days, followed by 2 capsules or 10 ml of syrup every 6 hours for days 3 to

5, and 1 capsule or 5 ml of syrup every 6 hours for days 6 through 9. Administration beyond day 9 is not recommended. The treatment for delirium tremens, status epilepticus, or toxemia of pregnancy requires injection or infusion of clomethiazole in an 0.8 percent solution. For delirium tremens and status epilepticus, the initial drip rate is 180 to 450 ml per hour, until shallow sleep is induced, after which the rate is reduced to 30 to 60 ml per hour, or the lowest possible rate required to achieve shallow sleep with good spontaneous breathing. For preeclamptic toxemia, the intravenous dosage usually recommended is 30 to 50 ml at a rate of 60 drops per minute until the patient feels drowsy, after which the rate is reduced to 10 or 15 drops per minute, depending upon the patient response.

**SOURCES**—Astra Pharmaceuticals Limited, St. Peter's House, 2 Bricket Road, St. Albans, Herts AL1 3JW, England; Astra Läkemedel AB, Strängnäsvägen 44, Södertälje, Sweden.

## Clomipramine Hydrochloride (Chlorimipramine Hydrochloride, Monochlorimipramine)—Anafranil

**ACTIONS AND USES**—Clomipramine hydrochloride is an antidepressant that is similar to amitriptyline, a widely used antidepressant. In the treatment of depression, clomipramine has been employed in cases of manic-depressive psychosis, involutional depression, periodic depression, reactive depression, neurotic depression, and all forms of endogenous depression. The drug also has been used in the treatment of anorexia nervosa, narcolepsy (and cataplexy associated with narcolepsy), obsessive states, pain, phobias, and premature ejaculation. Clomiprimine, like amitriptyline, is classed as a tricyclic antidepressant, so named because the chemical molecules of such drugs appear in structural formulas as three adjacent benzene rings. The tricyclic antidepressants act by interfering with the removal of two nerve-impulse transmitter substances, norepinephrine and serotonin, at nerve endings of segments of the autonomic nervous system. By preventing the natural removal of the nerve transmitter substances after they have been released, the tricyclic antidepressants create a condition at the nerve synapses that is approximately the same as if excessive amounts of nerve transmitter chemicals were being produced and released. For patients susceptible to depression, it is believed their nervous systems produce inadequate amounts of certain vital nerve transmitter substances, which accounts for their illness.

**PRECAUTIONS**—Clomipramine hydrochloride should not be given to patients suffering from severe liver disease, urinary retention, or recent myocardial infarction, heart failure, heart block, or heart arrhythmias. Use should also be avoided by patients with narrow-angle, or acute, glaucoma, or those using monoamine oxidase inhibitors. Clomipramine and monoamine oxidase inhibitors should not be used at the same time or within 14 days of each other. Clomipramine should be avoided by women during pregnancy, particularly during the first and third trimesters. The drug may result in ejaculatory disorders or impotence in men and orgasmic impotence in women. Elderly patients are particularly susceptible to such side effects as agitation, confusion, and a drop in blood pressure when arising from a sitting or reclining position. Caution should be observed in giving clomipramine to patients with an enlarged prostate, potential suicidal personalities, or nursing mothers. Because the full effects of clomipramine may not be observed during the first few weeks of treatment, the patients should be monitored closely during that period. Patients should be advised that alertness may be impaired by the drug, making it hazardous to operate motor vehicles or machinery. Clomipramine may interact with barbiturates, methylphenidate, clonidine, methyldopa, and other drugs administered for hypertension or nervous system disorders. Clomipramine also may increase the effects of alcohol and interact with anesthetics used in surgery. Common side effects of tricyclic antidepressants in general include dry mouth, blurred vision, rapid heartbeat, nausea, constipation, drowsiness, sweating, tremors, tingling or prickling sensations, skin rashes, blood pressure changes, and some difficulty in urinating. Sweating, insomnia, and irritability may occur as withdrawal symptoms.

**DOSAGE AND ADMINISTRATION**—Clomipramine hydrochloride is supplied in capsules containing 10, 25, and 50 mg of the drug, 2 and 8 ml injection ampules providing 12.5 mg per ml, and a syrup containing 5 mg per ml. The usual recommended adult dosage is 10 mg per day initially, with gradual increases to 30 or as much as 150 mg per day, if required. The drug may be taken in divided doses or a single dose at bedtime. The recommended maximum daily dose for patients over 60 years of age is 75 mg. For severe cases of depression, intramuscular injection of up to six 25 mg ampules a day may be administered. For intravenous infusion, the recommended initial dosage is 25 or 50 mg diluted to 200 to 500 ml of fluid to be infused over a period of two hours to assess patient tolerance. The intravenous therapy generally is used for a period of a week or more until acutely depressed patients can gradually change over to oral therapy. A dosage for children has not been established.

**SOURCE**—Geigy Pharmaceuticals, Horsham, West Sussex RH12 4AB, England; Geigy Pharmaceuticals, Division of Ciba-Geigy Canada Ltd., 6860 Century Ave., Mississauga, Ontario L5N 2W5, Canada.

## **Clopamide**—Brinaldix, Brinaldix K, Brinerdina, Brinerdine, Viskaldix

**ACTIONS AND USES**—Clopamide is a diuretic used in the treatment of hypertension and edema associated with disorders of the heart, kidney, or liver. It is recommended by some authorities for long-term management of hypertension. Clopamide is related chemically to thiazide diuretics and has actions similar to those of chlorothiazide, which inhibits the reabsorption of sodium and chloride ions in the kidney tubules so their excretion rate is increased and, as a result, water loss through the kidneys also is increased. Potassium loss also is increased by the effects of the diuretics, and some clopamide preparations contain potassium salts to compensate for the loss of the vital mineral. The onset of the diuretic effect of clopamide usually occurs within two hours after oral administration of the drug, and the effect lasts up to 24 hours. Clopamide is reported to have diuretic and sodium-excreting activity that is 25 to 50 percent greater than chlorothiazide and bendrofluazide. Clopamide has been used in the treatment of congestive heart failure and hyperammonemia (a severe liver disease marked by high blood levels of ammonia), in addition to its applications in hypertension therapy.

**PRECAUTIONS**—Clopamide should not be given to patients with a known sensitivity to sulfonamide drugs or to patients with impaired liver or kidney function, especially those with glomerulonephritis, a usually inflammatory kidney disease. Caution should be used in administration of clopamide to patients with diabetes and high uric acid levels or other gout symptoms. Patients receiving clopamide should be monitored periodically for signs of hypokalemia, indicating an excessive loss of potassium with symptoms of weakness, muscle cramps, drowsiness, gastrointestinal distention, or heart arrhythmias. Hypokalemia may be aggravated in patients with cirrhosis of the liver or in individuals on a diet that severely restricts sodium. Patients also receiving digitalis therapy may show an increased sensitivity to the heart medication when blood levels of potassium are abnormally low. Use of clopamide is not recommended during the first three months of pregnancy, and breast feeding should be suspended by nursing mothers while they are using clopamide. Side effects reported by patients using clopamide include nausea, headache, and skin rash. Clopamide may interact with other antihypertensive medications and with calcium blockers, such as verapamil, and drugs containing lithium.

**DOSAGE AND ADMINISTRATION**—Clopamide is supplied in 20 mg tablets and in 5 mg doses in preparations also containing reserpine and dihydroergocristine (which also have antihypertensive effects), as well as in tablets containing 20 mg of clopamide plus potassium salts. The usual recommended dosage for treatment of hypertension is 20 to 40 mg taken daily with breakfast. The recommended initial dosage for edema is 40 to 60 mg per day, taken with breakfast, followed by 20 or 40 mg taken on consecutive days or on an intermittent basis according to the response of the patient. The maximum recommended dose of clopamide is 80 mg per day.

**SOURCES**—Sandoz Products (Ireland) Ltd., Airton Road, Tallaght, Co. Dublin, Ireland; Sandoz de Mexico, S.A. de C.V., Amores No. 1322, Mexico 12, D.F., Mexico.

## Cobalt Edetate (Cobalt EDTA, Dicobalt Edeate)—Kelocyanor

**ACTIONS AND USES**—Cobalt edetate is used in the treatment of cyanide poisoning. While both cyanide and cobalt are toxic, the substances combine to form chemical complexes that reduce the poisonous effects of each. Cobalt edetate is recommended for use only in severe cases of cyanide poisoning; otherwise the patient may experience the toxic effects of cobalt due to the lack of cyanide ions for forming stable complexes. The use of cobalt edetate, therefore, requires an accurate diagnosis by the examining physician. It has been determined that the ratio of cobalt edetate to hydrocyanic acid required to neutralize the two toxic substances is 8:1, so that a measured amount of the cobalt compound will inactivate one-eighth of its weight of hydrocyanic acid.

**PRECAUTIONS**—Cobalt edetate should not be used except in cases of a confirmed diagnosis of cyanide poisoning. Administration of the drug should be done in a hospital setting where oxygen and resuscitative equipment are available, as well as qualified personnel for handling the equipment. Speed in diagnosis and treatment is important. Caution must be used in estimating the appropriate dosage of cobalt edetate. An overdosage may result in an anaphylactic reaction marked by acute shock, falling blood pressure, heart irregularities, breathing difficulty, pain, collapse, laryngeal and facial edema, and urticaria (hives). Side effects of cobalt edetate include similar signs and symptoms, such as a drop in blood pressure, vomiting, and rapid heartbeat.

**DOSAGE AND ADMINISTRATION**—Cobalt edetate is supplied in 20 ml ampules containing 300 mg of the product. It is recommended that intravenous injection of one 300 mg ampule be given at a steady rate over a period of one minute, followed immediately by the injection of 50 ml of a dextrose solution, using the same needle. If the response to the first injection is not adequate, it is recommended that the same procedure be repeated, with injection of a second ampule of cobalt edetate followed by 50 ml of dextrose solution. If a second ampule fails to produce a response after five minutes, it is recommended that a third injection be given. The side effects noted previously may follow the initial injection, but recovery should follow in about one minute.

**SOURCES**—Rona Laboratories Ltd., Caldwell Lane, Hitchin, Hertfordshire SG4 OSF, England; Laboratoires Laroche Navarron, 20, rue Jean-Jaures, 92800 Puteaux, France.

**Cyclofenil**—Ciclifen, Fertodur, Gyneuro, Ondogyne, Ondonid, Rehibin, Sanocrisin, Sexadieno, Sexovid

**ACTIONS AND USES**—Cyclofenil is a gonad-stimulating agent that is used primarily in the treatment of infertility. The drug also is used to treat amenorrhea, menopausal disorders, premenstrual syndrome, oligomenorrhea (scanty menstruation), functional sterility, and menstrual cycle disorders due to long-term use of oral contraceptives. The drug has been used in the treatment of scleroderma, characterized by a thickening and swelling of the fibrous tissues of the skin. Cyclofenil is similar to clomiphene citrate, another drug sometimes used to treat infertility, although it may be less effective in some patients.

**PRECAUTIONS**—The drug should not be used in patients with acute or chronic liver disorders because of a risk of jaundice from impaired bile flow. Hot flushes, ovarian enlargement, and gastrointestinal disorders have been reported as side effects. Other side effects may include headaches, loss of appetite, and nausea.

**DOSAGE AND ADMINISTRATION**—Cyclofenil is supplied in 100 and 200 mg tablets. The usual recommended therapy is 100 mg twice a day for three menstrual cycles, or three months if cycles are irregular. If regular cycles are not established at that time, the dosage is increased to 200 mg twice daily for 10 days, followed by 20 treatment-free days, for the next three months.

**SOURCES**—Laboratorios Promeco de Mexico, S.A. de C.V., Calle del Maiz No. 49, Mexico 23, D.F., Mexico; Schering Mexicana, S.A., Calz. Mexico Xochimilco No. 5019, Mexico 22, D.F., Mexico; Thames Laboratories Ltd., Thames Building, 206 Upper Richmond Rd. West, London SW14 8AH, England; AB Ferrosan, Box 839, 201 80 Malmö, Sweden.

**Debrisoquine Sulfate (Isocaramidine)**—Declinax, Equitonil, Tendor

**ACTIONS AND USES**—Debrisoquine sulfate is an antihypertensive drug used in the treatment of moderate to severe cases and in mild hypertension cases that have failed to respond to other medications. The product apparently is selective in effects on patients who have inherited a sensitivity to debrisoquine, and patients who possess an enzyme for metabolizing the substance may show no response to doses that produce a significant effect in patients who lack the inherited enzyme. It has a more significant effect in reducing blood pressure while the patient is standing rather than reclining. Debrisoquine acts by blocking the transmission of nerve impulses responsible for increasing the resistance to blood flow in peripheral areas of the body. Debrisoquine is similar in actions to guanethidine medications for hypertension, but it lacks the effect of guanethidine in depleting norepinephrine, a nerve impulse transmitter, in body tissues.

**PRECAUTIONS**—Debrisoquine should not be given to patients with a pheochromocytoma, an adrenal system tumor. Caution should be used in giving the drug to patients with impaired kidney function, to patients also taking tricyclic antidepressant drugs, which may inhibit the activity of debrisoquine, or to patients using levodopa, a drug often used in Parkinson's disease. Because patients using antihypertensive drugs may have lower blood pressure in a warm environment, dosage may need to be adjusted during summer months or when the patient lives in a hot climate. The drug should not be used concurrently with monoamine oxidase inhibitors. Patients with severe impairment of coronary or cerebral circulation may be hypersensitive to the profound blood pressure changes that may be produced by debrisoquine. Patients should be monitored periodically and instructed regarding steps to take if they experience dizzy spells that may lead to loss of consciousness. Patients who have a history of episodes of syncope (fainting or swooning) should not use debrisoquine. The safety of debrisoquine in pregnancy has not been established, and therefore the drug is not recommended for women of childbearing potential. The product also is not recommended for use in children.

**DOSAGE AND ADMINISTRATION**—Debrisoquine sulfate is supplied in 10 and 20 mg tablets. The usual recommended dosage for mild to moderate hypertension is 10 to 20 mg per day in divided doses. The dosage can be increased by 10 mg per day after an interval of three days, if necessary. For severe hypertension, the recommended initial dosage is 20 to 40 mg per day with gradual increases of 10 to 20 mg per day every three or four days up to a maximum of 120 mg per day. Blood pressure should be monitored closely, and patients should not attempt to get out of bed or rise suddenly from a reclining to a standing position without assistance while making a dosage adjustment. The patient also should not increase the dosage without supervision of the attending physician. Special care is required in helping the patient make the transition from diuretics to debrisoquine.

**SOURCES**—Hoffmann-LaRoche Ltd., 100, boulevard Roche, Vandreuil, Quebec J7V 6B3, Canada; Roche Products Ltd., P.O. Box 8, Welwyn Garden City, Hertfordshire AL7 3AY, England.

## Diamthazole Hydrochloride (Amycazolum, Diamzole Hydrochloride)—Asterol, Atelor

**ACTIONS AND USES**—Diamthazole hydrochloride is an antifungal drug used in the treatment of ringworm and related infections. It has been employed in the eradication of a wide variety of skin infections, including *Candida albicans* or moniliasis, tinea barbae or barber's itch, tinea capitis or ringworm of the scalp, tinea cruris or jock itch, tinea corporis or fungus of smooth skin surfaces, athlete's foot, pityriasis versicolor or fungus of the trunk, and erythrasma, a skin disease of the armpits and genital area. The drug acts by penetrating the skin and causing the infected outer layer to be shed at a faster than normal rate.

**PRECAUTIONS**—Diamthazole should not be applied during the acute phase of a fungal infection. The product should be used only on external surfaces and should not contact mucous membranes. Side effects include skin irritation and photosensitivity. The drug should not be applied to the skin of a child under 6 years of age because of a risk that absorption of diamthazole through the skin may result in symptoms of nervous system poisoning, with epilepsylike seizures and agitation. However, the central nervous system effects observed in small children treated with diamthazole also have been attributed by some authorities to oral contact, such as thumb sucking, rather than to absorption of the product through the skin.

**DOSAGE AND ADMINISTRATION**—Diamthazole usually is supplied in a 5 percent tincture, ointment, or dusting powder. The product is applied one or two times a day to the infected area, avoiding extensively inflamed or eroded skin areas. It is recommended that the powder be used for a daytime application and the ointment used at night or when the infected area is covered by a dressing.

**SOURCES**—Rivopharm Pharmaceutical Laboratories, Rivopharm SA, 6911 Manno, Lugano, Switzerland; Productos Roche, S.A., Avenida Principal de Los Ruices, Edif. Roche, Apartado 68.168, Altamira, Caracas 1.062-A, Venezuela; Cahill May Roberts Ltd., P.O. Box 1090, Chapelizod, Dublin 20, Ireland.

## **Domperidone**—Motilium

**ACTIONS AND USES**—Domperidone is an antiemetic used in the treatment of nausea, vomiting, dyspepsia, and to increase gastrointestinal motility. It also has been used in the treatment of heartburn and to correct severe cases of constipation. Patients using the drug have reported it reduces flatulence after meals. Domperidone appears to increase gastric emptying without affecting gastric secretions and without producing psychotropic or neurologic effects in most patients. The product has proved effective in stimulating spontaneous bowel movements in diabetic patients whose disease has resulted in gastroparesis, a condition in which gastrointestinal activity is so weak that bowel movements cannot be stimulated with diets and medications usually recommended for severe constipation.

**PRECAUTIONS**—Domperidone is not recommended for pregnant women. The product may interact adversely with certain antihistamines, antiemetics used to control nausea and vomiting in motion sickness, and medications prescribed for Parkinson's disease, with a result of reducing the effectiveness of domperidone. No serious side effects have been reported. Some patients, however, have complained of gastric distress, headache, or facial flushing after administration of domperidone.

**DOSAGE AND ADMINISTRATION**—Domperidone is supplied in tablets, oral solution, and ampules for injection. One tablet or one ml of solution contains 10 mg of domperidone. A 2 ml ampule also provides 10 mg of the drug. The usual recommended adult dosage is 10 mg three times daily, between 15 and 30 minutes after a meal. Doses for children are calculated at 300 mcg per kg of body weight, or approximately one-third the adult dose, three times daily, preferably after meals.

**SOURCES**—Janssen Farmaceutica, S.A. de C.V., Blvd. A. Ruiz Cortines No. 3453, Mexico 20, D.F., Mexico; Janssen Pharmaceutical Ltd., Janssen House, Marlow, Bucks SL7 1ET, England.

## Dothiepin Hydrochloride (Dosulepin Hydrochloride)—Prothiaden

**ACTIONS AND USES**—Dothiepin hydrochloride is an antidepressant with sedative properties. It has been used in the treatment of all types of mental depression but is reported to be particularly effective in cases of reactive depression associated with anxiety. The mode of action is uncertain, but it is believed that dothiepin, like other tricyclic types of antidepressants, blocks the natural process by which neurotransmitter substances are continuously removed from the synaptic area of nerve endings. As a result, transmission of nerve impulses vital for normal mental functions is allowed to continue. Some clinical studies suggest that dothiepin is as effective as impipramine and more effective than amitriptyline in relieving the symptoms of depression.

**PRECAUTIONS**—The safety of dothiepin in pregnancy has not been established, although animal studies in which doses 20 times greater than human doses were given showed no apparent adverse effects on the offspring. The drug appears in breast milk, and caution should be observed in administering the drug to nursing mothers. The drug also should not be given to persons suffering from epilepsy, patients who have recently recovered from myocardial infarction, persons with impaired liver function, and patients who are using monoamine oxidase (MAO) inhibitors or who have used MAO inhibitors within the past 14 days. The drug should be withdrawn before elective surgery, may provoke a shift toward the manic phase of manic-depressive psychosis, lowers the convulsive threshold and increases the hazard of electroconvulsive therapy, may provoke heart conduction defects and arrhythmias, can exacerbate glaucoma and urinary retention, and may interact with other psychotropic drugs. The most common side effects are drowsiness, dizziness, tremors, confusion and disorientation, blurred vision, nausea, vomiting, constipation, dryness of the mouth, sweating, urinary retention, and either increased or decreased libido. The effect of alcohol is increased by dothiepin, and the interaction may be fatal.

**DOSAGE AND ADMINISTRATION**—Dothiepin hydrochloride is supplied in 25 and 75 mg capsules. The usual recommended dosage is one 25 mg capsule three times daily or three 25 mg capsules at night for mild to moderate depression. For moderate to severe depression, the dosage is increased to 50 mg three times daily. For outpatients, the total daily dose should not exceed 200 mg. Higher doses have been used for hospitalized patients. Dothiepin medication is not recommended for persons under 16 years of age, and caution should be used in prescribing the drug for elderly persons.

**SOURCES**—The Boots Company (Australia) Pty Ltd., 21 Loyalty Road, North Rocks, N.S.W. 2151, Australia; The Boots Company Ltd., 1 Thane Road West, Nottingham NG2 3AA, England.

## Dropropizine—Catabex, Ribex, Troferit

**ACTIONS AND USES**—Dropropizine is a synthetic antitussive (used for the relief of cough). The product reportedly has a sedating effect on the tracheobronchial mucosa and depresses the activity of the cough reflex center in the medulla. It is used for a variety of cough conditions, including bronchospasm, pharyngitis, laryngitis, coughs due to irritation, bronchitis, tracheitis, and coughs associated with breathing difficulties.

**PRECAUTIONS**—Side effects include drowsiness, nausea and gastric distress, and depressed respiration.

**DOSAGE AND ADMINISTRATION**—Dropropizine is supplied in 45 mg suppositories, 30 mg tablets, and a syrup. The usual recommended adult dosage is one tablet or one tablespoonful of syrup every six to eight hours, or one suppository three or four times daily. For children a 20 mg suppository is available. It is administered three or four times a day. The child-size dose of syrup is one teaspoonful, or about 5 ml, three or four times a day.

**SOURCE**—Chinoin, Productos Farmaceuticos, S.A. de C.V., Lago Tangañica No. 18, Mexico 17, D.F., Mexico.

## Econazole Nitrate—Ecostatin, Epi-Pevaryl, Gyno-Pevaryl, Mycopevaryl, Pevaryl, Skilar

**ACTIONS AND USES**—Econazole nitrate is an antifungal agent usually applied to the skin or the vagina to treat a variety of fungal diseases. The product also has some antibacterial activity. It has been used to treat aspergillosis of the lung by intravenous injection. Econazole is believed to produce its fungicidal and bactericidal effects by penetrating the cell walls of the disease organisms, then interfering with the cell physiology so the microbes cannot reproduce. Among uses for econazole are treatment of infections by the yeastlike *Candida* strains of fungus, including the vaginal type of infection known as moniliasis, the ringworm effects of tinea, and pityriasis (branny eruptions on the surface of the body). In the treatment of moniliasis, econazole reportedly has produced cures in 80 percent of the cases in one treatment and 90 percent in two treatments. Econazole also is used to treat balanitis (when the penis or clitoris is affected by fungal infections), candidal vulvitis, and vaginal pruritus. Laboratory studies indicate the drug has some effect against bacterial strains of *Streptococcus*, *Staphylococcus*, and the organism responsible for the potentially fatal erysipelas skin disorder. However, the effects have not been demonstrated adequately thus far in clinical studies.

**PRECAUTIONS**—Econazole should not be used by a patient known to be hypersensitive to the drug. If marked irritation or sensitization develops during intravaginal use, the drug should be discontinued. Because small amounts of the product are absorbed from the vagina, econazole is not recommended for use during pregnancy. If use is advised by a physician, the pregnant patient should exercise caution in the use of vaginal applicators to avoid injury to cervical tissues. Because intractable moniliasis often is associated with diabetes, the patient should be examined for signs of that disorder if the infection does not respond to econazole treatment. Adverse effects may include temporary sensations of itching, burning, or other signs of irritation. If the signs persist, or are severe, consideration should be given to discontinuance of the therapy.

**DOSAGE AND ADMINISTRATION**—Econazole nitrate is supplied as topical or vaginal creams, vaginal pessaries, or vaginal ovules. For skin infections, a thin layer of the topical cream should be rubbed in gently two or three times daily until the lesions have healed. For vaginal infections, the patient should introduce one vaginal pessary, ovule, or applicatorful of cream high in the vagina while in a supine position. Each vaginal pessary or applicatorful of cream contains 50 mg of econazole nitrate. The treatment should be repeated daily for 14 days. An ovule and some pessaries contain 150 mg of econazole nitrate. It is recommended that the 150 mg ovules and pessaries be introduced in the vagina daily for three consecutive days. Some brands of ovules require an applicator while others do not. Some authorities advise that the sexual partner of a moniliasis patient receive simultaneous treatment. When the sexual partner is a male, the glans penis and prepuce areas should be cleaned with warm water and the cream applied once daily for two weeks.

**SOURCES**—Ortho-Cilag Pharmaceutical Ltd., P.O. Box 79, Saunderton, High Wycombe, Bucks HP14 4HJ, England; Squibb Canada Inc., 2365 Côte de Liesse Rd., Montreal, Quebec H4N 2M7, Canada; Cilag AB, Box 7073, 191 07 Sollentuna, Sweden.

## Etilefrine Hydrochloride (Ethylphenylephrine)—Circupon, Effoless, Effortil, Effortil PL, Efortil, Presotona, Pressoton, Sanlephrin, Tensio Retard, Tensofar, Tonus-Forte-Tablinen

**ACTIONS AND USES**—Etilefrine hydrochloride is a sympathetic nervous system stimulant that is used in the treatment of abnormally low blood pressure. It is employed in controlling orthostatic hypotension, a condition in which a person's blood pressure tends to fall dramatically when rising from a sitting or reclining to a standing position. Etilefrine also is used in controlling subnormal blood pressure in cases of shock or circulatory collapse, hypotension associated with pregnancy and premature birth, and hypotension due to intoxication, infection, or debility. Etilefrine produces its action by stimulating both alpha and beta pathways of the autonomic nervous system. In clinical tests, etilefrine hydrochloride reduced systolic blood pressure changes from an average of 26 to 4 percent and diastolic pressure from about 4 percent to 1.2 percent.

**PRECAUTIONS**—Etilefrine hydrochloride should not be administered to patients with arterial hypertension or thyrotoxicosis. The safety of etilefrine in pregnant women and nursing mothers has not been established, and the drug therefore is not recommended for patients in these groups. Etilefrine is likely to interact with beta-blocker drugs, resulting in a reduced effectiveness of etilefrine.

**DOSAGE AND ADMINISTRATION**—Etilefrine hydrochloride is supplied in 5 mg tablets, injection ampules of 10 mg per ml, a syrup containing 1 mg per ml, and drops providing 7.5 mg per ml. The usual recommended dosage is one or two tablets, or 10 to 20 drops, three times a day for adults and children over the age of 7. For children between the ages of 1 and 7 years, the usual recommended dose is one-half the adult dose. The dosage for the syrup is one teaspoonful three or four times a day and about one-half that amount for children.

**SOURCES**—Boehringer Mannheim GmbH, Sandhofer Strasse 116, Postfach: 310 120, 6800 Mannheim 31, West Germany; Ercopharm A/S, Skelstedt 13–15, 2950 Vedbaek, Denmark; Laboratorios Promeco de Mexico, S.A. de C.V., Insurgentes Sur No. 1457–80. piso-, Mexico 19, D.F., Mexico.

## Etofylline (Etofylline Clofibrate, Etofylline Nicotinate)—Bio-Phylline, De-Oxin, Dilaphyllin, Duolip, Hesotin, Hilyl, Oxyphylline

**ACTIONS AND USES**—Etofylline is a drug derived from theophylline, a caffeinelike substance present in tea leaves, and is used as a blood vessel dilator and diuretic. Etofylline also has been employed in the treatment of asthma and, in the clofibrate form, as a therapy for hyperlipidemia, or excess levels of fats in the blood. Some authorities have reported benefits in improving the blood flow to the brain through administration of etofylline, although the findings have been challenged by other medical scientists. In the treatment of cerebral ischemia, etofylline reportedly has corrected symptoms of dizziness, mild stroke, visual problems, and intellectual and behavioral deterioration attributed to a deficiency of blood flow to the brain. Etofylline has actions similar to aminophylline, another theophylline derivative that is used to stimulate the heart, lower venous blood pressure, and dilate the bronchial tubes leading to the air sacs of the lungs. Some preparations include theophylline in combination with etofylline.

**PRECAUTIONS**—Etofylline should not be given to patients with peptic ulcers. It is not recommended for children under the age of 15 years. Caution should be used in giving the drug to patients with heart disease, impaired liver function, hyperthyroidism, or a history of epilepsy. The drug should be avoided if possible during pregnancy, particularly during the last trimester, because of the risk of toxic effects on the fetus. Etofylline may interact with other medications, such as cimetidine and erythromycin, which can increase the effect of etofylline. Adverse effects of etofylline include insomnia, rapid heartbeat and, in excessive doses, convulsions.

**DOSAGE AND ADMINISTRATION**—Etofylline is supplied in 100 mg tablets and capsules, injection ampules providing 250 mg per dose, and 75, 250, 350, and 500 mg suppositories. The usual recommended adult dose is 300 to 500 mg per day by oral administration, 350 to 700 mg per day by suppository, or 250 to 500 mg per day by intravenous or intramuscular injection. The 75 mg suppositories are intended for infant use, and the 250 mg suppositories are designed for use by children between 1 and 12 years of age.

**SOURCES**—Kronans Lab., Box 33, 170 11 Drottningholm, Sweden; Bio-Chemical Laboratories, Inc., 2323 Montee St. Aubin, Ville de Laval, Quebec H7S 1Z7, Canada; Amido S.A., 65, rue du D'Jenner, 59 Lille, France; Laboratoires Bioserda, 42, av. Augustin Dumont, 92240 Malakoff, France.

## Etomidate—Hypnomidat, Hypnomidate

**ACTIONS AND USES**—Etomidate is used to induce anesthesia by intravenous injection. It is a nonbarbiturate drug and has no analgesic effects, but etomidate reportedly induces complete anesthesia in about 20 seconds with rapid recovery and with fewer of the side effects, such as cardiac depression, breathing difficulty, and residual headache, associated with other drugs used for the same purpose, such as thiopental. A single dose may last only a few minutes, and additional doses are required for continued anesthesia with the same drug. Narcotic analgesics and a muscle relaxant usually are administered with etomidate. Supplementary anesthetics, such as halothane, may be required for continued general anesthesia. Etomidate is quickly distributed to the brain, helping to account for its rapid, smooth anesthetic effect. Concentrations also decrease rapidly during the first 30 minutes, after which blood levels drop slowly through a half-life of slightly less than four hours.

**PRECAUTIONS**—Etomidate reportedly produces pain when injected in as many as one-third of the patients, even when anesthesia occurs within a few seconds. Involuntary muscle movements occur in about two-thirds of the anesthetized patients, requiring the concurrent use of analgesics and muscle relaxants. Some cases of venous thrombosis have been associated with injection of etomidate. Although animal studies have failed to demonstrate teratogenic (birth defect) effects, use of the drug should be avoided in pregnancy unless the potential benefits outweigh the risks. The use of large veins for injection is reported to reduce the incidence of painful side effects associated with administration of etomidate. Skin rash and postoperative nausea have been reported as side effects, but adverse effects other than those noted have been rare.

**DOSAGE AND ADMINISTRATION**—Etomidate is supplied in 10 ml ampules containing 2 mg per ml and in ampules containing a concentrate of 125 mg per ml. The concentrate should be diluted in at least 50 ml of infusion liquid before administration. The usual dosage is calculated at 300 mcg per kg of body weight, or approximately 20 mg for a 60 kg patient. The usual loading dose is 100 mcg per kg per minute for the first 10 minutes, followed by a reduced dose of 10 mcg per kg per minute until 5 minutes before the end of the surgical procedure. For short procedures, it is recommended that the duration of the loading dose be reduced to 5 minutes.

**SOURCES**—Janssen Pharmaceutical Ltd., Janssen House, Chapel Street, Marlow, Buckinghamshire SL7 1ET, England; Janssen Farmaceutica, S.A. de C.V., Blvd. Adolfo Ruiz Cortines No. 3453, Mexico 20, D.F., Mexico.

## Etoposide—Vepesid

**ACTIONS AND USES**—Etoposide is an anticancer drug that is used primarily to treat solid tumors of the lungs and testes. The drug also has been used in the treatment of leukemia, lymphoma, Hodgkin's disease, and cancer of the bladder, breast, kidney, esophagus, and thyroid. Etoposide is a cytotoxic agent, meaning it acts by destroying cells or preventing their multiplication. Laboratory studies indicate etoposide interferes with the production in cancer cells of DNA molecules, the chemical units needed for cell growth and reproduction, preventing the cells from reaching the early stages of replication. Like other anticancer drugs, etoposide can also affect some normal human tissue cells, such as those involved in the manufacture of new blood cells. This adverse effect in humans can result in leukopenia, or an abnormal decrease in white blood cells, and thrombocytopenia, an abnormal decrease in the number of blood platelets.

**PRECAUTIONS**—Etoposide should not be given to patients who may be hypersensitive to the drug, to patients with existing leukopenia or thrombocytopenia, or to those with impaired kidney or liver function. The drug is not recommended for women of childbearing potential unless they are exercising adequate contraceptive precautions. Any bacterial infection should be controlled before the start of etoposide therapy to reduce the risk of septicemia, or bacterial infection of the blood. Because of the effects of etoposide on white blood cell and blood platelet levels, patient blood counts should be monitored regularly. Blood marrow depression, including leukopenia and thrombocytopenia, may be observed after the first week of etoposide therapy. Side effects include nausea, vomiting, loss of appetite, constipation, gastric distress, changes in blood pressure and heart rate, and a feeling of weakness. Nearly one-fourth of the patients experience a temporary loss of hair, or alopecia, an effect associated with many of the cancer chemotherapy medications.

**DOSAGE AND ADMINISTRATION**—Etoposide is supplied in 100 mg capsules for oral administration and in 5 ml injection ampules containing 20 mg per ml of etoposide. Doses are adjusted according to individual patient requirements. The usual recommended dosage for small-cell cancer of the lungs is calculated at 60 mg per day per square meter of body surface; a 63-pound child 4 feet 2 inches in height would have approximately 1 square meter of body surface, a 119-pound person 5 feet in height would have a body surface of about 1.5 square meters, and a 175-pound person 6 feet tall would have a body surface area of 2 square meters. When used in combination with other chemotherapeutic agents, the dosage per square meter of body surface usually is reduced to 50 mg per day. The intravenous dosage is administered at a slow infusion rate over a period of 30 minutes, repeated daily for five days per course and with the course repeated in three- to four-week cycles. Other procedures are recommended for different types of cancer. The recommended oral dose is approximately double the intravenous dose.

**SOURCES**—Bristol Laboratories of Canada, Bristol-Myers Canada, Inc., 411 Roosevelt Ave., Ottawa, Ontario K2A 3X9, Canada; Bristol-Myers Pharmaceuticals, Bristol-Myers Co., Ltd., Station Rd., Langley, Slough SL3 6EB, England.

## **Fenclofenac**—Feclan, Flenac, Gidalon

**ACTIONS AND USES**—Fenclofenac is a nonsteroid drug derived from phenylacetic acid, with antiinflammatory, antipyretic, and analgesic activity. It has been used to treat symptoms of rheumatoid arthritis, ankylosing spondylitis, osteoarthritis, chronic synovitis, Reiter's syndrome, sciatica, psoriatic arthritis, and other disorders including pain associated with prolapsed intervertebral disks. Studies indicate that fenclofenac is about eight times as potent as aspirin in relieving symptoms of rheumatoid diseases. In some actions and effects, the product resembles ibuprofen. Fenclofenac is absorbed from the gastrointestinal tract, with peak plasma concentrations appearing 2 to 4 hours after a single oral dose. The half-life of fenclofenac is about 12 hours, compared with 2 hours for the half-life of ibuprofen.

**PRECAUTIONS**—Adverse effects of fenclofenac have included gastrointestinal disturbances, central nervous system reactions, and skin disorders. The product appears to alter thyroid function test results by resetting the concentrations of thyroid hormones without actually interfering with thyroid function. Miscellaneous side effects of edema, headache, drowsiness, dizziness, and tinnitus have been associated with the product. Central nervous system symptoms have included visual blurring or other ocular manifestations. Its use is contraindicated in cases of active peptic ulcer or a history of gastrointestinal lesions, in cases of renal or hepatic dysfunction, and in patients with eczema, asthma, or aspirin allergy. Fenclofenac is not recommended for children, and its safety has not been established for pregnant women or nursing mothers.

**DOSAGE AND ADMINISTRATION**—Fenclofenac is supplied in 300 mg tablets. The usual recommended dosage is two to four tablets daily in divided doses with food. The maintenance dosage is three tablets daily.

**SOURCES**—Reckitt & Colman Pharmaceuticals, UK, Dansom Lane, Kingston-upon-Hull, HU8 8DD, England; Scheramex, Av. 16 de Septiembre No. 301, Xochimilco Mexico 23, D.F., Mexico.

## **Fenoterol Hydrobromide**—Berotec, Dosberotec, Partusisten

**ACTIONS AND USES**—Fenoterol hydrobromide is a bronchodilator used in the treatment of bronchial asthma, bronchitis, and emphysema, including exercise-induced respiratory disorders. The product also has been used for the relief of symptoms of hay fever, silicosis, bronchial cancer, tuberculosis, and bronchiectasis. After inhalation of a mist of the fenoterol compound, the drug stimulates the beta nerve receptors in the lung area that are responsible for bronchodilation. However, the low doses used reportedly have little effect on the beta receptors of nerves influencing heart function. The drug is said to have greater potency and greater specificity for the nerve receptors of the beta network innervating respiratory tissue than other bronchodilator drugs that are not derived from epinephrine or other natural neurotransmitter substances. Also, because of fenoterol's chemical nature, it is not metabolized by naturally occurring enzymes in the lung tissue that would destroy epinephrine-type agents, and therefore fenoterol is allowed to remain longer in the respiratory tract. The prolonged action, in turn, reduces the number of times per day that medication must be administered. Because of its similarity to salbutamol as a beta-adrenergic stimulator, fenoterol has been used in efforts to prevent premature labor.

**PRECAUTIONS**—The safety of fenoterol in pregnancy has not been established. Because of its interaction with hormones involved in natural uterine contractions at childbirth, the use of fenoterol may prolong labor or inhibit the onset of labor. Caution should be exercised in administering fenoterol to patients afflicted with hypertension, thyrotoxicosis, or heart disorders such as angina pectoris, myocardial insufficiency, or arrhythmias. Fenoterol may interact with beta-blocking drugs to reduce effectiveness of the bronchodilator. The drug also may interact with monoamine oxidase inhibitors and other psychotropic drugs and with products that affect heart function. Patients should be advised against increasing the recommended dosage in an attempt to obtain relief of respiratory symptoms; accidental overdosage can result in the side effects of palpitations, rapid heartbeat, and tremors.

**DOSAGE AND ADMINISTRATION**—Fenoterol hydrobromide is supplied in pressurized, metered aerosol dispensers, each containing a 10 ml vial of the drug and a mouthpiece. Each metered dose contains approximately 0.2 mg of the product. The usual recommended dosage is one or two puffs of the product three times a day. The usual duration of action of fenoterol hydrobromide is six to eight hours. If necessary, the dosage can be increased to two puffs every four hours. The dosage for children usually is one puff three times a day, or one puff every four hours if necessary to control bronchospasms. A child's use of the pressurized inhaler should be supervised by an adult to help prevent accidental overdosage.

**SOURCES**—WB Pharmaceuticals Limited, P.O. Box 23, Bracknell, Berkshire RG12 4YS, England; Boehringer Ingelheim (Canada) Ltd., 977 Century Drive, Burlington, Ontario L7L 5J8, Canada; Boehringer Ingelheim s.p.a., Casella Postale 50100 Firenze, Italy.

## Fentiazac—Flogene, Norvedan, Ragilon

**ACTIONS AND USES**— Fentiazac is a nonsteroid analgesic used in the treatment of rheumatoid arthritis, synovitis, tendinitis, bursitis, gouty arthritis, spondylarthritis, and related muscle and joint disorders, including ankylosing spondylitis. The ability of fentiazac to reduce symptoms of fever, pain, and inflammation is believed to be due to an action that inhibits the prostaglandin activity associated with rheumatic and arthritic diseases. The drug also reportedly reduces the loss of function in the affected joints.

**PRECAUTIONS**—Fentiazac should not be given to patients with stomach or duodenal ulcers. Most of the reported side effects of the drug have consisted of various symptoms of gastric distress or irritation.

**DOSAGE AND ADMINISTRATION**—Fentiazac is supplied in sugar-coated pills containing 100 or 200 mg of the drug. The usual recommended dosage is one or two 100 mg pills once or twice daily or one 200 mg pill once or twice daily, depending upon the individual patient response and severity of symptoms.

**SOURCES**—Laboratorios Promeco de Mexico, S.A. de C.V., Calle del Maiz No. 49, Mexico 23 D.F., Mexico; LPB Instituto Farmaceutico s.p.a., Via dei Lavoratori 54, 20092 Cinisello Balsamo, Italy; Polifarma s.p.a., Via Tor Sapienza 138, 00155 Roma, Italy.

## Fentonium Bromide—Ketoscilium, Ulcesium

**ACTIONS AND USES**—Fentonium bromide is an atropinelike drug that is used in the treatment of peptic ulcers and spasms of the gastrointestinal tract. The drug acts on the three component factors of ulcer development—excessive gastric secretion, effects of stress, and hypermotility (excessive involuntary motion of the gastrointestinal tract). The product blocks the transmission of nerve impulses in pathways leading to muscles and glands of the gastrointestinal tract, thereby reducing the level of autonomic nerve activity associated with intestinal spasms and ulcer development. Because it inhibits activity of the cholinergic fibers of the sympathetic nervous system, which enervate certain glands and smooth muscles, fentonium bromide is classed as an anticholinergic drug. The product is used in the treatment of benign ulcers of the stomach and duodenum, gastric erosion of the esophagus, gastroduodenitis, recurrent ulcers, and ulcers that erode through the intestinal wall to produce abnormal connections between distant segments.

**PRECAUTIONS**—Atropinelike drugs produce a dryness of the mouth, thirst, and swallowing difficulty, accompanied by urination difficulties. Anticholinergic agents also affect the eye, dilating the pupil, increasing pressure within the eyeball, and causing blurred vision. Flushing and dryness of the skin have been reported as additional side effects. Large doses may cause heart palpitations and breathing difficulties. As a purpose of fentonium bromide is the reduction of gastrointestinal activity, the patient should be advised that constipation may develop. Individual sensitivities to anticholinergic drugs vary considerably, with some patients able to tolerate dosages that would prove toxic to other persons.

**DOSAGE AND ADMINISTRATION**—Fentonium bromide is supplied in tablets containing 20 mg of fentonium. The usual recommended dose for adults being treated for gastritis, gastroduodenitis, and related disorders is three tablets daily for three weeks. For treatment of gastroduodenal ulcers, the usual dosage is three to four tablets daily for the first week and three tablets daily for the next four weeks.

**SOURCE**—Bracco de Mexico, S.A. de C.V., Calzada de las Armas No. 110, Tlalnepantla, Edo. de Mexico.

## Floctafenine—Idarac, Idolon

**ACTIONS AND USES**—Floctafenine is an analgesic with antiinflammatory properties that is used in the treatment of mild to moderately severe acute pain. It has been employed in the relief of symptoms of dysmenorrhea, sciatica, arthrosis (joint) pain, arthritis, periarteritis, vertebral and vertebromuscular pain, bone and muscle pain associated with injury, pain associated with oral surgery, neck and shoulder pain, and pain associated with surgery of the abdomen and locomotor structures of the body, including joints, muscles, bones, and connective tissue. Floctafenine also has been used to alleviate the pain of cancer. The drug is believed to produce its analgesic and antiinflammatory effect by inhibiting the body's production of prostaglandins, hormonelike substances known to induce symptoms of pain and inflammation.

**PRECAUTIONS**—Floctafenine should not be given to patients with an active inflammatory disorder of the gastrointestinal tract, such as peptic ulcers. The drug is not recommended for women of childbearing potential, nursing mothers, children, or patients who may be sensitive to the drug. Floctafenine is not recommended for long-term use at this writing. Caution should be exercised in giving floctafenine to patients with impaired kidney function or difficulty in urination and to patients also taking anticoagulant medication. Side effects reported include nausea, diarrhea, headache, insomnia, drowsiness, dizziness, heartburn, constipation, gastrointestinal bleeding, urination difficulties, and skin rashes.

**DOSAGE AND ADMINISTRATION**—Floctafenine is supplied as 200 mg tablets, scored for division into smaller doses if required. The usual recommended dosage is 200 to 300 mg three to four times a day as required to relieve symptoms of pain and inflammation. The maximum recommended daily dose is 1,200 mg. The drug is recommended only for short-term relief of acute pain.

**SOURCES**—Roussel Laboratoria B.V., Bijenvlucht 30, 3871 JJ Hoevelaken, The Netherlands; Roussel Maestretti s.p.a., Viale Gran Sassa 18, 20131 Milano, Italy; Grupo Roussel, S.A., Av. Universidad No. 1738, Mexico 21, D.F., Mexico.

## **Flucloxacillin Sodium (Floxacillin Sodium)**—Culpen, Dumpikal, Flopen, Floxapen, Fluclox, Flupen, Heracillin, Penplus, Staphylex

**ACTIONS AND USES**—Flucloxacillin is an antibiotic that is used for the treatment of infections by strains of staphylococcal bacteria that are resistant to benzylpenicillin or penicillin G products. Flucloxacillin also is used to control infections of mixed staphylococci and streptococci when the staphylococcal strain is pencillin-resistant. The penicillin-resistant staphylococci produce an enzyme, called penicillinase, which destroys penicillin. Flucloxacillin is used in general practice in the treatment of tonsillitis, infections of the upper respiratory tract, quinsy, pharyngitis, sinusitis, and otitis media (middle ear infection). The antibiotic also has been used to treat boils, abscesses, carbuncles, furunculosis, the cellulitis of erysipelas, infected wounds, infected burns, pneumonia, empyema due to pus in the chest cavity, osteomyelitis, intestinal infections, endocarditis, urinary tract infections, septicemia, and meningitis.

**PRECAUTIONS**—Flucloxacillin should not be administered to patients who are hypersensitive to penicillin or other antibiotics. It should not be applied topically or otherwise to the conjunctiva or eye surfaces because the product can produce severe eye inflammation and lead to development of opaque corneas and loss of vision. Safety of flucloxacillin in pregnancy has not been established, and the product should be administered to pregnant women only when the benefits outweigh the risks. Flucloxacillin is found in small amounts in the breast milk, and nursing mothers are advised when using flucloxacillin to switch to other feeding methods to avoid the development of antibiotic sensitivity in the offspring. The drug should be used with extreme caution in premature infants or newborn infants with jaundice. Caution is recommended in administering flucloxacillin to patients with susceptibility to allergies. Adverse reactions include skin rash, nausea, gastric distress, diarrhea, constipation, and loss of appetite.

**DOSAGE AND ADMINISTRATION**—Flucloxacillin is supplied in 250 and 500 mg capsules, in a syrup containing 125 mg flucloxacillin per 5 ml dose, and in 250 and 500 mg ampules or vials for injection. The usual recommended adult oral dosage is 250 to 500 mg three times daily, taken 30 to 60 minutes before meals. By injection, the recommended dosage is 250 mg four times a day intramuscularly or 250 to 500 mg four times a day intravenously. For children 2 to 10 years of age, the dosage is one-half the adult rate; for children under 2 years of age, the daily dose is one-fourth the recommended adult dose.

**SOURCES**—Ayerst Laboratories, P.O. Box 6115, Montreal, Quebec H3C 3J1, Canada; Astra Läkemedel AB, Strängnäsvägen 44, 151 85 Södertalje, Sweden; Beecham Research Laboratories, Great West Road, Brentford, Middlesex TW8 9BD, England.

**Flunitrazepam (Flunidazepam)**—Darkene, Narcozep, Primun, Rohipnol, Rohypnol, Roipnol, Valsera

**ACTIONS AND USES**—Flunitrazepam is a hypnotic drug used to induce sleep. It also is employed occasionally as an anesthetic. Flunitrazepam reportedly is ten times as potent as diazepam, which is marketed under the brand name of Valium. However, clinical studies indicate flunitrazepam and diazepam are approximately equal in their speed of onset of anesthesia and effects on heart, blood pressure, and other physiological measurements in surgical patients who have received premedication sedatives. As a hypnotic, to induce drowsiness, reduce the level of physical activity, and sustain sleep, flunitrazepam was found in a large double-blind study to be more effective than other hypnotic drugs. Flunitrazepam also has been found to have anticonvulsant and muscle relaxant properties and to act as an anxiolytic, or antianxiety, drug in a manner similar to that of the minor tranquilizers.

**PRECAUTIONS**—Safety in pregnancy has not been established for flunitrazepam, and the drug therefore should not be administered to pregnant women. It also should not be administered to nursing mothers. And it should not be given to patients with a known sensitivity to drugs of the benzodiazepine category or to persons suffering from myasthenia gravis. The muscle relaxant properties of flunitrazepam can exacerbate the symptoms of myasthenia gravis. Caution should be used in administering the drug to patients with impaired liver or kidney function, to elderly patients who are likely to be sensitive to the product, and to persons prone to drug abuse. Patients should be warned that mental and physical abilities may be impaired for at least 18 hours after receiving a dose of flunitrazepam, and they may be in danger if operating motor vehicles or dangerous machinery and, in some cases, if being a pedestrian. Patients should be instructed that alcohol must be avoided and no other drugs should be taken with flunitrazepam unless prescribed by the attending physician. Side effects can include hangoverlike symptoms the day after taking the drug, tiredness, confusion, dizziness, involuntary muscle activity, headache, hiccups, sweating, slurred speech, rapid heartbeat, and blood pressure changes.

**DOSAGE AND ADMINISTRATION**—Flunitrazepam is supplied in tablets containing 2 mg each of the drug. For recent-onset insomnia, the recommended dose is one-fourth to one-half tablet, or 500 mcg to 1.0 mg, at bedtime. For insomnia of several weeks' duration, the usual recommended dose is one 2 mg tablet at bedtime. In cases of severe chronic insomnia associated with psychotic, neurotic, or depressive symptoms, the dose may be increased to 3 to 4 mg, but it should not exceed 6 mg, or three tablets, per day. The safety and efficacy of the drug have not been established for children under 15 years of age, and therefore the drug is not recommended for children in the younger age categories. In geriatric patients, regular adult doses may result in delirium or clouding of consciousness, and caution should be exercised in administering flunitrazepam to elderly persons.

**SOURCES**—Roche Products Pty Ltd., 4–10 Inman Road, Dee Why, N.S.W. 2009, Australia; Productos Roche, S.A. de C.V., Av. de la Universidad No. 902, Mexico 12, D.F., Mexico; Roche-Produkter AB, Storsätragränd 12, Skärholmen, Sweden.

## Fluocortin Butyl (Fluocortin Butylester)—Novoderm, Vaspid, Vaspide, Vaspit, FCB

**ACTIONS AND USES**—Fluocortin butyl is a corticosteroid agent with antiinflammatory properties used as a cream to treat skin disorders. The exact mechanism of action is unknown, but fluocortin butyl causes some constriction of surface blood vessels and relieves symptoms of itching, burning, and irritation associated with diseases of the skin.

**PRECAUTIONS**—The safety of fluocortin butyl in pregnancy and in nursing mothers has not been established. No reports of adverse effects on offspring have been found at this writing, but use of the product in pregnancy or in nursing mothers is not recommended unless the benefits outweigh the risks. The drug should not be applied to skin surfaces with infective bacterial or fungal diseases present, to skin afflicted with acne, or to wounds, cuts, abrasions, or ulcerations. Corticoid preparations can retard healing of wounds. The product also should not be applied to the external ear canal if the patient has a perforated eardrum, and it should not be applied to or near the eyes. Corticosteroid preparations can be absorbed through the skin and may affect normal steroid hormone functions, such as inhibiting bone growth in children. Care should be exercised in administering corticosteroid drugs to patients with impaired liver or kidney function. Care also should be exercised in the use of occlusive dressings, such as plastic sheeting, that prevent air from reaching the area being treated. Occlusive dressings increase the absorption of corticosteroids through the skin. Side effects reported after application of fluocortin butyl include local irritation and stinging sensations. Treatment should be discontinued if severe skin reactions occur or if there is no improvement in symptoms after one week of therapy.

**DOSAGE AND ADMINISTRATION**—Fluocortin butyl is supplied in 15 g tubes of cream. The cream is applied as a thin film to the irritated skin area two or three times daily. An occlusive dressing may be required in treating chronic skin disorders that resist usual treatment; but as noted under "Precautions," care should be exercised, and when possible the occlusive dressing should be applied to only one portion of the affected area at a time.

**SOURCES**—Schering Pty Ltd, Wood Street, Tempe N.S.W. 2044, Australia; Schering AG, Müllerstrasse 170, Postfach 650311, 1000 Berlin 65, West Germany.

## **Fluocortolone**—Ficoid, Plastoderm, Topodil, Ultradil, Ultradilan, Ultralan, Ultralanum, Ultraproct

**ACTIONS AND USES**—Fluocortolone preparations are used in the treatment of inflammatory skin disorders, including eczema, dermatoses, burns, sunburn, insect bites, and other skin conditions that usually respond to steroid medications. In various preparations, fluocortolone has been used to relieve symptoms of hemorrhoids, proctitis, superficial anal fissures, neurodermatitis, psoriasis, lichen planus, chronic lupus erythematosus, vulvar pruritus, and complications of varicose veins. Stronger concentrations of fluocortolone are designed to treat skin disorders that fail to respond to less potent corticosteroids. An oral preparation is used in the treatment of rheumatoid arthritis, pemphigus (a skin condition characterized by blebs or blisters), and atopic dermatitis.

**PRECAUTIONS**—Fluocortolone should not be given to pregnant patients unless directed by a physician. The product should not be used in the presence of bacterial, tubercular, viral, or fungal infections unless those conditions also are being treated appropriately. Nor should fluocortolone be applied in skin conditions complicated by acne vulgaris or acne rosacea, nor in skin disorders near the mouth. Caution is advised in using any corticosteroid medications for prolonged periods, in large amounts over short periods, or with occlusive dressings that seal the medicated skin area against the surrounding air. Corticosteroid drugs can be absorbed through the skin and cause suppression of normal pituitary and adrenal gland functions, this effect depending upon such factors as the area of skin, the condition of the skin, and the length of time of use and potency of the drug. Because of the risk of adrenocortical and growth suppression, the drugs should not be used for more than three weeks of continuous treatment in children under the age of 3 years. Continuous application of the drugs also can result in atrophy of the skin or the development of streaks and enlarged blood vessels in the skin, particularly on the face.

**DOSAGE AND ADMINISTRATION**—Fluocortolone is supplied as fluocortolone hexonate or fluocortolone pivalate in 0.1 percent and 0.25 percent concentrations and as 0.25 percent fluocortolone alone. It is available in creams, ointments, tablets, lotions, and suppositories. The creams and ointments generally are applied in a thin layer two or three times daily at first, with a single daily application following if there is a good initial response. The tablets, supplied in 5 and 20 mg units, are intended primarily for systemic disorders responding to corticosteroids, and are taken in amounts of 20 to 60 mg of fluocortolone in a single dose initially. The daily dose is reduced to 5 to 20 mg after optimal improvement is noted. A children's oral dose calculated at 1 to 2 mg per kg of body weight, with subsequent dosage reduction, has been used. Children's use of fluocortolone ointments, creams, and lotions is not recommended. The lotion is applied twice daily to the inflamed skin area and is used mainly for certain forms of eczema. The recommended dosage for the suppositories is two or three the first day, followed by one daily. As response to treatment of hemorrhoids, proctitis, or anal fissure is noted, the manufacturer suggests using a suppository on alternate days while applying the ointment daily.

**SOURCES**—Schering Mexicana, S.A., Calz. Mexico-Xochimilco

No. 5019, Mexico 22, D.F., Mexico; Schering s.p.a., Via Cassanese, 20090 Segrate (M1), Italy; Schering AG, Pharmaceutical Division, Postfach 650311, D-1000 Berlin 65, West Germany.

## Flupentixol (Flupenthixol, Flupentixol Decanoate, Flupentixol Dihydrochloride)—Depixol, Emergil, Fluanxol, Fluanxol Depot, Fluanxol Retard, Metamin, Siplarol, Viscoleo

**ACTIONS AND USES**—Flupentixol is a tranquilizer used in the treatment of depression (with and without anxiety), of obsessive-compulsive neuroses, and of schizophrenia in patients who are considered unreliable in taking oral medications prescribed for them. Flupentixol is reported to be of particular benefit in schizophrenic patients who exhibit apathy, inertia, withdrawal, anxiety, hallucinations, and paranoid delusions. It has been recommended for the treatment of paranoid psychosis in elderly patients, nonagitated anxiety states, and other psychoses, except those characterized by mania and psychomotor hyperactivity. Flupentixol has actions similar to those of chlorpromazine, a major tranquilizer, and fluphenazine, a related tranquilizer, causing less sedation and abnormally low blood pressure but with a greater risk of tremors and other involuntary muscle activity than other tranquilizers in its category. However, side effects associated with flupentixol are fewer when low doses are used.

**PRECAUTIONS**—Flupentixol should not be given to patients known to be sensitive to the drug or to other antipsychotic drugs that are chemically related to it; there is a risk of cross-sensitivity between certain tranquilizers. Flupentixol also should not be given to patients with central nervous system depression due to subcortical or cerebrovascular brain damage, or due to other causes, as well as to patients with impaired kidney or liver function, blood diseases, severe heart disease, or pheochromocytoma, a type of adrenal tumor associated with hypertension. It should not be administered to severely agitated psychotic patients, psychoneurotic patients, or elderly patients afflicted with confusion or agitation. Safety in pregnancy has not been established for flupentixol; therefore it should not be administered to women of childbearing age unless expected benefits outweigh the potential risks. The drug also is not recommended for children. Caution should be used in giving the drug to patients with arteriosclerosis, glaucoma, susceptibility to convulsive disorders, or parkinsonism. Like certain other tranquilizers, flupentixol has an antiemetic effect which may suppress symptoms of nausea and vomiting, thereby masking signs of another underlying illness. The lowered blood pressure effect of flupentixol should be considered when administering anesthetics or other central nervous system depressants to patients using the drug. Ambulatory patients using flupentixol should be advised that while the drug is relatively lacking in sedative effects, it may impair mental alertness and motor coordination so that operating motor vehicles or machinery may be hazardous. The drug also may interact with alcohol or other psychotropic drugs to have an additive effect. The most common side effects are those involving involuntary muscle activity, such as tremors and parkinsonlike activity, which usually appear in the first few days and are controlled by adjusting the drug dosage. Other side effects include restlessness, insomnia, headache, drowsiness, fatigue, weight change, dry mouth, blurred vision, constipation, excessive salivation, and changes in libido. Various skin disorders, ranging from pruritus to eczema, have been reported among users of flupentixol and similar drugs.

**DOSAGE AND ADMINISTRATION**—Flupentixol is supplied in 500 mcg and 3 mg sugar-coated tablets or in injection ampules containing 10, 20, and 100 mg per ml. The tablets contain the dihydrochloride and the injection ampules the decanoate form of flupentixol. The usual oral dosage is 3 to 9 mg taken twice daily, according to the desired response, up to a maximum of 18 mg daily. The decanoate salt is administered by deep intramuscular injection in the upper, outer buttock or lateral thigh in doses of 20 to 40 mg at intervals of two to four weeks. Larger doses may be required to achieve the desired response in some patients. For patients being transferred from other antipsychotic medications, it is recommended that a test injection of 20 mg be administered and the patient's response monitored for about a week, including observation of side effects.

**SOURCES**—H. Lundbeck & Co., Ottilivaje 7, 2500 Valby, Denmark; Dow Pharmaceuticals, Down Chemical Canada, Inc., 380 Elgin Mills Road East, Rochmond Hill, Ontario L4C 5H2, Canada; Laboratoires Labaz, B.P. 599–33003 Bordeaux Cedex, France.

## Flurbiprofen—Cebutid 100, Froben

**ACTIONS AND USES**— Flurbiprofen is a nonsteroidal analgesic with antiinflammatory and antipyretic properties used in the treatment of rheumatoid arthritis, osteoarthrosis, and ankylosing spondylitis. Like indoprofen, flurbiprofen is derived from phenylpropionic acid and is believed to produce its effects by inhibiting the synthesis of pain-producing and inflammatory prostaglandins by the body's tissues. Flurbiprofen is reported to be slightly more effective than naproxen, often recommended as the drug of choice among nonhormonal analgesics.

**PRECAUTIONS**—Flurbiprofen is reported to produce slightly more gastrointestinal side effects than ibuprofen or naproxen analgesic drugs. The drug should be used with caution in patients with impaired liver or kidney function, in pregnancy, and in patients with peptic ulcers or allergies, particularly hypersensitivity to aspirin and other salicylate medications. Side effects may include nausea, occasional gastrointestinal bleeding, dizziness, and a ringing or buzzing in the ears.

**DOSAGE AND ADMINISTRATION**—Flurbiprofen is supplied in 50 and 100 mg tablets. The usual recommended dosage is 150 to 200 mg per day in three to four divided doses for most painful and inflammatory rheumatic or musculoskeletal disorders, and up to 300 mg per day for acute or severe cases. It is recommended that the medication be taken after meals.

**SOURCES**—Laboratoires Boots-Dacour, 49, rue de Bitche, B.P. 66, 92404 Courbevoie Cedex, France; The Boots Company, Ltd., 1 Thane Road West, Nottingham NG2 3AA, England.

## Fluspirilene—Imap, Redeptin

**ACTIONS AND USES**—Fluspirilene is a tranquilizer used as a maintenance drug for schizophrenia and related psychotic conditions. Fluspirilene has fewer sedative effects than most other major tranquilizers and fewer side effects that involve interference with functions of the nerve transmitter substance acetylcholine in the autonomic nervous system. However, fluspirilene produces greater side effects characterized by involuntary muscle activity and marked by restlessness and excitement. Fluspirilene is related chemically to haloperidol, another antipsychotic drug, but has pharmacological action similar to the chlorpromazine tranquilizers. In addition to its uses in the management of acute and chronic schizophrenia, fluspirilene has been used in the treatment of depression, anxiety state, anxiety neuroses, and anorexia nervosa. Because it is a long-acting agent, it is used as a substitution for other major tranquilizers in certain psychotic patients who have been stabilized on short-acting psychotropic drugs. Also, as an injectable tranquilizer, fluspirilene often is used as a substitute for oral tranquilizers in patients who cannot be relied upon to follow the physician's advice about using oral medications.

**PRECAUTIONS**—Fluspirilene should not be given to patients in a comatose state or to patients with a known sensitivity to fluspirilene or chemically related drugs, patients with impaired kidney or liver function, blood diseases, parkinsonism, or subcortical brain damage. The safety of fluspirilene in pregnancy has not been established, and the drug therefore should not be given to women of childbearing age unless the potential benefits outweigh the risks. The drug also is not recommended for children. Because fluspirilene, like other tranquilizers, has an antiemetic effect, it may suppress the symptoms of nausea and vomiting that might be diagnostic of another illness. Fluspirilene also may interact with other drugs, particularly alcohol and other central nervous system depressants, causing an additive effect. Fluspirilene alone can impair mental alertness and motor coordination, making it dangerous for the patient to operate a motor vehicle, machinery, or perform other tasks that require normal mental and physical abilities. Fluspirilene can lower the convulsive threshold in patients subject to epileptic seizures, making them more vulnerable to attacks. Fluspirilene tends to produce hypotension, or abnormally low blood pressure, in some patients, requiring caution in the use of anesthetics and preoperative medications in patients undergoing surgery. Adverse effects include autonomic nervous system aberrations, such as involuntary muscle activity and powerful muscle contractions resulting in rigid postures. Such reactions usually occur or peak about two days after the start of fluspirilene therapy and subside after adjustment of dosages. Other side effects include tiredness, gastrointestinal distress, blurred vision, lowered blood pressure, dizziness, skin rashes, and electrocardiographic changes.

**DOSAGE AND ADMINISTRATION**—Fluspirilene is supplied in 1 and 3 ml ampules and 6 ml vials, each containing 2 mg fluspirilene per ml. The usual initial dosage is 2 mg weekly by deep intramuscular injection, followed by increased doses in increments of 2 mg per week until an adequate response is achieved. Most patients respond to doses between 2 and 8 mg per week, but some may require larger weekly doses. The recommended maximum is 20 mg per week.

**SOURCES**—Janssen Pharmaceutica, Turnhoutsebaan 30, 2340 Beerse, Belgium; McNeil Laboratories (Canada) Ltd., 600 Main Street West, Stouffville, Ontario LOH 1LO, Canada.

## Fonazine Mesylate (Dimethothiazine Mesylate)—Alius, Banistyl, Bisbermin, Bonpac, Calsekin, Migrethiazin, Migristene, Neomestin, Normelin, Promaquid, Yoristen

**ACTIONS AND USES**—Fonazine mesylate is an antihistamine drug with properties that make it effective in the treatment of a wide range of allergic reactions and other histamine-related disorders, including migraine headache, hay fever, and rhinitis. The product also is used to relieve symptoms of urticaria, allergic eczema, pruritus, seborrheic and atopic dermatitis, prurigo, and itching of the anogenital area. It is reported to be of limited value in maintenance therapy of some mild cases of bronchial asthma. Laboratory studies indicate that fonazine mesylate reduces or abolishes the actions of histamine, which are responsible for most of the symptoms of allergic reactions. It also shows a greater antiserotonin effect (which accounts for its headache-reducing effects) than promethazine, a prototype antihistamine drug. Fonazine mesylate, meanwhile, causes less drowsiness than other antihistamines and has a greater antiemetic effect in controlling motion sickness.

**PRECAUTIONS**—The safety of fonazine mesylate in pregnant women and nursing mothers has not been established, and the drug therefore is not recommended for patients in these groups. The patient should avoid alcoholic beverages while taking fonazine mesylate and should not operate machinery or motor vehicles when starting use of the drug until it has been demonstrated that fonazine mesylate will not produce drowsiness, confusion, or other dangerous effects in the individual. Side effects reported include blurred vision, dryness of the mouth, dizziness, tiredness, skin rash, and nervousness. Adverse effects generally are controlled by reducing the dosage or discontinuing the medication. The product should be administered only under close supervision to children under 6 years of age. There is no specific antidote for overdosage, and centrally acting emetics are not recommended because of the antiemetic effect of the drug. Gastric lavage and treatment of symptoms are advised in the event of an overdose.

**DOSAGE AND ADMINISTRATION**—Fonazine mesylate is supplied in 20 mg capsules and in some areas also is available in suppositories. The usual recommended adult oral dosage is one 20 mg capsule three times daily, initially, with a gradual increase up to a total daily intake of 120 mg in three divided doses if necessary. For children between the ages of 6 and 12, the usual dosage is 10 mg twice daily, and for adolescents, 20 mg two or three times daily.

**SOURCES**—May & Baker Limited, Dagenham, Essex RM 10 7XS, England; Rhone-Poulenc Pharma Inc., 8580 Esplanade, Montreal, Quebec H2P 2R9, Canada; Rhodia Mexicana, S.A. de C.V., Jose Ma. Rico No. 611, Mexico 12, D.F., Mexico.

## **Framycetin Sulfate**—Framycort, Framygen, Isoframicol, Sofradex, Soframycin, Soframycine, Sofratul, Sofra-Tulle, Tuttomycin

**ACTIONS AND USES**—Framycetin sulfate is an antibiotic used primarily in the treatment of bacterial infections of the skin and mucous membrane surfaces of the body. It is closely related to neomycin in actions and uses and usually contains small amounts of one or more of the various forms of neomycin. Framycetin is considered safe for topical application—to infections of the skin, eye, ear, and certain mucous membranes—but too potent for general internal use. It is used for pyoderma, folliculitis, paronychia, sycosis barbae, and impetigo, all involving bacterial infections of the skin, and for secondary infections of eczema, burns, contact dermatitis, acne, psoriasis, varicose ulcers, neurodermatitis, seborrhea, and fungal disorders. A nebulizer spray preparation of framycetin is used in the treatment of rhinitis, sinusitis, sore throat, pharyngitis, and laryngitis. Framycetin also is prepared as ophthalmic drops and ointments for corneal abrasions, burns, and ulcers, conjunctivitis, styes, blepharitis due to bacterial infection of the eyelid, and as a preventive against infection due to a foreign body in the eye. Framycetin is sometimes combined with other drugs or used alone to reduce the bacterial population by direct instillation in specific internal sites, such as the urinary bladder or the intestine. Because of the sensitivity of the kidney to framycetin, the drug usually is introduced by catheter to irrigate the bladder. The procedure also may be used to control potential infection following prostate surgery.

**PRECAUTIONS**—Framycetin should not be administered to patients who are sensitive to the drug or related antibiotics, such as neomycin. The nebulizer spray form of the drug should not be administered to small children or to patients using monoamine oxidase inhibitors. The drug should never be administered by intravenous or intramuscular injection because of the risk of kidney damage or ototoxicity (a condition characterized by deafness due to sensitivity of the sensory organs of the inner ear to certain drugs). Deafness has developed in patients several weeks after antibiotics of the framycetin type have been discontinued. Ototoxicity can develop from absorption of framycetin through the skin, particularly where there are breaks in the skin, as a result of excessive or prolonged use of the drug. Prolonged use of antibiotics also can encourage the overgrowth of bacteria that are not susceptible to the drug used. When used in the treatment of infections of the external ear canal, caution should be used in determining whether the eardrum is intact because of the risk of framycetin spreading into the middle and inner ear regions. Side effects generally are limited to allergic reactions in the skin areas treated with framycetin.

**DOSAGE AND ADMINISTRATION**—Framycetin is supplied as 0.5 percent drops, creams, and ointments for application to the eye, external ear, and skin areas. It also is prepared as a 1.5 percent cream also containing gramicidin, an antibiotic with a mode of action that differs from that of framycetin. The nasal spray contains a 1.25 percent framycetin sulfate solution. The ointments and creams usually are applied to the infected area two to four times daily, limiting the area of application so as to reduce the risk of absorption through the skin. The ophthalmic drops are applied at a rate of one or two drops every one to two hours in acute infections or one to two drops three or four times daily for mild to moderate infections. For most nose and throat infections, the recommended nebulizer dosage is four or five sprays into each nostril every two or three hours. Framycetin also is supplied as a sterile powder to be administered for infections of the bladder or the cornea, for the preservation of corneal grafts, and for similar purposes at a rate not exceeding 500 mg per day. Framycetin is available as a 1 percent impregnated sterile dressing for immediate use in the protection of lesions caused by burns, scalds, lacerations, bites, puncture wounds, crush injuries, and similar emergency conditions.

**SOURCES**—Roussel de Venezuela, S.A., Calle 7 cruce con Calle 4, Edif. Roussel, La Urbina, Apartado 75.770, Caracas 1/070-A, Venezuela; Laboratoires du Docteur E. Bouchara, 8, rue Pastourelle, 75003 Paris, France; Roussel Canada, Inc., 4045 Côte Vertu, Montreal, Quebec H4R 2E8, Canada; Roussel Laboratories Ltd., Roussel House, Wembley Park, Middlesex HA9 ONF, England.

## Fusidic Acid (Diethanolamine Fusidate, Sodium Fusidate) —Fusidin, Fusidine, Fusidin H

**ACTIONS AND USES**—Fusidic acid is an antibiotic that is used primarily in the treatment of staphylococcal infections, particularly in cases that have failed to respond to other kinds of antibiotics. It has been used to treat staphylococcal septicemia, burns, endocarditis, pneumonia, peritonitis, impetigo, osteomyelitis, enteritis, infected wounds, furunculosis, skin grafts, infections of skin lesions originating as abrasions, acne, varicose ulcers, eczema, soft tissue abscesses, and infections complicating cystic fibrosis. Fusidic acid is derived from a fungus and is related to the cephalosporin antibiotics. The antibiotic and its salts have an unusual ability to penetrate tissue and reach deep infections, particularly infections in bones. It acts against bacteria by preventing them from assembling protein molecules needed for their own survival and growth; laboratory studies show bacterial cells stop dividing within two minutes after contact with fusidic acid or its salts. Fusidic acid has been recommended for treatment of staphylococcal infections caused by strains that have become resistant to penicillin, but resistance to fusidic acid also is possible and has been observed in hospitals using the antibiotic in the treatment of skin disorders.

**PRECAUTIONS**—Fusidic acid should not be administered to patients with a known hypersensitivity to the drug or its salts. The drug is excreted mainly in the bile, so caution should be exercised in administering the drug to patients with impaired liver function. Liver function tests also are recommended for patients receiving large doses of fusidic acid, when the drug is used for prolonged periods, or when the drug is administered concurrently with other medications that are excreted in the bile. Fusidic acid may interact synergistically or antagonistically with other antibiotics, depending upon such factors as their mode of action. For example, fusidic acid inhibits protein synthesis but penicillin requires bacterial cell growth in order to produce its own antibiotic activity. The safety of fusidic acid in pregnancy has not been established. The drug is believed to cross the placental barrier and also has been detected in breast milk, although the significance for nursing mothers has not been determined. Side effects reported among patients using fusidic acid include nausea, vomiting, epigastric distress, diarrhea, and loss of appetite, as well as skin rashes, blurred vision, headaches, and dizziness. Some local inflammation and blood vessel spasms have been associated with intravenous injection of the drug.

**DOSAGE AND ADMINISTRATION**—Fusidic acid is supplied in 250 mg capsules and tablets, in a suspension providing 250 mg of fusidic acid per 5 ml dose, in vials containing 580 mg of diethanolamine fusidate (equivalent to approximately 500 mg of fusidic acid), and as 2 percent ointments and gels. The antibiotic also is available in a single-dose Caviject applicator that injects a sodium fusidate gel and in Intertulle sterile gauze squares impregnated with sodium fusidate ointment. The usual oral dosage for severe infections is 500 mg taken three times daily as capsules or tablets or 15 ml (about one-half ounce) of the suspension form taken three times a day. For children, the recommended dosage is 10 ml three times daily for those between 5 and 12 years of age and 5 ml (the equivalent of one teaspoonful) three times daily for those between 1 and 5 years of age. For infants, the dosage is calculated at 1 ml per kg of body weight per day divided into three equal doses. The recommended intravenous dosage for adults and children weighing more than 50 kg (110 pounds) is one vial (580 mg) three times a day, and for those weighing less than 50 kg, the intravenous dosage is 6 to 7 mg per kg of body weight three times daily. The gels and ointments are applied gently three or four times a day to uncovered lesions and less frequently to lesions covered by dressings. The Caviject gel is injected into an abscess that has been incised and curetted, after which the lesion is covered by a dressing and the tube and nozzle of the device discarded. The Intertulle impregnated dressing usually is replaced once a day. Fusidic acid preparations may contain other drugs, such as corticosteroids or other antibiotics.

**SOURCES**—Laboratoire Leo, 38, avenue Hoche, 75008 Paris, France; Sigma Tau s.p.a., Via Pontina Km. 30,400, 00040 Pomezia (Roma), Italy; Pennwalt of Canada Limited, 393 Midwest Road, Scarborough, Ontario M1P 3A6, Canada; Løvens kemiske Fabrik, Industriparken 55, DK-2750 Ballerup, Sweden; Leo Laboratories Ltd., Longwick Rd., Princes Risborough, Aylesbury, Bucks HP17 9RR, England.

## Gangliosides—Cronassial

**ACTIONS AND USES**—Gangliosides are presently used for the treatment of various types of peripheral neuropathies (diseases of nervous tissue outside the brain and spinal cord; conditions sometimes identified as neuritis or neuralgia are examples of peripheral neuropathies). The gangliosides used in the treatment of peripheral neuropathies are extracted with a high degree of purity from the brain tissues of cattle. They act by accelerating and improving the healing process of damaged or diseased nerves. The pharmaceutical product is a mixture of four major types of gangliosides. It is reported to have been particularly successful in the treatment of diabetic neuropathy and is being evaluated as a possible treatment for diseases of the central nervous system.

**PRECAUTIONS**—No serious adverse effects have been reported from the use of gangliosides to date. Because it is an injected medication, some patients have experienced local pain or discomfort commonly associated with injected drugs.

**DOSAGE AND ADMINISTRATION**—The usual recommended dosage is 10 to 40 mg of gangliosides daily administered as a single intramuscular injection.

**SOURCE**—Fidia s.p.a., Via Ponte della Fabbrica, 3/A, 35031 Abano Terme, Italy.

## Gliclazide—Diamicron, Dramion

**ACTIONS AND USES**—Gliclazide is a drug for the treatment of maturity-onset diabetes in patients who do not require insulin injections but whose symptoms cannot be controlled by diet alone. Gliclazide is similar to other oral diabetic medications derived from sulfonylurea compounds, but it is believed to cause fewer long-term complications. Gliclazide has fibrinolytic properties and related actions that reduce the risk of blood clotting and circulatory disorders associated with diabetic therapy. The product acts primarily by increasing the release of natural insulin from the beta cells of the pancreas. Thus, a certain amount of beta-cell function must be present in the patient in order for the drug to be effective. Sulfonylurea drugs in general are ineffective in patients with juvenile-onset diabetes or in patients whose pancreas has been removed. Gliclazide may stimulate an overgrowth of beta cells in patients treated with the drug.

**PRECAUTIONS**—There is a lack of information about the effects of gliclazide use in pregnancy or in breast milk, so the drug is not recommended for pregnant women or nursing mothers unless the benefits outweigh the risks. Gliclazide should not be given to patients whose diabetes is complicated by acidosis, an abnormal acid-base balance in the individual's body chemistry; in ketosis, associated with incomplete metabolism of food fats; or in diabetic coma. It is not recommended for children, for patients with juvenile-onset diabetes, for persons with brittle diabetes due to unpredictable variations in the individual's glucose tolerance, or for patients with severe liver or kidney impairment. The drug should be avoided by persons known to be sensitive to other types of oral diabetic drugs and by diabetic patients undergoing surgery, after severe trauma, or during infections. Gliclazide may interact with other drugs that can alter the patient's diabetic state or the effectiveness of gliclazide, such as certain sulfa drugs, salicylates, beta-blocking agents, monoamine oxidase inhibitors, diuretics, and steroid hormones. Side effects may include headache, nausea, gastrointestinal distress, and skin rashes.

**DOSAGE AND ADMINISTRATION**—Gliclazide is supplied in tablets containing 80 mg each of the drug. The tablets are scored so they can be divided into even portions if needed. The usual initial dose is 40 to 80 mg of gliclazide, or one-half to one tablet, daily, followed by gradually increased doses until a satisfactory level of control is reached. The usual maximum daily dose in 320 mg.

**SOURCES**—Laboratoires Servier, 22 rue Garnier, 92200 Neuilly, France; Laboratorios Kriya, S.A., Ave. Jose Maria Rico No. 317, Mexico 12, D.F., Mexico; Servier Laboratories (Aust) Pty Ltd., 2–8 Lynch Street, Hawthorn Vic., Australia.

## **Gliquidone**—Glurenor, Glurenorm

**ACTIONS AND USES**—Gliquidone is an oral hypoglycemic drug for the treatment of maturity-onset diabetes in patients who fail to maintain control of the disease with diet. Gliquidone is similar to chlorpropamide, a commonly prescribed drug that stimulates the cells of the pancreas to secrete more insulin. It is believed the drugs also may reduce the amount of blood sugar released by the liver. Gliquidone requires that the patient still has a certain amount of active insulin-synthesizing and secreting cells in the pancreas. Gliquidone is given alone and when necessary in combination with a biguanide type of oral hypoglycemic medication, which can increase the effectiveness of the insulin a diabetic patient may be able to produce.

**PRECAUTIONS**—Gliquidone should not be given to juvenile-onset diabetics, as the medication does not replace insulin. It is recommended that patients undergoing surgery, pregnant patients, and those with an acute infection or impaired kidney or liver function be transferred temporarily to insulin medication. Patients should be advised that physical exercise, consumption of alcoholic beverages, and certain medications such as psychotropic drugs, antibiotics, and beta-blockers can increase the effects of oral hypoglycemic drugs. The most common side effects reported are gastrointestinal distress and skin reactions.

**DOSAGE AND ADMINISTRATION**—Gliquidone is supplied in 30 mg tablets. While dosage varies according to individual patient requirements, most maturity-onset diabetes patients respond to 45 to 60 mg per day. The medication is taken in two to three divided doses, with the largest of unequal doses taken in the morning before breakfast. It is recommended that all doses be taken at least 30 minutes before a meal. The maximum daily dose recommended is 180 mg.

**SOURCE**—Winthrop Laboratories, Sterling-Winthrop House, Surbiton-upon-Thames, Surrey KT6 4PH, England.

## Glyburide (Glibenclamide, Glybenclamide)—Adiab, Daonil, Diabeta, Euglucon, Gilemal, Gliben, Glibenclamida McKesson, Glibenil, Gliboral, Glidiabet, Glucolon, Glucoven, Miglucan, Pira

**ACTIONS AND USES**—Glyburide is an oral hypoglycemic drug used by patients with diabetes mellitus of a mild, stable, maturity-onset or adult type, which cannot be controlled adequately by dietary management and exercise. It also is used when insulin therapy is not appropriate or when a diabetic patient is not ketosis-prone, a condition that results from incomplete metabolism of fats used as body fuel by diabetics when carbohydrates cannot be utilized as a source of energy. The principal action of glyburide is an increased release of insulin from cells in the pancreas, leading to a more effective carbohydrate metabolism. Use of glyburide requires a certain capacity of the pancreas to produce insulin, although the amounts produced may not be adequate for normal health. In most cases of maturity-onset diabetes, the pancreas is still able to produce some insulin. Other mechanisms leading to a reduction of blood sugar are also believed to be influenced by glyburide. Studies show that blood sugar levels fall within 3 hours after a single dose of glyburide, and a reduced blood sugar concentration continues for approximately 15 hours. Laboratory experiments with pancreatic cells from animals showed they released insulin continuously in the presence of 500 micrograms of glyburide per milliliter of fluid. Glyburide is completely metabolized in the human body, and the metabolites are excreted via the bile in urine and feces.

**PRECAUTIONS**—Glyburide should not be given to patients with juvenile diabetes mellitus or those with unstable or insulin-dependent diabetes, ketoacidosis, coma, or other metabolic complications. The use of glyburide will not prevent the development of complications peculiar to diabetes mellitus. The safety of glyburide in pregnancy has not been established, and like other oral antidiabetic drugs, it should not be given during pregnancy or to a woman who is contemplating pregnancy. It should not be used by patients with impaired liver or kidney function or during stressful conditions, including severe infections, injury, or surgery; in the event of accidents or emergency surgery, the patient should be given insulin rather than an oral hypoglycemic drug. Over a period of time, patients may become progressively less responsive to therapy with oral antidiabetic agents because of deterioration of their condition. If a loss of adequate blood-glucose-lowering response to glyburide is detected, the product should be discontinued. Severe hypoglycemia can be induced by sulfonylurea drugs, including glyburide; particularly susceptible are elderly persons, patients with impaired liver or kidney function, and those with adrenal insufficiency or who are malnourished or debilitated. Patients who develop maturity-onset diabetes after the age of 65 may be at greatest risk of developing hypoglycemia. Hypoglycemia also is most likely to occur when the calorie intake is inadequate or after strenuous physical exertion, including exercise. Like other sulfonylurea drugs, glyburide may react adversely with alcoholic beverages, corticosteroid medications, oral contraceptives, certain diuretics, phenylbutazone, monoamine oxidase inhibitors, beta-blockers such as propranolol, and other drugs. Overdosage with glyburide can result in hypoglycemia, but the dosage level that causes the effect varies with different individuals. The use of glyburide is intended as a therapy to supplement a proper diabetic diet and not as a substitute for a dietary regimen.

**DOSAGE AND ADMINISTRATION**—Glyburide is supplied in 2.5 and 5 mg tablets, scored for division into smaller doses. The usual dose for persons under 60 years of age is 5 mg daily; for those over 60 years, the initial dose is 2.5 mg daily. The initial dose is continued for five to seven days, then adjusted upward in increments of 2.5 mg daily according to individual patient needs. The maximum recommended dose is 20 mg daily; higher doses rarely have added benefit.

**SOURCES**—Hoechst Pharmaceuticals, Canadian Hoechst Limited,

.5 Côte Vertu Blvd., Montreal, Quebec H4R 1R6, Canada; Novo .dustri A/S, Gamle Drammensv. 48, 1320 Stabekk, Norway; Laboratorios Calox, C.A., Callejon Gutierrez Francisco Miranda, Apartado 62.483, Caracas, Venezuela.

**Gonadorelin (Gonadoliberin, Luliberin)**—HRF Ayerst, Lutamin, Relefact LH-RH, Relefact LH-RH/TRH, Relisform L, Stimu-LH

**ACTIONS AND USES**—Gonadorelin is a sex hormone occurring both naturally and as a synthetic agent used in the treatment of male and female sterility. It also is employed in the treatment of cryptorchidism in males, due to the failure of one or both testes to descend into the scrotum. Gonadorelin stimulates the natural synthesis and release of the follicle-stimulating and luteinizing hormones in the anterior lobe of the pituitary gland. Those hormones aid in the maturation and release of the ovum and the production of estrogen in the female and the development of spermatozoa and production of testosterone in the male. By correcting deficiencies of the sex hormones in both sexes, infertility also is corrected. However, because of the short half-life of gonadorelin, repeated doses often are necessary. Other uses of gonadorelin include growth hormone deficiency treatment, diagnosis of pituitary and hypothalamic disorders, and, through a variation in the gonadorelin molecule, a contraceptive that can be administered as a nasal spray.

**PRECAUTIONS**—Adverse effects reported from the use of gonadorelin include increased menstrual bleeding, abdominal pain, headache, and nausea. A case of temporary visual difficulty has been observed following administration of the drug.

**DOSAGE AND ADMINISTRATION**—Gonadorelin is supplied in 100 and 500 mcg vials of powder to be diluted or 1 ml ampules containing 100 mcg of the drug for administration by injection. The usual dose is 100 mcg, intravenously. Smaller doses have been used to treat amenorrhea, or absence of menses, and larger doses have been employed to correct cryptorchidism.

**SOURCES**—Ayerst Laboratories Ltd., South Way, Andover, Hants SP10 5LT, England; Hoechst UK Ltd., Pharmaceutical Division, Hoechst House, Salisbury Rd., Hounslow, Middx TW4 6JH, England.

**Heptabarbital (Heptabarbitone)**—Medapan, Medomin, Medomina, Medomine

**ACTIONS AND USES**—Heptabarbital is a sedative used mainly for insomnia, for management of anxiety-tension states, and as a premedication for minor surgical procedures. Heptabarbital is one of the intermediate-acting barbiturates, so classified because its duration of action is less than eight hours. It is preferred by some authorities for the treatment of chronic insomnia because the drug makes it easier for the patient to fall asleep and also tends to increase total sleep time. In most cases, heptabarbital produces from three to six hours of uninterrupted sleep when used at a hypnotic dose level.

**PRECAUTIONS**—Heptabarbital should not be given to patients with severe respiratory or circulatory depression, to patients with a known addiction for sedative drugs, or to patients with a personal or family history of acute intermittent porphyria. The porphyria is an inherited disorder that may not produce symptoms until precipitated by infection, starvation including crash diets, sex hormones, and certain drugs, including barbiturates, leading to acute nervous system dysfunction which can be fatal. Barbiturates also tend to induce the liver to produce enzymes that increase the body's tolerance for alcohol and other depressant drugs. The drug should not be given to patients with impaired liver function. Patients should be advised that heptarbarbital may interact with alcohol and other drugs, producing an additive effect when used concurrently with other depressants. When used concurrently with oral contraceptives, heptabarbital may reduce the effectiveness of the hormonal drugs or cause breakthrough bleeding. The drug should not be used during the first trimester of pregnancy unless the potential benefits outweigh the risks. Prolonged use of heptabarbital or other barbiturates, even at prescribed dosages, may result in addiction and withdrawal symptoms of delirium and convulsions if the drug is suddenly discontinued. Side effects may include nausea, vomiting, gastrointestinal distress, paradoxical excitement and restlessness, and skin rashes.

**DOSAGE AND ADMINISTRATION**—Heptabarbital is supplied in 200 mg tablets cross-scored to facilitate division into smaller doses. The usual adult dose for insomnia is 200 to 400 mg taken with a warm milk drink about 30 minutes before retiring. The recommended dosage for daytime sedation is 50 to 100 mg, taken as one-fourth to one-half tablet, three or four times during the day. The maximum recommended children's dose is 200 mg for those over 10 years of age, 100 mg for children between 2 and 10 years, and 50 mg for younger children.

**SOURCES**—Geigy Pharmaceuticals, Ciba-Geigy Canada Ltd., 6860 Century Ave., Mississauga, Ontario L5N 2W5, Canada; Ciba-Geigy Lakemedel AB, Box 605, 421 26 V Frolunda, Sweden; Geigy Pharmaceuticals, Horsham, West Sussex RH12 4AB, England; Laboratoires Ciba-Geigy, 2–4, rue Lionel-Terray, 92506 Rueil-Malmaison, France.

## Hexamethylomelamine (Trimethylomelamine)—Hexastat

**ACTIONS AND USES**—Hexamethylomelamine is an anticancer drug used primarily in the treatment of cancer of the ovaries and other solid tumors. It has been used in the treatment of lung cancer and cancer of the cervix. Hexamethylomelamine is related chemically to triethylenemelamine and tretamine, agents that also have been used in the treatment of cancer. Hexamethylomelamine acts by interfering with the production of nucleic acid molecules in cancer cells, thereby inhibiting their growth and proliferation. The drug also acts as an antimetabolite by disrupting the normal enzyme activity of cancer cells. In clinical studies, hexamethylomelamine reportedly produced a regression rate of 20 percent in cancers of the cervix and respiratory tract.

**PRECAUTIONS**—Hexamethylomelamine should not be given to women of childbearing potential unless the potential benefits outweigh the risks. Patients using the product should be monitored closely for signs of blood count changes, particularly reduced levels of white cells and platelets. Adverse effects include nausea and vomiting, moderate but reversible blood count changes, and skin reactions in the form of rash, pruritus, or eczema. With prolonged or high doses of hexamethylomelamine, neurological effects have been observed, including numbness, tingling or prickling sensations, depression, confusion, drowsiness, and occasional hallucinations. The neurological effects have generally been reversible, but in a few cases peripheral neuropathy symptoms continued after the drug was discontinued.

**DOSAGE AND ADMINISTRATION**—Hexamethylomelamine is supplied in 100 mg capsules. The usual dosage for treatment of lung cancer is 400 to 500 mg per day, taken in three or four divided doses between meals and at bedtime. The dosage is continued for five days, followed by an interval of three weeks, after which the five-day course is repeated. For cancers of the reproductive tract, the recommended dosage is 400 to 500 mg per day for a course of 21 days each month.

**SOURCE**—Laboratoire Roger Bellon, B.P. 105–159, av. du Roule, 92201 Neuilly-sur-Seine Cedex, France.

## Hexetidine—Buchex, Bucosept, Collu-Hextril, Drossadin, Duranil, Givalex, Glypesin, Hexocil, Hexoral, Hextril, Oraldene, Oraldine, Oraseptic, Sterisil, Steri/Sol

**ACTIONS AND USES**—Hexetidine is a drug used in a variety of antiseptic procedures because it is active against strains of bacteria, protozoa, and fungi. It is recommended in the treatment of mouth and throat infections, including gingivitis, pharyngitis, pyorrhea, stomatitis, dental ulcers, halitosis, pre- and post-dental surgery, oral thrush, aphthous ulcers of the mouth, and tonsillitis. It has been used in combating infections caused by penicillin-resistant *Staphylococcus*, anaerobic *Staphylococcus* and *Streptococcus*, *Candida albicans*, and *Trichophyton* strains of skin fungus, in addition to other infectious microorganisms. In addition to mouth, throat, and skin applications, hexetidine has been used in a gel form for the treatment of vaginitis, cervicitis, vulvar pruritus, and endometritis.

**PRECAUTIONS**—Except for occasional mild irritation of the mucosal lining of the mouth, adverse effects of hexetidine when used as a mouth rinse or gargle have not been reported in the medical literature. However, precautions should be taken in administering hexetidine to small children because of the menthol or other substances also contained in the preparation. Caution also should be used to avoid swallowing the product, even though the ingredients in the solution are not present in toxic amounts.

**DOSAGE AND ADMINISTRATION**—Hexetidine is supplied as a 1 percent solution with 9 percent alcohol. For infections of the mouth and throat, it is recommended that the patient use the solution at full strength as a mouthwash, gargle, or spray each morning and night. The recommended amount per application is 15 ml, or approximately one-half ounce. The solution also can be applied by swab to local ulcers or other lesions in the oral cavity. For vaginal and uterine treatment, hexetidine is supplied in 10 mg ovule inserts and as a 50 g container of gel with applicator. The recommended dosage is daily use of the gynecological preparation for about two weeks.

**SOURCES**—Vister s.p.a., Via Don Rossi, 22064 Castenovo Brianza (Como), Italy; Parke, Davis Canada, Inc., Box 633, Station A, Scarborough, Ontario M1K 5C5, Canada; William R. Warner & Co., Limited, Usk Road Pontypool, Gwent NP4 OYH, England; Laboratorios Substancia, C.A., Avenida Principal de Los Ruices, Apartado 11.439, Caracas 101, Venezuela; Cia. Medicinal "La Campana," S.A. de C.V., Av. Division del Norte No. 3443, Mexico 21, D.F., Mexico; Laboratoires Norgan, 21, rue de Madrid, 75008 Paris, France.

## **Hydrocortisone 17-Butyrate**—Alfason, Locoid, Locoid C, Locoidon, Plancol

**ACTIONS AND USES**—Hydrocortisone 17-butyrate is a corticosteroid used in the treatment of eczema, psoriasis, dermatitis, and other skin disorders. It has been used for the relief of symptoms of anogenital pruritus, lichen planus, intertrigo, seborrhea capitis with or without severe dandruff, otitis externa, systemic lupus erythematosus, skin disorders caused by radiation or sunlight, neurodermatitis, burns, and various allergies. It is a class II, or potent, corticosteroid for skin applications and requires greater care than moderately potent or mild corticosteroids to avoid effects resulting from absorption of the medication through the skin layers. Hydrocortisone 17-butyrate usually is used to treat inflammatory skin disorders that fail to respond to the less potent corticosteroid drugs.

**PRECAUTIONS**—The more potent corticosteroids used in treating skin disorders carry the risk of absorption through the skin resulting in severe suppression of pituitary and adrenal gland hormone functions. The risk of hormonal imbalance may be affected by the area of the body treated, the length of treatment, the amount of raw surface area treated, application of the medicine in skin folds, and use of occlusive dressings such as plastic sheeting that seal the treated area from the surrounding air. The product should not be used during pregnancy unless directed by a physician. It should not be used in the presence of bacterial infections without specific antibiotic therapy. Nor should the product be used in the presence of viral, fungal, tuberculous, or treponemal (syphilis, yaws, pinta) infections. Caution should be exercised in the administration of corticosteroid creams or ointments to children, particularly children under the age of 3 years, who should not receive continuous treatment for more than three weeks. The product should not be applied near the eyes or in the external ear canal of a patient with a perforated eardrum. Prolonged use, particularly with occlusive dressings, can result not only in skin atrophy but in suppression of pituitary and adrenal gland functions.

**DOSAGE AND ADMINISTRATION**—Hydrocortisone 17-butyrate is supplied as 0.1 percent ointments, creams, and lotions. The creams or ointments are applied evenly in a thin layer to affected skin areas two to four times a day. The lotion, intended primarily for scalp treatment, also is applied two to four times daily. Some authorities advise that class II corticosteroids should not be used longer than 14 days at a time, nor that more than 60 g of the product be applied during that period. Studies indicate that use of more than 50 g of hydrocortisone 17-butyrate products in a short period of time may affect normal adrenal functions.

**SOURCES**—Brocades s.p.a., Viale Spagna 45, 20093 Cologno Monzese (M1), Italy; Gist-Brocades Farmaca Nederland B.V., Frijdastraat 7–9, 2288 EX Rijswijk, The Netherlands; Mycofarm de Mexico, S.A., Blvd. W.C. Buchanan No. 125, Naucalpan de Juarez, Edo. de Mexico, Mexico.

## Hydroxytryptophan (L-5-Hydroxytryptophan, 5-Hydroxytryptophan)—Pretonine, Quietim, Telesol

**ACTIONS AND USES**—Hydroxytryptophan is a substance from which the body manufactures serotonin, a chemical that enhances motor nerve functions in animals. When hydroxytryptophan is given by mouth to patients, there is a significant increase in the level of serotonin in their central nervous systems. A deficiency of serotonin is associated with a variety of nervous system disorders, including schizophrenia, myoclonus, depression, parkinsonism, and the self-mutilation symptoms of Lesch-Nyhan syndrome. Hydroxytryptophan also has been used in the treatment of Gilles de la Tourette syndrome, which is marked by tics as well as self-mutilation. The several forms of myoclonus, characterized by involuntary jerky muscle movements, seem to have in common a deficiency of brain serotonin.

**PRECAUTIONS**—Because of the tendency of hydroxytryptophan to trigger excess serotonin formation in tissues other than the target organ, the product usually is administered with carbidopa to reduce gastrointestinal side effects. The side effects of hydroxytryptophan medication include nausea, diarrhea, loss of appetite, occasional vomiting, and breathing difficulty. Some neurological side effects have been observed with large doses. They include dilation of the pupils, abnormally sensitive reflexes, loss of muscle coordination, and blurring of vision. Changes in heart rhythm also have been reported.

**DOSAGE AND ADMINSTRATION**—Hydroxytryptophan can be administered orally or by intravenous injection. Dosages have ranged from 100 mg to 2 g daily in divided doses, depending upon the condition treated and the patient response. For the treatment of myoclonus, oral doses of 400 mg to 2 g with carbidopa in amounts of 100 to 300 mg daily have been administered in divided doses.

**SOURCES**—Laboratoires Arkodex, 58 rue de la Glaciere, 75013 Paris, France; Lasa Laboratorios SA, Plaza Centenario 5, San Sebastian, Spain.

**Hyoscine Butylbromide (Butylscopolamine Bromide)—** Algo-Buscopan, Anafen, Antidol, Aristan, Buscapina, Buscobrax, Buscopan, Buscopax, Butibol, Butilamina, Butylmido, Colepren, Diaste-M, Escapin, Escopina, Espanal, Espasantral, Hiofenil, Hyospan, Lobon, Nolotil, Pascopan, Reladan, Retodol Compositum, Salfalgin, Scordin-B, Selpiran, Spasmania

**ACTIONS AND USES**—Hyoscine butylbromide is an antispasmodic drug used primarily to control spasms in the smooth muscles of the hollow abdominal organs. It is given in the treatment of gastrointestinal spasms, spasms of the gallbladder and biliary tract, urinary tract spasms, spasmodic dysmenorrhea, and in certain obstetrical procedures. Hyoscine butylbromide also is used in x-ray examinations of the abdominal organs; in certain types of surgery, such as eye operations, when it is necessary to suppress reflexes; and in instrumentation procedures, such as endoscopy of the stomach and duodenum. Other uses include the treatment of motion sickness, Meniere's disease, positional vertigo, peptic ulcer, headaches, polyarteritis, burns, toothache or odontalgia, neuralgia, and the management of fractures and dislocations. Hyoscine butylbromide is related chemically to atropine but with effects that are of shorter duration. Like atropine, hyoscine, which also is known as scopolamine, occurs naturally in a number of plants in the potato family, including belladonna and jimsonweed. The drug produces its action by blocking the nerve impulse transmitter substance acetylcholine at receptor sites in smooth muscles and other tissues. In very large doses, atropinelike drugs can block the activity of serotonin and norepinephrine, which also help transmit nerve impulses. Hyoscine is eight to ten times as potent as atropine in effects on the central nervous system.

**PRECAUTIONS**—Hyoscine butylbromide should not be administered to patients with a known sensitivity to atropine, hyoscine, or related drugs. The product also should not be given to patients with glaucoma and should not be administered by intramuscular or intravenous injection to patients with enlarged colon, enlarged prostate with urinary retention, rapid heartbeat, or lesions that cause blockage of the gastrointestinal tract. Side effects can include dry mouth, blurred vision, and abnormally rapid heartbeat, effects that usually can be controlled by reducing the dosage. Hyoscine medications also may cause drowsiness and loss of mental alertness. Patients using hyoscine butylbromide should be advised to avoid consumption of alcoholic beverages and the operation of motor vehicles or machinery, because attention difficulties can result in accidents. Hyoscine, like atropine, can cause dilation of the pupils and sensitivity of the eyes to bright light. Because of the effect of the drug on smooth muscles controlling glandular secretion, the patient may expect decreased production of saliva and an absence of perspiration in warm, humid environments.

**DOSAGE AND ADMINISTRATION**—Hyoscine butylbromide is supplied in 10 mg coated tablets, injection ampules containing 20 mg per ml, and 20 mg suppositories. In some areas, hyoscine butylbromide is supplied in preparations containing other medications, such as amebicides (when gastrointestinal spasms may be due to dysentery) or analgesics. The usual recommended dosage is 20 mg orally four times daily or one or two 20 mg suppositories four times daily, or one injection ampule administered intravenously or intramuscularly and repeated at 30- to 60-minute intervals as necessary to control spasms. Hyoscine butylbromide is not always recommended for children, but some authorities suggest an oral dose of 10 mg three times daily if needed.

**SOURCES**—Boehringer Ingleheim KG, Binger Strasse, Postfach: 200, 6507 Ingleheim am Rhein, West Germany; Farmaquila, S.A., Lago Rodolfo No. 58, Mexico 17, D.F., Mexico; Chemil, Chemioterapici s.r.l., Via Cavour 41/43, 20026 Novate Milanese (M1), Italy; Bequim, C.A., Avenida Nueva Granada, Los Rosales, Apartado 40.150, Caracas, Venezuela; Laboratoires Delagrange, 39, bd de Latour-Maubourg, 75340 Paris Cedex 07, France.

## Ifosfamide—Holoxan, Mitoxana

**ACTIONS AND USES**—Ifosfamide is an anticancer drug used in treatment of tumors of the lung, ovary, breast, testis, uterus, kidney, pancreas, gastrointestinal tract, bone, ear, nose, and throat. It also has been used for soft tissue sarcomas and lymphomas, or tumors of the lymphatic system. Ifosfamide is a cytotoxic alkylating agent, a name given anticancer drugs that act by killing tissue cells by damaging the DNA molecules which contain the genetic information for producing more cells through cell division. Although cytotoxic alkylating agents are more likely to affect rapidly reproducing tissue cells, such as those in tumors, they are generally nonselective and may also damage dividing cells of vital tissues, such as those in blood-forming bone marrow and in the gonads, where female ova and male spermatozoa are produced. Cytotoxic alkylating agents also have an immunosuppressive effect, which is beneficial when used to suppress rejection of organ transplants, but which also makes the patient vulnerable to infectious diseases. Ifosfamide is often used together with other anticancer drugs, such as vincristine or methotrexate, and is used alone or with other drugs and radiation therapy.

**PRECAUTIONS**—Ifosfamide should not be administered to patients with a known hypersensitivity to the drug or to similar products, such as cyclophosphamide. It also should not be given to patients with severe kidney or liver disorders or bleeding in the urinary bladder. Urinary tract disorders are among the more common side effects of ifosfamide use. The drug should not be given to women of childbearing potential unless they use adequate contraception. The drug also should not be given to nursing mothers. Women can expect to experience amenorrhea, and men are likely to experience azoospermia (absence of spermatozoa), because of effects of the drug on reproductive organs. Central nervous system side effects may include confusion, lethargy, restlessness, disorientation, and mood changes. Among other side effects observed are temporary hair loss, irritation of the mouth, and diarrhea. Nausea and vomiting usually associated with the use of anticancer drugs may be controlled with antiemetic drugs. Patients can expect some temporary changes in blood cell counts and an increased susceptibility to infections while using ifosfamide.

**DOSAGE AND ADMINISTRATION**—Ifosfamide is supplied in dry powder vials of 500 mg, 1 g, and 2 g. The drug is dissolved in water in a ratio of 1 g per 12.5 ml of fluid and further diluted in sodium chloride and dextrose solutions to 4 percent (1 g per 25 ml) for direct intravenous injection or slow infusion over a period of 30 minutes to 2 hours. The usual course of therapy consists of single daily doses over a period of three to ten days to a total administration of 8 to 10 g per square meter of body surface. The courses may be repeated after intervals of two to four weeks, depending upon such factors as patient blood counts and response.

**SOURCES**—WB Pharmaceuticals Ltd., P.O. Box 23, Bracknell, Berkshire RG12 4YS, England; Laboratoires Lucien, 3, rue des Ecoles, 92704 Colombes Cedex, France; Schering s.p.a., Via Cassanese, 20090 Segrate (M1), Italy.

## Indapamide—Fludex, Ipamix, Natrilix

**ACTIONS AND USES**—Indapamide is a diuretic and antihypertensive drug used primarily for the treatment of essential hypertension, or high blood pressure that is not secondary to another disorder. It is used either alone or in combined therapy with other antihypertensive drugs. It is similar to chlorothiazide and furosemide, acting to increase the excretion of sodium and chloride ions by inhibiting their reabsorption in the kidney tubules. By reducing the levels of sodium and chloride electrolytes in the body tissues, excess water also is excreted. In addition to its effects on blood pressure, indapamide is used to control edema (the accumulation of fluid) in congestive heart failure and kidney and liver disorders.

**PRECAUTIONS**—Indapamide should not be given to patients who have recently experienced a cerebrovascular accident (stroke) or who may have impaired kidney or liver function. Although no evidence of birth defects has been reported as a result of animal tests, indapamide should not be used during pregnancy. The use of indapamide in high doses may result in an excessive excretion of potassium, leading to symptoms of hypokalemia, a condition marked by muscular weakness or paralysis, muscle spasms, and postural hypotension (a severe drop in blood pressure on suddenly arising from a reclining position). Indapamide should not be used concurrently with other antihypertensive medications that may cause potassium depletion. The action of indapamide develops gradually over a period of several months, and maximum effects may not be observed until after a relatively long period of therapy. Uric acid levels may rise as a result of water depletion but should not pose a problem except in sensitive individuals, such as gout patients. Side effects may include nausea, headache, and occasionally muscular cramps.

**DOSAGE AND ADMINISTRATION**—Indapamide is supplied in 2.5 mg sugar-coated tablets. The usual recommended dosage is one 2.5 mg tablet taken each morning. The manufacturers advise that a larger dose than 2.5 mg daily is not recommended because an added dose will not increase antihypertensive benefits. It is suggested instead that another antihypertensive agent be combined with indapamide if additional antihypertensive activity is needed. There is no recommended dosage for children because of a lack of pediatric experience with the product.

**SOURCES**—Servier Laboratories Ltd., Fulmer Hall, Windmill Road, Fulmer, Slough, Buckinghamshire SL3 6HH, England; L.B.F. Biopharma, Eutherapie Distrib., 27, rue du Pont, 92201 Neuilly-sur-Seine, France; Laboratorios Grossman, S.A., Calzada de Tlalpan No. 2021, Mexico 21, D.F., Mexico; Instituto Gentili s.p.a., Via Mazzini 112, 56100 Pisa, Italy.

## Indoprofen—Flosint, Flosinte, Reumofene

**ACTIONS AND USES**—Indoprofen is an analgesic used primarily for the relief of pain and inflammatory symptoms in rheumatic and arthritic diseases. It has been used in the treatment of rheumatoid arthritis, bursitis, tendinitis, myositis, periarthritis marked by inflammation of the area surrounding a joint, ischialgia or sciatica of the hip, and osteoarthritis (degenerative joint disease) involving the spinal column, knee, hip, or shoulder. Because indoprofen is derived from phenylpropionic acid rather than a corticosteroid hormone, it reportedly can be tolerated better in the long-term management of arthritic and rheumatic disorders by patients who are hypersensitive to hormonal remedies. Like other nonsteroidal analgesics, indoprofen is believed to act by inhibiting the body's synthesis of prostaglandins, which are associated with the symptoms of pain and inflammation.

**PRECAUTIONS**—Adverse effects reported by patients using indoprofen include gastrointestinal distress, headache, dizziness, insomnia, drowsiness, skin rash, ringing or buzzing in the ears, and blurred vision or other visual abnormalities. Some cases of gastrointestinal bleeding or peptic ulcers have been reported.

**DOSAGE AND ADMINISTRATION**—Indoprofen is supplied in 200 mg tablets. The usual recommended dosage is 200 to 800 mg per day in divided doses of 200 mg each. The higher doses usually are recommended for the relief of symptoms of rheumatoid arthritis and osteoarthrosis, a noninflammatory form of arthritis.

**SOURCES**—Farmitalia Carlo Erba s.p.a., Gruppo Montedison, Via Imbonati 24, 20159 Milano, Italy; Von Boch Arzneimittel s.r.l., Instituto Farmacobiologico, Via Rovigo 1, 00161 Roma, Italy; Montedison Farmaceuticos, S.A., Apdo. Postal 233, Av. Miguel Angel de Quevado No. 555, Mexico 21, D.F., Mexico.

## **Indoramin**—Baratol

**ACTIONS AND USES**—Indoramin is used primarily for the treatment of hypertension. As an antihypertensive medication, it usually is combined with a diuretic or a beta-blocking drug. Indoramin is believed to act as an alpha-receptor antagonist, interfering with the transmission of nerve impulses along the alpha pathways of the autonomic nervous system; this action can change a hypertensive (high blood pressure) signal into a hypotensive (low blood pressure) response. Indoramin has been used for the control of all grades of hypertension, usually in combination with a thiazide diuretic. In addition to its hypertensive applications, indoramin has been used in the treatment of exercise-induced asthma, migraine headaches, and Raynaud's disease.

**PRECAUTIONS**—Adverse effects reported in patients using indoramin include drowsiness, particularly in early stages of treatment and in high doses, dry mouth, nasal congestion, weight gain, dizziness, depression, skin rash, and failure of ejaculation. The drug should not be administered to patients with heart failure, and caution should be observed in giving the drug to patients with impaired kidney or liver function or Parkinson's disease. The drug should not be used in pregnancy unless the physician believes the benefits may outweigh the risks. Indoramin can interact with monoamine oxidase inhibitors and should not be given to patients using these antidepressants.

**DOSAGE AND ADMINISTRATION**—Indoramin is supplied in 25 and

50 mg tablets. The usual initial dosage is 25 mg taken twice daily, with gradual increases of 25 to 50 mg daily every two weeks, up to a maximum of 200 mg daily. The medication should always be taken in two or three divided doses, with the largest of unequal doses taken before retiring because of the sedating effect of the drug. When used in combination with diuretics and beta-blocking drugs, the daily dosage of indoramin should be adjusted gradually, as when indoramin is used alone.

**SOURCE**—Wyeth Laboratories, Huntercombe Lane South, Taplow, Maidenhead, Berkshire SL6 OPH, England.

## **Inosiplex (Methisoprinol)**—Delimmun, Isoprinosine, Viruxan

**ACTIONS AND USES**—Inosiplex is an antiviral drug that is used to increase the patient's normal immune response to several strains of virus, but primarily the infectious agent that is the cause of subacute sclerosing panencephalitis, which usually attacks children and adolescents. This form of encephalitis, sometimes called "measles of the brain," causes gradual dysfunction of the brain and death within a year. Inosiplex also has been used in various countries in the treatment of herpes zoster, type A infectious hepatitis, measles, chickenpox, and cold sores or fever blisters. Inosiplex is believed to act by stimulating activity of macrophages (cells that destroy invading organisms) and B and T lymphocytes. The B (for bone) and T (for thymus) lymphocytes are a part of the body's immune response system which defend against viruses, fungi, and certain bacteria.

**PRECAUTIONS**—Inosiplex tends to increase tissue levels of uric acid and may therefore aggravate gout or other conditions associated with uric acid excess. The drug is not recommended for use during the first trimester of pregnancy. Side effects of nausea and vomiting have been reported at the start of inosiplex therapy by mouth but not by intravenous injection. With few exceptions, the drug is reported to be well tolerated.

**DOSAGE AND ADMINISTRATION**—Inosiplex is supplied in 500 mg tablets and in a syrup containing 5 g per 100 ml or 6 g per 120 ml. Adult dosage is calculated at 100 mg per kg of body weight per day initially, followed by a maintenance dose of 40 mg per kg of body weight per day. For children 5 years of age and younger, the initial dosage is the same as for adults, but the maintenance dose for children is 50 mg per kg of body weight per day. When administered in syrup, one teaspoonful provides approximately 250 mg of inosiplex.

**SOURCES**—Sigma Tau s.p.a., Via Pontina Km. 30,400, 00040 Pomezia (Roma), Italy; Laboratorios Sanfer, S.A., Calz. de Tlalpan No. 550, Mexico 13, D.F., Mexico; Laboratoires Delalande, 16, rue Henri-Regnault, 92400 Courbevoie, France.

### **Inositol Niacinate (Inositol Nicotinate)**—Dilcit, Dilexpal, Esantene, Evicil, Hämovannad, Hexanicit, Hexanicotol, Hexopal, Hexopal Forte, Linodil, Mesonex, Mesotal, Palohex, Vasodil

**ACTIONS AND USES**—Inositol niacinate is used to cause dilation of the blood vessels, particularly vessels involved in blood circulation at the extremities of the body. It is used as a treatment for restless legs syndrome, night cramps, Raynaud's disease, intermittent claudication, chilblains, Buerger's disease, acrocyanosis (marked by hands or feet that are constantly blue and cold), erythrocyanosis (characterized by the limbs that become red and swollen when exposed to cold temperatures), dysmenorrhea, migraine, and peripheral and cerebral arteriosclerosis. The product also has been used in the treatment of hyperlipoproteinemia and hyperlipidemia, caused by excessive fatty substances in the blood, and necrobiosis lipoidica, a disorder marked by shiny leg lesions due to atrophy of the skin. It is believed that inositol niacinate is slowly converted in the body to nicotinic acid, or niacin, a part of the vitamin B complex. Nicotinic acid is a known dilator of peripheral blood vessels, mainly in the skin. It also reduces levels of most fatty substances in the blood by inhibiting the release of free fatty acids from lipid molecules.

**PRECAUTIONS**—Side effects include flushing, dizziness, nausea, vomiting, headache, itching skin, and blood pressure changes. Caution is recommended in giving the product to persons who may be hypersensitive to the drug, pregnant women, or patients who have recently recovered from a heart attack or stroke. The product is generally well tolerated, and manufacturers note that inositol niacinate has been used for more than 20 years without a reported case of poisoning or overdosage.

**DOSAGE AND ADMINISTRATION**—Inositol niacinate is supplied in 200, 250, 300, 500, 600, and 750 mg tablets, as well as in 25 mg units compounded with other medications. The drug also is available in suspensions containing 1,000 mg per 5 ml dose. The usual recommended adult dosage varies with the condition treated but, for most complaints, begins with an intake of 400 to 500 mg three times daily, gradually increasing the amount as necessary to a total daily dose of 3,000 to 4,000 mg. For night cramps or restless legs, the usual recommended dose is 200 to 600 mg given at night. Initial doses of 1,000 mg three times daily have been used in the treatment of cerebrovascular insufficiency.

**SOURCES**—IBIS-Instituto Biochimica Sperimentale s.p.a., Viale Machiavelli 29–31–33, 50125 Firenze, Italy; A/S Dumex (Dumex Ltd.), Prags Boulevard 37, 2300 Copenhagen S, Denmark; Winthrop Laboratories, Sterling-Winthrop House, Surbiton-upon-Thames, Surrey KT6 4PH, England.

## Ipratropium Bromide—Atem, Atrovent

**ACTIONS AND USES**—Ipratropium bromide is a bronchodilator used in the treatment of chronic bronchitis and other reversible obstructive diseases of the respiratory system. Ipratropium bromide is employed in moderate asthmatic attacks, chronic asthma, asthma in patients with heart disease, and bronchospasms, particularly bronchospasms that accompany surgical procedures. Ipratropium acts by blocking the reflexes of the vagus nerve that are the source of nerve signals causing constriction of the bronchial pathways. The bronchodilator action of ipratropium bromide usually is observed within three to five minutes after administration, and the effects of a single dose may last up to six hours. The drug reportedly provides partial protection against histamine- and allergen-caused bronchospasms, but without significantly altering the volume, viscosity, or clearance of sputum.

**PRECAUTIONS**—Ipratropium should not be given to patients with a known sensitivity to the drug or to aerosol propellants used to administer the product. It should not be given to patients with glaucoma or an enlarged prostate gland. Although animal studies have failed to show adverse effects in pregnancy, ipratropium bromide is not recommended for use in pregnancy, particularly during the first trimester. Caution also should be used in giving the drug to nursing mothers, although no reports of adverse effects have been published to indicate a hazard of the drug in breast milk. No interactions with beta-blocking agents or other drugs have been reported. The most common side effect reported from the use of ipratropium bromide is a dry mouth sensation. The patient should be advised to exercise care in administering the aerosol-propelled medication to prevent the product from contacting the eyes, although the effect may be only a mild and reversible blurring of vision.

**DOSAGE AND ADMINISTRATION**—Ipratropium bromide is supplied in 10 ml vials providing approximately 200 metered doses of 20 micrograms per puff. The usual adult dosage is one or two puffs (20 to 40 micrograms) three to four times daily. For children between the ages of 6 and 12, the recommended dosage is one or two puffs three times daily; and for children under 6 years of age, a maximum dosage of one puff three times per day is advised. Ipratropium bromide also is available in a nebulizer solution containing 250 micrograms per 1 ml, or 12.5 mcg per drop (1 ml = 20 drops). The nebulizer solution, which allows the patient to inhale the medication without use of the propelled spray, is recommended for children who may be unable to use an aerosol spray properly or for patients sensitive to fluorocarbon or other chemicals used in aerosol sprays.

**SOURCES**—Boehringer Ingleheim Ltd., Southern Industrial Estate, Bracknell, Berkshire RG12 4YS, England; Chiese Farmaceutici s.p.a., Via Palermo 30, 43100 Parma, Italy.

## Iprindole Hydrochloride—Prondol

**ACTIONS AND USES**—Iprindole hydrochloride is an antidepressant drug used in the treatment of psychotic depression, the depressive phase of manic-depressive psychosis, neurotic depression, and anxiety and agitation that may be accompanied by depression. The drug also is employed in the treatment of mild depression, elderly patients with symptoms of depression, and as an auxiliary therapy to electroconvulsive therapy for severe suicidal depression. Iprindole is believed to act primarily by interfering with the activity of the nerve impulse transmitter norepinephrine in the brain. Iprindole shows some similarities to amitriptyline, a commonly prescribed antidepressant drug, but less potency than mianserin in inhibiting norepinephrine activity.

**PRECAUTIONS**—Iprindole hydrochloride should not be given to patients with impaired liver function or a history of liver disease. Reports of reversible jaundice within the first 4 to 21 days of use of iprindole have been published. Other adverse effects, including dry mouth, blurred vision, sweating, urination difficulty, and cardiovascular disorders, are reported to be less frequent or less severe than with an alternative antidepressant medication, imipramine. Caution should be used in giving iprindole to patients with diabetes, heart disease, epilepsy, thyroid disease, glaucoma, or urinary difficulty. The drug may interact with alcohol and anesthetics. Some patients may experience a sedative effect that could impair the ability to operate motor vehicles or machinery with safety. However, authorities advise that sedative effects of iprindole hydrochloride are milder than with amitriptyline medications.

**DOSAGE AND ADMINISTRATION**—Iprindole hydrochloride is supplied in 15 and 30 mg tablets. The usual recommended dosage is 15 to 30 mg three times daily as an initial procedure, gradually increasing the dosage if necessary to a maximum of 180 mg per day, given in divided doses. The usual maintenance dose is 90 mg per day in three divided doses. The drug is not recommended for children.

**SOURCE**—Wyeth Laboratories Limited, 765 South Circular Road, Islandbridge, Dublin 8, Ireland.

## Iproniazid Phosphate—Marsilid

**ACTIONS AND USES**—Iproniazid phosphate is an antidepressant that acts by inhibiting monoamine oxidase, an enzyme that destroys amine types of nerve transmitter substances, such as norepinephrine; iproniazid allows them to accumulate so that their stimulating effect on the nervous system is extended. Iproniazid is related in pharmacological activity to phenelzine, which has been classified as less stimulating and therefore safer than some of the alternative forms of monoamine oxidase inhibitors used in treating depression. The drug also reportedly promotes appetite and weight gain and may have the effects of reducing blood pressure and blood sugar levels in some patients. Some authorities have reported benefits in treating cardiovascular disorders, such as angina pectoris, intermittent claudication, and arterial circulation problems, with iproniazid phosphate.

**PRECAUTIONS**—Iproniazid should not be given to patients with a history of liver disease or impairment. Monoamine oxidase inhibitors may cause jaundice in some patients. Patients using iproniazid should be monitored periodically for signs of liver impairment, and the drug should be withdrawn if evidence of a toxic reaction is observed. Caution should be used in giving the drug to patients with impaired kidney function. Patients should be advised to avoid alcohol and foods and drugs that are likely to interact with monoamine oxidase inhibitors. Common food items that may contain tyramine, a substance that may react with iproniazid to produce severe adverse effects, include Chianti wine, cheese, pickled herring, broad bean pods, meat or yeast extracts, and certain other fermented or matured food products. Iproniazid also may interact with pethidine and other depressant drugs, amphetamine and other stimulants, levodopa, imipramine derivatives, reserpine, and certain tranquilizers and diuretics. Because effects of monoamine oxidase inhibitors may persist for two weeks, a two-week interval should elapse between the end of iproniazid therapy and the start of administration of a different antidepressant. In the treatment of mental illness, iproniazid should be used only in patients who have failed to respond to other forms of antidepressant therapy. Iproniazid is a potent monoamine oxidase inhibitor developed originally as a drug for the treatment of tuberculosis; its antidepressant properties were discovered as a side effect. Because of its potency and occasional toxic liver effects in certain patients, the use of iproniazid has been discontinued in some countries.

**DOSAGE AND ADMINISTRATION**—Iproniazid phosphate is supplied in 25 and 50 mg tablets. The usual initial therapy for adults is 100 to 150 mg in a single daily dose until a beneficial response is noted, after which the dosage may be reduced to a maintenance level of 25 to 50 mg per day.

**SOURCES**—Roche Products Ltd., P.O. Box 8, Welwyn Garden City, Hertfordshire AL7 3AY, England; Produits Roche S.A., 52, bvd du Parc, 92521 Neuilly-sur-Seine Cedex, France.

## **Josamycin (Yosamicina)**—Jomybel, Josacine, Josamy, Josaxin, Yosaxin

**ACTIONS AND USES**—Josamycin is an antibiotic used in the treatment of a wide range of respiratory infections. The drug has been used for pharyngitis, pharyngolaryngitis, tonsillitis, sinusitis, infections of the middle and external ear, bronchitis, bronchiectasis, bronchopneumonia, and pneumonia. Josamycin has also been used in the treatment of certain infections of the skin and soft tissues. Josamycin is reported to be similar to erythromycin in activity and to have greater activity, on the basis of laboratory studies, against some strains of bacteria.

**PRECAUTIONS**—Josamycin should not be given to patients who are hypersensitive to the product and should be administered with caution to patients sensitive to other antibiotics. Like other antibiotics, also, it should be used with caution in patients with impaired liver or kidney function. Studies with laboratory animals indicate josamycin does not cause birth defects or chromosome defects. The drug is found in breast milk, but its effect on nursing infants has not been established. Side effects reported include nausea, diarrhea, loss of appetite, and flatulence; less frequent are constipation, headache, inflammation of the mouth, pruritus, and other skin disorders.

**DOSAGE AND ADMINISTRATION**—Josamycin is supplied in 500 mg tablets and in 125, 250, and 500 mg doses in fluid suspensions. A 60 ml container of a suspension provides approximately 12 doses at 5 ml per dose. The adult dose is one 500 mg tablet every six to eight hours for mild to moderate infections and up to two or three tablets, or 1,000 to 1,500 mg, every six to eight hours for severe infections. For children over the age of 5 years, the usual dose is one teaspoonful of the 250 mg suspension every six to eight hours, and for children 5 years and younger, 125 mg of josamycin suspension every six to eight hours. Children's dosages also may be calculated at 30 to 50 mg per kg of body weight per day in divided doses.

**SOURCES**—Laboratoires Spret-Mauchant Pharmuka, 49, quai du Moulin de Cage, 92231 Gennevilliers, France; Laboratorios Endo de

Mexico, S.A., Amores No. 1734, Mexico 12, D.F., Mexico; Yamanouchi Pharmaceutical Co., Ltd., 5 Nihonbashi-Honcho 2-chome, Chuo-ku, Tokyo, Japan.

**Ketazolam**—Anxon, Contamex, Loftran, Solatran, Unakalm

**ACTIONS AND USES**—Ketazolam is a drug used primarily in the treatment of anxiety, although it also has muscle relaxant properties and is often prescribed for that purpose. Ketazolam has been administered for the treatment of anxiety neurosis, tension, irritability, and similar stress-related symptoms. Its muscle relaxant activity is used in the management of spasticity associated with spinal cord injuries, stroke, and multiple sclerosis. Ketazolam is a benzodiazepine type of minor tranquilizer, distinguishing it from barbiturates and propranolol, which may be used as anxiolytic drugs. It also is related chemically to diazepam, a minor tranquilizer used in the treatment of anxiety, insomnia, and acute alcohol withdrawal symptoms. Ketazolam is reported to be superior to barbiturates and meprobamate in reducing anxiety. While ketazolam itself has a metabolic half-life of only 2 hours, its metabolites (including diazepam) have half-lives of up to 54 hours. The metabolites accumulate in the tissues during the first two weeks and eventually reach a steady state of activity, leading to a sustained antianxiety effect.

**PRECAUTIONS**—Ketazolam should not be given to patients with a known hypersensitivity to benzodiazepine drugs. The product also should not be given in pregnancy, to infants, or to patients with myasthenia or glaucoma. The safety of ketazolam in persons under the age of 18 years has not been established, and its use therefore should be avoided in such patients. Use also should be avoided in patients with depressive or psychotic disorders. Animal studies show that ketazolam is excreted in breast milk, and it is assumed that the same effect occurs in humans. Therefore, the drug should not be given to nursing mothers. Ketazolam should not be given to persons prone to drug abuse and should be used with caution in patients with a potential for psychological dependence as well as in elderly or debilitated patients or those with organic brain disease. Ketazolam interacts with alcohol, monoamine oxidase inhibitors, phenothiazines, butyrophenones, and other drugs that affect the central nervous system. Patients should be advised that ketazolam may affect their mental alertness and physical reactions, with the result that they should avoid operating motor vehicles or machinery until it has been established that use of the drug does not present an accident risk. Side effects include drowsiness, dizziness, blurred vision, loss of muscular coordination, loss of depth perception, headache, seizures, agitation, and irritability.

**DOSAGE AND ADMINISTRATION**—Ketazolam is supplied in 15 and 30 mg capsules. Dosage is generally individualized but for most patients the initial recommended dose is 30 mg at bedtime. The dosage usually is adjusted in a range between 15 and 60 mg daily, taken as a single dose at bedtime or in divided doses. For elderly and debilitated patients, it is recommended that the initial dosage be 15 mg per day until tolerance and efficacy can be established. Ketazolam is not recommended for children.

**SOURCES**—Beecham Research Laboratories, Great West Road, Brentford, Middlesex TW8 9BD, England; Beecham Laboratories, Inc., 115 Brunswick Blvd., Pointe Claire, Quebec H9R 1A4, Canada.

## **Ketoprofen (Ketoprofene, Ketoprophen)**—Alreumat, Alreumun, Alrheumat, Alrheumun, Alrhumat, Anaus, Artrosilen, Capisten, Fastum, Flexen, Iso-K, Kefenid, Ketalgin, Keto, Kevadon, Lertus, Orudis, Profenid, Remauric, Rofenid, Salient, Sinketol

**ACTIONS AND USES**—Ketoprofen is an antiinflammatory, analgesic, and antipyretic drug used in the treatment of rheumatoid arthritis, ankylosing spondylitis, and osteoarthritis. Clinical studies indicate the drug reduces joint swelling, pain and duration of morning stiffness, increases grip strength, and improves functional capacity. Peak blood concentrations of ketoprofen have been observed 30 minutes to 2 hours after administration of a dose by mouth. The product also can be administered by rectal suppository.

**PRECAUTIONS**—The safety of ketoprofen has not been established for pregnant or nursing women, or children under 12 years of age, and its use for persons in these groups is not recommended. The product should be used with caution in patients with a history of gastrointestinal inflammatory disorders or peptic ulcers; suppositories as well as oral doses are capable of causing gastrointestinal effects in sensitive individuals. Ketoprofen also should be used with caution in patients with impaired liver or kidney functions. Because of its potency in reducing pain and fever, ketoprofen may mask signs of infectious diseases. The drug should not be given to patients known to be sensitive to aspirin or other nonsteroidal antiinflammatory drugs because of the possibility of cross-sensitivity. Gastrointestinal reactions account for most of the adverse effects observed. The complaints include abdominal pain, nausea, constipation, vomiting, dyspepsia and flatulence, diarrhea, loss of appetite, and a bad taste in the mouth. Other adverse effects have included allergies and skin rashes, ringing in the ears, headache, fatigue, dizziness, depression, drowsiness, and heart palpitation.

**DOSAGE AND ADMINISTRATION**—Ketoprofen is supplied in 50 mg capsules and 100 mg suppositories. The usual recommended oral dosage is 150 to 200 mg per day in three or four divided doses. For rectal administration, the recommended dosage is one suppository in the morning and one in the evening. One suppository at bedtime supplemented by divided oral doses during the day is a plan favored by some patients. However, the total daily combined dose should not exceed 200 mg of ketoprofen unless directed by the physician when a satisfactory response cannot be achieved with a lower dose. However, the maximum dose under such circumstances should not exceed 300 mg per day.

**SOURCE**—Rhone-Poulenc Pharma Inc., 8580 Esplanade Avenue, Montreal, Quebec H2P 2R9, Canada.

## Ketotifen Fumarate—Zaditen

**ACTIONS AND USES**—Ketotifen fumarate is a drug with antiallergic and antihistamine properties that is used in the treatment of asthma. It has actions similar to those of sodium cromoglycate, an older antiasthma drug that stabilizes cell membranes of the respiratory tract and suppresses the release of the cell substances that trigger episodes of bronchospasm. Ketotifen fumarate is recommended by some authorities as having the advantage of oral administration rather than requiring inhalation of an aerosol or powdered medication. Ketotifen also may allow a reduction in the use of corticosteroid or bronchodilator drugs in the treatment of respiratory disorders. However, the prophylactic effect of ketotifen fumarate may require as long as four weeks to develop, and the drug therefore is not recommended for acute attacks.

**PRECAUTIONS**—Because of the antihistamine properties of ketotifen fumarate, it may cause drowsiness and can impair the ability of the patient to operate motor vehicles or machinery without danger to himself or others. The drug is not recommended for use during pregnancy or by nursing mothers. If the patient has been using another antiasthma drug in long-term therapy, the previous medication should be continued for at least two weeks after ketotifen fumarate therapy has begun; abrupt withdrawal of antiasthma drugs, particularly those containing corticosteroids, which may mask a condition of adrenocortical hormone insufficiency, should be avoided. Patients should be advised that ketotifen fumarate may interact with alcohol, sedative or hypnotic drugs, or antihistamines to increase the impairment of physical or mental abilities. In addition to drowsiness, side effects may include dry mouth and dizziness. Caution should be observed in giving the drug to patients who are sensitive to sedation-producing medications. Overdosage symptoms may include confusion, disorientation, headache, visual difficulties, abnormally slow heartbeat, and depressed breathing.

**DOSAGE AND ADMINISTRATION**—Ketotifen fumarate is supplied in 1 mg tablets and capsules as well as in an elixir providing 1 mg per 5 ml of fluid. The usual recommended adult dosage is 1 mg taken twice daily with food. The dosage may be doubled to 2 mg per dose, if necessary. The recommended dosage for children weighing over 30 kg is 1 mg taken twice daily. For easily sedated patients, the recommended daily dosage is 500 mcg to 1 mg at bedtime.

**SOURCES**—Wander Pharmaceuticals, 98 The Centre, Feltham, Middlesex TW13 4EP, England; Sandoz De Mexico, S.A. de C.V., Amores No. 1322, Mexico 12, D.F., Mexico; Division Wander Pharma, Laboratoires Sandoz S.A.R.L., 14, bvd Richelieu, 92500 Rueil-Malmaison, France.

## **Labetalol Hydrochloride**—Trandate

**ACTIONS AND USES**—Labetalol is an antihypertensive agent with both alpha- and beta-blocking properties. It is unrelated chemically to other beta-blockers and is the first drug to offer both alpha- and beta-blocking activity. By blocking transmission of nerve impulses along the autonomic nervous system pathways at beta receptors, blood pressure is lowered by reducing the response of the heart to stress and exercise. Blocking transmission of nerve impulses along alpha receptor pathways helps reduce blood pressure by decreasing resistance in the blood vessels in the peripheral areas of the body. The product is used for all grades of hypertension. Labetalol is used with diuretics and alone.

**PRECAUTIONS**—Because labetalol has both alpha- and beta-blocking properties, some patients may experience hypotension, or abnormally low blood pressure, particularly after initial doses and in interactions with anesthetics, such as halothane. Beta-blocking drugs in general should be administered with caution in patients susceptible to respiratory disorders, such as bronchospasm, because the products tend to increase airway resistance in the bronchial tree. Beta-blockers also may depress normal contractility of the heart muscle, leading to heart failure. Labetalol should be used with caution in diabetic patients because beta-blockers can mask the initial signs of acute hypoglycemia. The safety of labetalol in pregnancy and breast milk has not been established, and use of the drug by pregnant women or nursing mothers is not recommended. Adverse reactions include dizziness, hypotension, fatigue, nausea, vomiting, difficulty in urinating, depression, and allergic rhinitis.

**DOSAGE AND ADMINISTRATION**—Labetalol hydrochloride is supplied in tablets containing 100 or 200 mg each of the drug. The recommended initial dose is 100 to 200 mg taken twice daily. The dosage should then be increased at weekly intervals until satisfactory control of blood pressure is achieved. The effective daily dose for some patients may be as little as 200 mg or as much as 2,400 mg. For severe cases, the maximum may be still higher. It is recommended that the daily medication intake be in divided amounts after meals. High daily amounts should be divided into three or four doses. A children's dosage has not been established at this writing. For geriatric patients, caution is advised because of possible effects on liver function or other body systems.

**SOURCES**—Allen & Hanburys Ltd., Horsenden House, Oldfield Lane North, Greenford, Mddx UB6 OHB, England; Glaxo de Mexico, S.A. de C.V., Centeno No. 132, Col. Granjas Esmeralda, Mexico 13, D.F., Mexico.

## Levamisole Hydrochloride (Tetramisole Hydrochloride)—Decaris, Ergamisol, Ketrax, Levasole, Meglum, Nemicide, Solaskil, Tramisol

**ACTIONS AND USES**—Levamisole hydrochloride is an antihelmintic used primarily for the treatment of infestations of intestinal nematodes and other types of worms. Because the product also stimulates activity of the body's natural immune functions, levamisole has been used in the treatment of systemic lupus erythematosus, rheumatoid arthritis, leishmaniasis, toxoplasmosis, warts, aphthous ulcers of the mouth associated with herpes infections, warts, and a respiratory disease called tropical eosinophilia. Levamisole also has been used with varied results in different types of cancer, reportedly producing beneficial results in Hodgkin's disease and apparently increasing the survival rate when used in conjunction with other cancer drugs in treatment of other forms of cancer. When used as an antihelmintic, levamisole is effective against hookworms (*Ancylostoma* and *Necator*) and roundworms (*Ascaris*), paralyzing or killing the worms so they can be expelled through the rectum.

**PRECAUTIONS**—A single dose of levamisole may produce side effects of nervousness, insomnia, gastrointestinal distress with possible nausea and vomiting, and changes in taste and smell. Prolonged use of the drug has been associated with skin rash, mouth ulcers, and blood disorders in certain sensitive patients. Reports of photosensitivity and vasculitis (blood vessel inflammation) have been associated with levamisole use. Treatment of adverse effects is generally directed toward relief of symptoms.

**DOSAGE AND ADMINISTRATION**—Levamisole hydrochloride is supplied in 30, 50, and 150 mg tablets and as a syrup containing 8 mg per ml, or 40 mg per teaspoonful. Dosage varies according to the disease treated and the body weight of the patient. The dosage for treatment of roundworms usually is 150 mg per day for adults and 3 mg per kg of body weight for children, and for hookworms 300 mg for adults and 6 mg per kg of body weight for children. The drug usually is administered as a single dose, which may be repeated in a second single dose the following day. For other conditions, dosages employed have ranged between 50 and 150 mg per day in continuous or intermittent courses of therapy.

**SOURCES**—Specia, 16, rue Clisson, 75646 Paris Cedex 13, France; Janssen Farmaceutici s.p.a., Viale Caravaggio 107, 00147 Roma, Italy.

## Lidoflazine—Clavidene, Clinium, Corflazine, Klinium

**ACTIONS AND USES**—Lidoflazine is a coronary artery dilator used in the long-term management of angina pectoris and related heart disorders. Lidoflazine, in addition to its action in dilating the coronary arteries, has calcium-blocking properties that relieve coronary artery spasms. Calcium blockers inhibit the flow of calcium ions across the membranes of smooth muscle cells. Calcium is important for smooth muscle contractions. By reducing the calcium flow, the drug has the effect of relaxing the smooth muscle tone and reducing the risk of spasms. Lidoflazine increases exercise tolerance so that the patient can exert an increased amount of physical effort before the symptoms of angina pectoris are experienced. The drug also reduces the incidence of heart flutter or fibrillation. Although the risk of abnormal heart rhythms is reduced, lidoflazine is not recommended as a primary drug for the treatment of heart arrhythmias.

**PRECAUTIONS**—Lidoflazine is not recommended for use by women of childbearing potential or for patients with myocardial infarction or cardiac insufficiency. Caution should be used in administration of lidoflazine in patients with impaired liver function and patients with abnormally low blood calcium levels. The response to lidoflazine develops gradually over a period of several weeks to several months, with the result that the patient's increased exercise tolerance may not be experienced for a similar time period. Adverse effects resulting from the use of lidoflazine include gastric distress, dizziness, headache, and a ringing or buzzing in the ears. The side effects reportedly diminish after dosage adjustments are made.

**DOSAGE AND ADMINISTRATION**—Lidoflazine is supplied in 60 and 120 mg tablets. The usual recommended dosage is 120 mg a day as a single dose for the first week, with increases to 120 mg twice daily the second week and 120 mg three times a day as a maintenance dose beginning with the third week. It is recommended that the drug be taken with or after meals.

**SOURCES**—Janssen Pharmaceutical Ltd., Janssen House, Chapel Street, Marlow, Buckinghamshire SL7 1ET, England; Laboratoires Syntex, 20, rue Jean-Jaures, 92800 Puteaux, France; Camillo Corvi s.p.a., Viale dei Mille 3, 29100 Picacenza, Italy.

## Lymecycline—Ciclisin, Ciclolysal, Lisinbiotic, Lisinciclina, Tanclina, Tetralysal, Tralisin

**ACTIONS AND USES**—Lymecycline is an antibiotic that is similar to tetracycline but is more completely absorbed from the gastrointestinal tract so that smaller doses can be used to effect control of an infection. It has been used in the treatment of chronic bronchitis, undulant fever, genital tract infections (including lymphogranuloma venereum), psittacosis, trachoma, rickettsial infections such as Q fever, sinusitis, otitis, mouth infections, biliary tract infections, gastrointestinal infections, and skin infections, including severe acne vulgaris. Lymecycline exerts its effects against bacteria by suppressing the ability of the microorganism to build necessary protein molecules from amino acids in its environment. The drug also is believed to disrupt the ability of the bacterium to build cell membranes from the chemical complexes with essential minerals available to it.

**PRECAUTIONS**—Lymecycline forms complexes with calcium in the body and becomes bound to growing bones and teeth, causing teeth stains and occasionally pitting of tooth surfaces. The drug is not recommended for children under 12 years of age or for pregnant women or nursing mothers. The calcium-binding effect on teeth and bones is most likely to occur by exposure of the fetus from about the third month of pregnancy until about one year of age. The effect on permanent teeth can result from exposure to the antibiotic from the sixth month of pregnancy until about 12 years of age. Pitting and discoloration of the nails can occur following use of the antibiotic at any age. The drug should not be given to patients with impaired kidney function. Side effects may include gastrointestinal complaints, such as nausea, vomiting, and diarrhea. However, the side effects are reported to be fewer and less serious than with other tetracycline-type antibiotics. Caution should be used to prevent the development of superinfections and overgrowth of strains of bacteria that are resistant to lymecycline.

**DOSAGE AND ADMINISTRATION**—Lymecycline is supplied in 150 and 300 mg capsules and tablets. The 150 mg dose is approximately equivalent to 250 mg of tetracycline and many times more soluble. The usual adult dosage of lymecycline is 300 mg taken in the morning and again in the evening. For severe infections, a total daily dosage of 1.2 g has been recommended.

**SOURCES**—Farmitalia Carlo Erba s.p.a., Via Imbonati 24, 20159 Milano, Italy; Fabo Farmindustria s.a.s., Via del Borghetto 3B, 40122, Bologna, Italy; Farmacosmici s.r.l., Via A. Volta 24, 22100 Como, Italy.

## Lynestrenol—Anacyclin, Exultena, Exulton, Exultona, Franovul, Lindiol, Linseral, Lyndiol, Lyndiolett, Micro-Ovostat, Minilyn, Mini Pregnon, Ministat, Neo-Lyndiol, Nonovulet, Noracyclin, Normofasico, Orgamentril, Ovamezzo, Ovanon, Ovanone, Ovariostat, Ovoresta, Ovostat, Physiostat, Restovar, Yermonil

**ACTIONS AND USES**—Lynestrenol is an oral contraceptive for women who are unable to tolerate other kinds of hormonal contraceptives for various reasons. The drug also is used for functional and other forms of dysmenorrhea, irregular menstruation, premenstrual syndrome, mastodynia or breast pain, amenorrhea, menorrhagia, and endometriosis. Lynestrenol is similar in action to the natural hormone progesterone but is reported to be a more potent inhibitor of ovulation. Lynestrenol also may have some weak properties of estrogen and the androgenic male sex hormones. Lynestrenol may be combined with an estrogen for use as an oral contraceptive and with mestranol, a form of estrogen, for the treatment of menstrual irregularities.

**PRECAUTIONS**—Lynestrenol should not be administered to a patient who is pregnant or is suspected of being pregnant or a patient with undiagnosed vaginal bleeding or a known suspected mammary or genital tumor that is estrogen-dependent. The drug should also not be given to a patient with a history of thrombophlebitis or a related condition, a cerebrovascular or heart disorder, a blood disorder such as sickle-cell anemia, jaundice or a history of jaundice during pregnancy, impaired liver function, porphyria, or hyperlipoproteinemia. The patient should be examined periodically, preferably at least twice a year, for signs of changes in body weight, blood pressure, breasts, legs, skin, and pelvic organs. Caution should be used in administration of oral contraceptives to diabetic patients because the drugs tend to reduce glucose tolerance. The risk of thrombosis in users of oral contraceptives increases with age and cigarette smoking. A few side effects, such as acne, increased hair growth, and deepening of the voice in some patients, have been attributed to the androgenic hormonal influence of lynestrenol. Other side effects observed include nausea, headache, and breast tenderness, particularly during the first few cycles of lynestrenol use.

**DOSAGE AND ADMINISTRATION**—Lynestrenol is supplied in 22-day calendar packets, each pill containing 2.5 mg of lynestrenol and 50 mcg of ethinyl estradiol, or an alternative preparation of 1.0 mg of lynestrenol and 50 mcg of ethinyl estradiol or 750 mcg of lynestrenol and 37.5 mcg of ethinyl estradiol. Lynestrenol also is supplied in 500 mcg and 5 mg tablets. When used as an oral contraceptive, the first course of one tablet daily for 22 days should be started on the fifth day of the menstrual cycle. It is recommended that a nonhormonal form of contraception also be used for the first 14 days of the first course. Subsequent courses should follow 6 tablet-free days after the last tablet of the previous course. Somewhat different procedures are recommended for patients using lynestrenol after childbirth or abortion, or when changing from the use of a different oral contraceptive.

**SOURCES**—Organon Laboratories Ltd., Crown House, London Road, Mordem, Surrey SM4 5DZ, England; Organon Mexicana, S.A., Calz. de Camarones No. 134, Mexico 16, D.F., Mexico; Erco Läkemedel AB, Grevgatan 34, 114 53 Stockholm, Sweden; Francia Farmaceutici s.r.l., Industra Farmaco Biologica, Via del Pestagalli 7, 20138 Milano, Italy.

**Meclofenoxate (Centrophenoxine, Clofenoxine)**—Analux, Brenal, Cellative, Cerebron, Clocete, Helfergin, Licidril, Lucidril, Luncidril, Lutiaron, Marucotol, Methoxynal, Proserout, Proseryl, Ropoxyl

**ACTIONS AND USES**—Meclofenoxate is a psychotropic drug used in the treatment of stroke, mental retardation, and other brain disorders associated with an impaired flow of oxygen to tissues of the cerebral cortex. It has been used in the treatment of brain disorders due to alcoholism, drug abuse, toxic chemicals, oxygen deprivation at birth or during surgical procedures, cerebral ischemia (insufficient oxygenation of brain tissues), and accidents involving blood vessels of the brain. The product also has been employed in the therapy of a variety of visual disorders linked to nervous system structures, such as the retina, optic nerve, and optic disc, leading to loss of normal visual perception. Studies indicate the drug improves the metabolic activity of brain cells under conditions of hypoxia (oxygen deprivation) which otherwise would result in impaired mental performance and, in older individuals, signs of senility.

**PRECAUTIONS**—Meclofenoxate should not be administered to persons who are easily excitable, patients with severe arterial hypertension, or those subject to convulsions or involuntary musculoskeletal movements. The drug also should not be given to nursing mothers. Adverse effects include hyperexcitability, insomnia, tremors, motion sickness, paradoxical drowsiness, and depression.

**DOSAGE AND ADMINISTRATION**—Meclofenoxate is supplied in 500 mg coated tablets for oral administration and in 250 and 500 mg doses in 10 ml ampules for injection. The usual recommended dosage is two to six tablets daily or slow intravenous injection of one to four ampules of the injectable product. The drug also has been administered by intramuscular injection. Because of the risk of insomnia, it is recommended that the drug not be given late in the day.

**SOURCE**—Bracco de Mexico, S.A. de C.V., Calzada de las Armas No. 110, Tlalnepantla, Edo. de Mexico.

## Medaxepam—Anxitol, Azepamid, Benson, Elbrus, Lerisum, Megasedan, Metonas, Narsis, Navizil, Nivelton, Nobrium, Raporan, Resmit, Siman, Templane, Tranquilax

**ACTIONS AND USES**—Medazepam is an anxiolytic, or antianxiety, drug used in the treatment of cases of anxiety that threaten the well-being of the patient. It has been used in the treatment of mentally retarded children to correct their behavioral disturbances. The product is believed to act on the central nervous system in the automatic pathways that influence emotions and behavior. It is chemically and pharmacologically related to diazepam (Valium), oxazepam (Serax), and other minor tranquilizers.

**PRECAUTIONS**—The drug is not recommended for pregnant women, nursing mothers, children, patients afflicted with myasthenia gravis, persons known to be hypersensitive to benzodiazepine antianxiety drugs, or some glaucoma patients. Medazepam may interact with alcohol or other psychotropic drugs and can impair the ability of the patient to drive a motor vehicle, be a pedestrian, or operate machinery. The drug should not be given to persons prone to drug abuse nor to severely disturbed schizophrenic patients. The drug also should be used with caution in patients with epilepsy, in elderly patients, and in debilitated patients. Adverse reactions reported include drowsiness, involuntary muscular movements, dizziness, fatigue, depression, headache, blurred vision, and skin rash.

**DOSAGE AND ADMINISTRATION**—Medazepam is supplied in 5 mg tablets and 10 mg capsules. The usual initial dosage is 5 mg two or three times a day, gradually increasing to 10 mg twice daily. For severe cases, the dosage may be increased to a total of 30 mg daily. Lower doses are recommended for elderly patients and those with impaired liver or kidney function. The product is not recommended for children.

**SOURCES**—Roche Products Pty. Limited, 4-10 Inman Road, Dee Why, N.S.W., Australia; Roche Products Limited, P.O. Box 8, Welwyn Garden City, Hertfordshire, AL7 3AY, England.

## Medigoxin—Lanitop

**ACTIONS AND USES**—Medigoxin is a form of digitalis, a drug used as a heart tonic with certain reported advantages over digoxin, a commonly prescribed heart medication. The advantages are a more rapid onset of action and a somewhat longer duration of effect. When administered orally or intravenously, medigoxin has been observed to produce effects in as little as 5 minutes, with a maximum effect on the heart muscle 15 minutes after administration, compared with an average onset of action time of 2 hours for digoxin and up to 12 hours for maximum effect. A half-life of 54 to 60 hours for medigoxin has been reported, as compared with some estimates of 48 hours for digoxin. Medigoxin has been used for all types of heart disease in which digitalis therapy is indicated, including congestive heart failure, atrial fibrillation, and certain other heart arrhythmias.

**PRECAUTIONS**—Medigoxin should not be administered to patients with signs or symptoms of digitalis intoxication or excessive blood levels of calcium. Caution should be used in giving the drug to patients who may have experienced potassium loss, who have normally slow heartbeats, who have disorders involving conduction of heart contraction signals from the atria to the ventricles, or who have been using another type of heart tonic. Caution also should be used in treating patients with impaired kidney or liver function and elderly patients, who may require a smaller dose of the drug. Side effects may include gastric distress, visual disturbances, and heart arrhythmias. Use of the drug should be avoided if possible during pregnancy, particularly during the first trimester.

**DOSAGE AND ADMINISTRATION**—Medigoxin is supplied in 100 mcg tablets and 2 ml injection ampules containing 200 mcg of the drug. The usual dosage for most patients during digitalization (establishment of an optimum individual dosage) is 400 mcg per day for three to five days. The dosage for oral or intravenous administration is the same and interchangeable, that is, either two tablets twice daily or two ampules per day. The maintenance dosage is 200 to 300 mcg per day in divided doses. The recommended emergency dosage for digitalization is 200 mcg three times daily for two to four days, of which the first 200 mcg may be by intravenous injection. The dosage for children under 14 years of age is calculated at 10 mcg per kg of body weight repeated at six-hour intervals for digitalization, followed by a maintenance dose of 10 mcg per kg per day. The recommended dosages are based on experience with a great majority of patients, but individual requirements may vary.

**SOURCE**—Roussel Laboratories Ltd., Roussel House, North End Road, Wembley Park, Middlesex HA9 ONF, England.

## Medroxyprogesterone Acetate—Depo-Provera

**ACTIONS AND USES**—Medroxyprogesterone acetate is a substance closely related to the female sex hormone progesterone and is used as a short-term contraceptive administered by intramuscular injection. The same drug is used in the United States in the treatment of cancer of the uterus and urinary tract; it also has been used in some countries in the treatment of cancer of the prostate gland. In countries where medroxyprogesterone acetate is used as a contraceptive, the drug is administered at the beginning of the menstrual cycle as a progestogen antifertility agent. A single injection is reported to be effective for at least three months, and large doses are reported to have provided protection against conception for periods of six months. The contraceptive injections have been as effective as oral contraceptives or intrauterine devices in a two-year test of nearly 1,000 women. Medroxyprogesterone acetate has been recommended for use when oral contraceptives or contraceptives containing estrogen may be inappropriate; some estrogen-free oral contraceptives are progestogen-only drugs similar to medroxyprogesterone acetate. The injectable contraceptive is favored in some countries to prevent pregnancy in women who have been exposed to or immunized against rubella (German measles) virus or whose husbands have recently undergone vasectomies. For wives of husbands undergoing vasectomy, a second injection may be administered three months after the first if the husband's sperm count has not fallen to zero.

**PRECAUTIONS**—Medroxyprogesterone acetate should not be administered to patients with thrombophlebitis, a history of pulmonary embolism, impaired liver function, or a known or suspected cancer of the breast or reproductive organs. The drug also should not be administered to a patient with uterine bleeding of unknown cause. Because of animal studies showing the development of breast nodules, some cancerous, and male sex hormone effects, caution should be used and patients should be monitored closely for such possible adverse effects. Side effects include a delay in returning to normal menstrual cycles after discontinuing the use of medroxyprogesterone acetate, temporary infertility lasting 18 months or longer, and amenorrhea. The side effects have occurred most frequently in women using the injectable contraceptive for prolonged periods.

**DOSAGE AND ADMINISTRATION**—Medroxyprogesterone acetate is supplied in 1, 3, and 5 ml injection ampules containing 50 mg of the drug per ml. For short-term protection against pregnancy, the recommended dosage is a single injection of 150 mg given deeply in the gluteal muscle. For menstruating women, it is recommended that the drug be administered during the first three to five days of the menstrual cycle. For women who have just given birth, it is recommended that the injection be given during the first week after delivery, but the drug can be administered up to six weeks after delivery. Although medroxyprogesterone acetate is not recommended for long-term use as a contraceptive, doses of 300 to 450 mg have been used to provide effective protection against pregnancy for periods of six months.

**SOURCES**—Upjohn Ltd., Fleming Way, Crawley, West Sussex RH10 2NJ, England; Upjohn International, Inc., Bostboks 10, 1310 Blómmenholm, Norway; Upjohn AB, Box 289, 433 25 Partille, Sweden.

## Metformin—Devian, Diaberit, Diabetosan, Diabex S.R., Diabiphage, Glafornil, Glucadal, Glucinan, Glucisulfa, Glucofagos, Glucophage, Islotin, Mellitin, Mellitron, Metiguanide, Obinese, Orabet, Stagid

**ACTIONS AND USES**—Metformin is an oral antidiabetic drug used in the management of maturity-onset diabetes in patients who have some insulin function but are overweight and unable to control their condition with diet. Metformin is a biguanide type of oral hypoglycemic agent that differs from the sulfonylurea drugs, such as tolbutamide, which produce a stimulant action upon the insulin-secreting cells of the pancreas. Metformin is believed to increase the efficiency of the available insulin in the body, whether injected as a therapy or produced by the body's own pancreas. Metformin does not enter into any reaction with insulin and is not metabolized, but is instead excreted as the intact molecule in the patient's urine. Metformin and the sulfonylurea drugs are not necessarily interchangeable. Metformin is most commonly prescribed for obese diabetics who cannot or will not lose weight as required for successful control of diabetes. Metformin may be used alone, in combination with a sulfonylurea drug, or in combination with insulin.

**PRECAUTIONS**—Metformin should not be given in cases of diabetic coma or ketoacidosis due to incomplete metabolism of fats in the diet. The drug also should not be given to patients with serious kidney disorders, particularly elderly patients, patients with heart failure or recent myocardial infarction, or those with impaired liver function, acute or chronic alcoholism, or conditions associated with respiratory dysfunction leading to lactic acidosis, a disorder that may develop when body tissues are deprived of oxygen. Metformin should not be given in pregnancy unless the benefits are likely to outweigh the risks, in patients suffering from a severe infection or injury, or in conditions associated with dehydration. When a patient receiving metformin is scheduled to undergo surgery or instrumentation, such as intravenous angiography or urography, the drug should be discontinued two days before the procedure and restarted after the procedure has been completed. Metformin can cause a decrease in the body's absorption of vitamin $B_{12}$, which is necessary to prevent pernicious anemia, and patients on continuous metformin therapy should be monitored at least once a year for $B_{12}$ levels. Vitamin $B_{12}$ deficiencies are most likely to occur in vegetarians. Although metformin alone is rarely a cause of hypoglycemia, the condition can develop when metformin is used with alcohol, insulin, or sulfonylurea drugs. Patients receiving combined antidiabetic medications should therefore be monitored periodically for signs of abnormal blood sugar readings. Metformin can interact with anticoagulants and other drugs, requiring a dosage adjustment.

**DOSAGE AND ADMINISTRATION**—Metformin is supplied in 500 and 850 mg tablets and also in combinations with other drugs, such as chlorpropamide, a sulfonylurea. The usual recommended dosage is 500 mg three times daily or 850 mg twice daily, taken with meals. The dosage may be increased to a maximum of 3.0 g per day if necessary and gradually reduced if possible once adequate control has been established. It may take as long as three weeks for control of diabetes with metformin to be established. Other therapeutic regimens are recommended for patients also receiving sulfonylurea drugs or insulin, for ketotic and nonketotic diabetes, and so on.

**SOURCES**—Lab. Farmacologico Milanese s.n.c., Via Monterosso 273, 21042 Caronno Perusella (VA), Italy; Difrex (Aust.) Laboratories, 13–19 Glebe St., Glebe N.S.W. 2037, Australia; Laboratorio Palenzona y Palenzona & Cia., Urbanizacion La Trinidad, Caracas 1.081, Venezuela; Rona Laboratories Limited, Cadwell Lane, Hitchin, Herts SG4 OSF, England; S.N.E. Laboratoires Aron, 116, rue Carnot, 92152 Suresnes Cedex, France; Productos Gedeon Richter (America), S.A., Miguel Angel de Quevedo No. 247, Mexico 21, D.F., Mexico.

## **Metopimazine**—Vogalen, Vogalene

**ACTIONS AND USES**—Metopimazine is an antiemetic used in the prevention and treatment of nausea and vomiting, particularly when associated with surgical procedures. The drug also has been used to relieve nausea and vomiting due to reactions to cancer chemotherapy and nausea-vomiting symptoms associated with heartburn, hiccups, stomach ulcers, duodenal ulcers, hiatus hernia, liver diseases including viral hepatitis, gallbladder disturbances, radiation therapy, and reactions to digitalis, estrogens, phenylbutazone, salicylates, and other medications. Metopimazine is reported to be as effective as prochlorperazine in the relief of nausea and vomiting symptoms from most causes, but in studies of metopimazine in the treatment of motion-sickness symptoms, the drug was found to be not effective. Metopimazine also is reported to be less effective than antihistamines in controlling nausea and vomiting associated with vertigo. Metopimazine is believed to produce its action by blocking nerve impulses to the vomiting center when the stimulus originates in the gastrointestinal tract. The drug produces a mild sedating effect and temporary reduction of blood pressure, but it does not show a depressive effect.

**PRECAUTIONS**—Metopimazine should not be administered to patients who are known to be sensitive to phenothiazine drugs, nor to those with liver impairment, blood disorders, severe central nervous system depression, or signs of circulatory collapse. It is not recommended for women of childbearing age or children under the age of 12. The drug should not be given to patients susceptible to convulsive disorders unless they are receiving treatment for the condition. Metopimazine may cause a temporary drop in blood pressure and can interact with phenothiazines and other blood-pressure-lowering drugs, including anesthetics, to increase the hypotensive effect. Side effects are generally dose-related and due to individual sensitivities to the product. They may include drowsiness, impaired motor nerve functions, insomnia, sleep inversion, agitation, photosensitivity, asthma, and sex hormonal changes such as delayed ovulation, menstrual irregularities, and ejaculation difficulties.

**DOSAGE AND ADMINISTRATION**—Metopimazine is supplied in 1 ml injection ampules containing 10 mg, in 5 mg suppositories, in sugar-coated 2.5 mg tablets, and in citrus-flavored drops containing 100 mcg per drop. The usual adult dosage for surgical patients is 10 to 20 mg by deep intramuscular injection, repeated every 8 to 12 hours as needed. The recommended oral dosage is 5 to 15 mg in two or three divided doses per day. For rectal administration, the usual dosage is one to three suppositories daily as needed.

**SOURCES**—Theraplix S.A., 46-52, rue Albert, 75640 Paris Cedex 13, France; Rougier, Inc., 8480 St. Lawrence Blvd., Montreal, Quebec H2P 2M6, Canada.

## Metronidazole + Nystatin—Flagyl Compak, Flagystatin

**ACTIONS AND USES**—Metronidazole + nystatin is a combination product that is used for a wide range of infections by bacteria and fungi, but is employed primarily for the treatment of mixed vaginal infections of *Trichomonas vaginalis* and *Candida albicans*. Metronidazole has selective action against certain anaerobic bacteria and in laboratory studies has been found to kill up to 99 percent of the organisms in a culture of *Trichomonas vaginalis* within 24 hours, even when diluted to a ratio of 1:400,000. It was found that mice injected with a culture of trichomonads and treated with a daily dose of metronidazole were free of the disease organism after seven days, whereas a control group of animals that did not receive metonidazole developed extensive abscesslike lesions swarming with trichomonads. Mystatin possesses little or no antibacterial activity but is active against fungi. It is produced from cultures of *Streptomyces noursei, Streptomyces aureus*, and other *Streptomyces* species. Nystatin is not absorbed from mucous membranes, and no systemic adverse effects have been observed as a result of local applications of the antifungal product. Nystatin has a fungistatic, or growth-inhibiting, effect against *Candida albicans*, the cause of moniliasis, at a concentration of approximately 3 micrograms per milliliter of fluid. *In vitro*, or test tube, studies have shown a fungicidal activity after a 5-hour contact with 1 mg per milliliter and fungicidal activity after 24 hours at a concentration 10 times smaller. Oral administration of nystatin in rabbits infested with 250 million *Candida albicans* cells showed the number of *Candida* cells per gram of feces reduced from millions to fewer than 20 after three days of treatment. Metronidazole and nystatin do not show antagonism in laboratory tests, and the presence of excessive amounts of either product apparently does not alter the specific effectiveness of the other.

**PRECAUTIONS**—Metronidazole + nystatin may not be effective in all bacterial infections of the vagina and should not be used unless there is a direct evidence of *Trichomonas* infestation. When there is trichomonal infection in a patient, the sexual partner should be concurrently treated with the oral product. Patients should be advised to avoid consumption of alcoholic beverages while oral doses of the product are administered because of the risk of an Antabuse or disulfiram type of reaction, characterized by falling blood pressure, nausea, vomiting, and diarrhea. Oral treatment should be discontinued if ataxia (marked by loss of muscular coordination) or other symptoms of central nervous system dysfunction develop. Metronidazole crosses the placental barrier, and use of the oral product should be avoided in pregnancy, particularly during the first trimester. The use of metronidazole + nystatin should be avoided in patients with a history of neurological disorders, blood diseases, hypothyroidism, or hypoadrenalism, unless the physician believes the benefits outweigh the risks. Side effects are reported to be minor and infrequent, but include vaginal burning and a granular sensation and unpleasant taste in the mouth. Vaginal inserts of metronidazole + nystatin every day for 30 days in monkeys resulted in no significant adverse effects when compared with use of placebo inserts.

**DOSAGE AND ADMINISTRATION**—Metronidazole + nystatin is supplied in vaginal inserts or ovules each containing 500 mg of metronidazole and 100,000 units of nystatin, as a vaginal cream delivering the same dosage, and as vaginal inserts of 100,000 units of nystatin plus 200 mg metronidazole tablets. The vaginal inserts and creams are administered daily for ten days. If a cure has not been achieved after ten days, a second ten-day course of treatment is recommended. When administered separately, the recommended procedure is one tablet three times daily for seven days while a vaginal insert is placed high in the vagina each morning and evening for seven days.

**SOURCES**—Rhône-Poulenc Pharma Inc., 8580 Esplanade, Montreal, Quebec H2P 2R9, Canada; Rhône-Poulenc Medisinsk Informasjonkontor, Skårevn. 150, Postboks 20, 1473 Skårer, Norway; May & Baker Ltd., Dagenham, Essex RM10 7XS, England.

## Mexenone—Uvistat, Uvistat-L

**ACTIONS AND USES**—Mexenone is a sunscreen that is used to protect the skin and lips from sunburn, acute solar dermatitis, keratosis, or precancerous conditions caused by exposure to ultraviolet light. Mexenone acts by absorbing a wide range of ultraviolet wavelengths that are responsible for sunburn and other abnormal skin effects. It has been used to control the chloasma, or skin pigmentation patches, induced by pregnancy or oral contraceptives and exacerbated by exposure to sunlight. It also has been used to prevent aggravation of the skin signs of systemic lupus erythematosus caused by sunlight and has been used in herpes simplex, urticaria, acne rosacea, erythema multiforme, and drug-induced photosensitivity reactions precipitated or exacerbated by sunlight. Mexenone is a nontoxic agent which when applied to the skin is held in the superficial layers of the epidermis to prevent abnormal responses to ultraviolet radiation.

**PRECAUTIONS**—With the possible exception of individual hypersensitivities to the ingredients, there are no warnings or recommendations against the use of mexenone as a sunscreen to be applied to the skin or lips. The medical literature at this writing contains no reports of serious adverse effects or cases of overdosages.

**DOSAGE AND ADMINISTRATION**—Mexenone usually is supplied as a 4 percent cream for skin application or as a 4 percent solid stick for lip application. The cream is applied twice daily, or more frequently if needed because of extended exposure to sunlight, and rubbed liberally into all skin areas likely to be exposed to the sun, including scalp areas where hair may be sparse. Additional applications may be required if there is profuse sweating or the skin becomes wet. The first application should be made before exposure to sunlight. The solid stick form of mexenone also should be applied to the lips before exposure to sunlight. Additional applications should be made after meals, swimming, or washing. Cosmetic lipsticks can be applied over the mexenone layer.

**SOURCES**—WB Pharmaceuticals Limited, P.O. Box 23, Bracknell, Berkshire RG12 4YS, England; Boehringer Ingelheim Pty Ltd., 50 Broughton Rd., Artarmon N.S.W. 2064, Australia.

## Mexiletine Hydrochloride—Mexitil

**ACTIONS AND USES**—Mexiletine hydrochloride is an antiarrhythmic drug used primarily for the management of abnormal heart rhythms originating in the ventricles and for ectopic beats, which originate at a point beyond the usual location in the heart muscle. The drug has been found in clinical studies to be effective in suppressing abnormal heart rhythms associated with myocardial infarction, toxic reactions to digitalis medications, artificial heart valves, and ischemic heart disease (due to an inadequate supply of oxygen to the heart muscle). It also has been found useful in the treatment of abnormally rapid heartbeats, flutter, and fibrillation. Unlike lignocaine, an alternative antiarrhythmic drug, mexiletine can be administered orally. It is prescribed on the basis of careful assessment of electrocardiograms.

**PRECAUTIONS**—Mexiletine hydrochloride is not recommended for pregnant women or nursing mothers and should be used with extreme caution in patients with kidney, liver, or heart failure, abnormally low blood pressure, abnormally slow heartbeat, or abnormalities of the heart's natural pacemaker or impulse conduction mechanism. It also should not be administered to children. Patients with parkinsonism may experience an increase in tremors as a result of using the product. In addition to heart palpitations, blood pressure changes, slower heartbeat and other side effects involving the circulatory system, patients may experience hiccups, nausea, vomiting, gastric distress, drowsiness, dizziness, confusion, tremors, or blurred vision after administration of the drug. The symptoms of side effects also may be signs of overdosage.

**DOSAGE AND ADMINISTRATION**—Mexiletine hydrochloride is supplied in capsules of 50 and 200 mg each and in 10 ml ampules containing 250 mg of the drug for intravenous injection. The smaller capsules are used for adjusting the maintenance dosage to a satisfactory response level. The usual initial, or loading, oral dose is two or three 200 mg capsules, followed two hours later by a maintenance dose of 200 to 250 mg three times daily. A lower maintenance dose may be desirable if side effects are serious. The intravenous loading dose is 200 to 250 mg administered at a rate of 25 mg per minute. A suggested maintenance dose is 0.5 mg per minute, until the oral dosage can be started or as long as needed to achieve a satisfactory patient response.

**SOURCE**—Boehringer Ingelheim Ltd., Southern Industrial Estate, Bracknell, Berkshire, England; Boehringer Ingelheim AB, Bredholmsgatan 10, Skärholmen, Sweden.

## Mianserin Hydrochloride—Athymil, Bolvidon, Lantanon, Lerivon, Norval, Tolvin, Tolvon

**ACTIONS AND USES**—Mianserin hydrochloride is an antidepressant used in the treatment of depression and involutional melancholia, a depressive psychosis experienced by some menopausal women and older men. The drug also has been employed in the management of anxiety, agitation, and insomnia associated with depression and in the treatment of phobias. Mianserin has antihistamine properties and produces a marked sedative action. Its pharmacological activities include a blocking effect in nerve receptors of the alpha pathways of the autonomic nervous system, and it is regarded by some authorities as an inhibitor of activity by serotonin, one of the body's nerve impulse transmitters that is associated with sleep, schizophrenia, and depression. It also is involved in norepinephrine activity in the brain and other areas. Mianserin is compatible with most antihypertensive drugs and is often the drug of choice in the treatment of patients suffering from both hypertension and depression.

**PRECAUTIONS**—Caution should be used in giving mianserin to patients with epilepsy, diabetes, or impaired kidney or liver function. Care also should be exercised in administering the drug to patients with heart disease. Although no evidence of birth defects has been reported as a result of animal tests, mianserin is not recommended for use in human pregnancy. Mianserin is reported to be generally free of adverse interactions with other medications, but caution should be observed in giving mianserin to patients also taking monoamine oxidase inhibitors, clonidine antihypertensive medications, barbiturates, or coumarin types of anticoagulants. The patient should be advised that mianserin may impair mental or physical abilities, particularly during the first few days of therapy, and caution should be used in operating motor vehicles or machinery until it has been determined whether the patient's alertness has been affected. The patient also should be warned that consumption of alcoholic beverages while using mianserin can result in increased intoxication effects. Like other antidepressants, mianserin hydrochloride can trigger episodes of mild mania or excitement in sensitive individuals. Other side effects may include a mild degree of jaundice, an abnormally low white blood cell count, dizziness, skin rash, postural hypotension, and breast disorders such as nipple tenderness and development of enlarged and sometimes functioning mammary glands in male patients.

**DOSAGE AND ADMINISTRATION**—Mianserin hydrochloride is supplied in 10, 20, and 30 mg tablets. The usual recommended dosage is 30 mg initially, taken either in divided doses or as a single dose before retiring. The dosage may be increased gradually after the first week to 60 mg daily, if necessary, or higher. The recommended maximum is 200 mg per day in divided doses. The mianserin tablets should be taken between meals and swallowed without chewing.

**SOURCES**—Bencard, Great West Road, Brentford, Middlesex TW8 9BE, England; Organon Laboratories Ltd., Crown House, London Road,

Morden, Surrey SM4 5DZ, England; Ravasini Dr. R. & Cia. s.p.a., Via Ostilia 15, 00184 Roma, Italy; Organon, B.P. 144, 03204 Saint-Denis Cedex 01, France.

## Midecamycin—Midecaine, Midecamycine Meiji

**ACTIONS AND USES**—Midecamycin is an antibiotic used in the treatment of respiratory tract infections and skin diseases that are suppurative (associated with pus formation). Midecamycin is particularly active against strains of *Staphylococcus*, *Streptococcus*, pneumococcus, and *Mycoplasma* pneumonia agents. Although midecamycin is an oral drug, it is selective in reaching infections in the skin and lungs, as well as other internal organs. It is recommended for treatment of infections by *Staphylococcus* strains that have developed resistance to penicillin, streptomycin, tetracycline, chloramphenicol, and other antibiotics. Midecamycin also does not induce resistance to antibiotics as do erythromycin and oleandomycin products. Midecamycin, like erythromycin, is believed to act by forming bonds with amino acids and RNA molecules to disrupt the normal cellular activity of building protein molecules within the bacterial cell. Midecamycin is used in the treatment of such skin diseases as furuncles, carbuncles, impetigo, erysipelas, subcutaneous abscesses, infectious atheromas, felons (infections of the terminal finger joint), and phlegmons (infections of the subcutaneous connective tissue). The drug also has been used in the treatment of pharyngitis, laryngitis, tonsillitis, bronchitis, pneumonia, cystitis, urethritis, otitis media, sinusitis, mastitis, osteomyelitis, lymph node infections, inflammations of the tear sacs and glands of the eyelids, and infections involving the teeth and jaws.

**PRECAUTIONS**—Midecamycin is a macrolide antibiotic, a term that identifies the structural shape of its molecule and a type that frequently is associated with gastrointestinal side effects. Administration of midecamycin causes loss of appetite, nausea, vomiting, abdominal pain, stomach discomfort, loose stools, and diarrhea. However, midecamycin reportedly causes fewer gastrointestinal side effects than other macrolide antibiotics because of treatment of the drug with a cellulose derivative. Other side effects may include an inflammation or coating of the tongue.

Some individuals may be hypersensitive to midecamycin; if signs of sensitivity occur, the drug should be discontinued.

**DOSAGE AND ADMINISTRATION**—Midecamycin is supplied in 200 mg capsules and 400 mg tablets, as well as a pediatric formulation that contains 200 mg of the drug in a powder form. The usual daily dosage for adults is 800 mg to 1.2 g taken in three to four divided doses. It is recommended that the medication be taken with meals. For children under the age of 6 years and infants, the recommended dosage is 30 mg of the powder per kg of body weight taken orally in three to four divided doses. The 400 mg tablets are not recommended for use in children under the age of 6 years.

**SOURCES**—Maiji Seika Kaisha, Ltd., 4-16, Kyobashi 2-chome, Chuo-ku, Tokyo Japan; Laboratoires Clin Midy, 20, rue des Fosses-Saint-Jacques, 75240 Paris Cedex 05, France.

## **Morinamide (Morfazinamide)**—Felder, Piazofolina, Piazolin, Piazolina, Piazoline, Tiepolo

**ACTIONS AND USES**—Morinamide is an antituberculosis drug that can be taken orally or be administered intravenously. Morinamide has been used in conjunction with other antituberculosis drugs and as an alternative therapy when a strain of the disease agent resistant to usual drugs is encountered. The product also has been used as a drug to be administered to tuberculosis patients before and after surgery.

**PRECAUTIONS**—Morinamide should not be given to patients who are sensitive to nicotinamide-type medications. Morinamide is chemically similar to pyrazinamide, and cross-resistance between the two drugs has been reported. Adverse effects reported include nausea, vomiting, and other forms of gastric distress.

**DOSAGE AND ADMINISTRATION**—Morinamide is supplied in 500 mg tablets. The usual recommended adult dosage is 50 mg per day per kg of body weight, or four to six tablets daily for a 60 kg adult. For children, the recommended dose is 25 to 50 mg per kg of body weight daily. The drug should be taken after meals and at regular intervals.

**SOURCE**—Bracco de Mexico, S.A. de C.V., Calzada de las Armas No. 110, Tlalnepantla, Edo. de Mexico.

## Netilmicin Sulfate—Certomycin, Netillin, Netromycin

**ACTIONS AND USES**—Netilmicin is an antibiotic used in treating infections caused by strains of bacteria that are resistant to another antibiotic, gentamicin. It is used in controlling infections of the respiratory tract, kidney and genitourinary tract, skin, and soft tissues; septicemia due to bacterial infections of the blood; bone and joint infections; abdominal infections including peritonitis; burns; wounds; infections of the uterus; and infections associated with surgical procedures. Netilmicin has been found effective in treating bacteria that are resistant to kanamycin, tobramycin, amikacin, and sissomicin, in addition to gentamicin. Netilmicin acts against certain strains of bacteria by blocking their synthesis of normal protein molecules from amino acids in the environment. The bacteria instead build defective protein molecules which render the microorganisms nonfunctional.

**PRECAUTIONS**—The safety of netilmicin in pregnancy and lactation has not been established, and the drug therefore should not be given to pregnant women or nursing mothers. Netilmicin also should not be given to persons who have experienced toxic reactions or sensitivity to netilmicin or antibiotics that are chemically related. The most serious adverse effects are kidney disorders and problems associated with the inner ear, including the senses of both hearing and balance. Among effects reported are dizziness, various degrees of deafness, ringing or buzzing in the ears, a sense of pressure in the ears, disorientation, and nystagmus (marked by involuntary movements of the eyeballs). Other side effects include headache, abdominal pain, vomiting, drug fever, skin rash, diarrhea, heart palpitations. Kidney function changes and abnormalities in blood coagulation have been reported. The drug should be used with caution in patients with neuromuscular disorders such as parkinsonism or myasthenia gravis because netilmicin can exacerbate such conditions. It also is not recommended for infants because of the risk of damage to their immature kidneys. Netilmicin may interact with other drugs, particularly certain diuretics, which can increase the risk of adverse effects on the senses of hearing and balance.

**DOSAGE AND ADMINISTRATION**—Netilmicin is supplied in ampules for use in intramuscular or intravenous injection. The ampules come in 1, 1.5, and 2 ml sizes, and in concentrations of 10, 25, 50, or 100 mg of netilmicin per ml. The usual dosage for adults is about 150 mg twice daily or an equivalent amount given in three divided doses eight hours apart. Doses generally are calculated at 4 to 6 mg per kg of body weight per day for urinary tract or systemic infections, and the dose is increased to 7.5 mg per kg of body weight for life-threatening infections. For children, the usual dose is 6.0 to 7.5 mg per kg of body weight per day. When administered to infants more than one week old, the usual dosage is 2.5 to 3.0 mg per kg every eight hours, for a total of 7.5 to 9.0 mg per kg of body weight per day.

**SOURCES**—Kirby-Warrick Pharmaceuticals Ltd., Mildenhall, Bury St. Edmunds, Suffolk IP28 7AX, England; Schering Canada, Inc., 3535 Trans-Canada, Pointe Claire, Quebec H9R 1B4, Canada.

## **Nicofuranose (Pyridine Fructose)**—Bradilan, Buclidan, Vasperdil

**ACTIONS AND USES**—Nicofuranose is a nicotinic acid derivative that is used in the treatment of peripheral vascular disease. It also has been used to reduce blood cholesterol levels. The product has properties similar to those of nicotinic acid, or the B vitamin niacin, which is produced in the metabolism of nicofuranose. It acts on the capillary microcirculation to increase the bore of the blood vessels, reduce circulatory resistance, and thereby improve the peripheral blood circulation. It is used in the treatment of intermittent claudication (restricted blood flow to the legs), deficient kidney blood flow, and insufficient blood circulation to the brain and its associated organs, particularly the eyes and ears. Nicofuranose has been used in the therapy of diabetic, senile, and arteriosclerotic retinopathies and other microcirculation disorders of the eye.

**PRECAUTIONS**—Nicofuranose should not be given to patients who suffer from arterial hypotension (low blood pressure) or who have recently recovered from a stroke or other form of cerebral hemorrhage. Side effects may include a sensation of warmth and flushing, particularly about the face. The effects are transient and are related to the influence of nicotinic acid, which also may produce symptoms of hypotension, dizziness, and some gastric distress when administered in large doses.

**DOSAGE AND ADMINISTRATION**—Nicofuranose is supplied in coated 250 mg tablets. The usual recommended dose is 500 mg twice a day, once in the morning and once in the evening, but not with meals.

**SOURCE**—Bracco de Mexico, S.A. de C.V., Calzada de las Armas No. 110, Tlalnepantla, Edo. de Mexico.

## Nicotine Gum—Nicorette

**ACTIONS AND USES**—Nicotine chewing gum is used as a partial or complete substitute for cigarette or other tobacco sources of nicotine. It is intended to be a temporary aid in cushioning the patient against the psychological and/or pharmacological trauma of withdrawal from cigarette smoking. When the gum is chewed, nicotine is slowly released into the mouth and absorbed through the mucous membranes lining the mouth. A significant portion of the nicotine is swallowed with saliva and inactivated in the digestive tract. The product is not recommended as a permanent replacement, but rather as a step toward abandonment of all forms of tobacco smoking and nicotine use.

**PRECAUTIONS**—Nicotine gum should not be used by pregnant women or nursing mothers because of nicotine's known adverse effects on the fetus or infant. It should be used with caution in patients with angina pectoris, coronary artery disease, peripheral vascular disease, or similar disorders of the heart or circulatory system. Caution also should be exercised in use of nicotine gum by persons with disease or inflammation of the mouth or throat and by individuals afflicted with peptic ulcers or gastritis. Adverse effects reported include ulcers of the mouth, throat irritation, excessive salivation, and hiccups. Dependence is a possible side effect, but less of a risk and less harmful than dependence through smoking. Persons with dentures may experience difficulty in chewing the nicotine gum.

**DOSAGE AND ADMINISTRATION**—Nicotine gum is supplied in square pieces containing either 2 or 4 mg of nicotine per piece. Chewing a 4 mg piece usually results in nicotine blood levels that are equivalent to those produced by inhaling while smoking a standard filter cigarette. A

2 mg piece of nicotine gum results in blood levels of nicotine comparable with those reached by a person who smokes a standard filter cigarette without inhaling. All the available nicotine in a piece of the gum usually is released after 30 minutes of chewing, but the rate of chewing and swallowing affects the amount of nicotine absorbed through the mucous membranes of the mouth.

**SOURCES**—Lundbeck Limited, Lundbeck House, Hastings Street, Luton, Bedfordshire LU1 5BE, England; Dow Pharmaceuticals, Dow Chemical Canada, Inc., 380 Elgin Mills Road East, Richmond Hill, Ontario L4C 5H2, Canada; AB Leo, Box 941, 251 09 Helsingborg, Sweden.

## **Nifurtoinol**—Urfadyn, Urfadyne

**ACTIONS AND USES**—Nifurtoinol is an antibacterial medication used in the treatment of urinary tract infections. The drug produces its antimicrobial activity through a mechanism whereby nifurtoinol becomes concentrated in the patient's urine rather than in the blood or other tissues. It has been recommended for use in the treatment of cystitis, pyelitis, pyelonephritis, hydronephrosis, and infections of the prostate gland and ureters. Nifurtoinol also is used to prevent infections during surgical procedures involving the kidney, urinary bladder, or associated tissues.

**PRECAUTIONS**—Nifurtoinol should not be used in patients with severely impaired kidney function. Caution should be used in administering the drug to patients who may be sensitive to nifurtoinol and related substances and to patients with certain abnormal levels of substances found in the blood and urine. The drug should not be given to small children or women in the first trimester of pregnancy. Side effects are mainly those of gastrointestinal distress, including nausea and loss of appetite.

**DOSAGE AND ADMINISTRATION**—Nifurtoinol is supplied in 40 mg tablets. The usual recommended adult dosage is 160 mg per day taken in divided doses with meals. For children, the recommended dosage is calculated at 3 to 5 mg per day per kg of body weight.

**SOURCES**—Inpharzam-Nederland N.V., De Paal 41, 1351 JH Almere, The Netherlands; Inpharzam S.A., 6814 Cadempino, P.O. Box 6812, Switzerland.

**Nitrazepam**—Apodorm, Dormicum, Dormigen, Dumolid, Mitidin, Mogadon, Nitrados, Noctem, Onirem, Paxisyn, Persopir, Prosonno, Quill, Solium, Somnite, Sonnolin, Surem, Tri, Unisomnia

**ACTIONS AND USES**—Nitrazepam is a sedative that is also used as a hypnotic and an anticonvulsant. It is a member of the benzodiazepine family of drugs that have replaced barbiturates in such uses as inducing sleep, while a smaller dose produces a calming effect. Nitrazepam is believed to produce its sedative-hypnotic action by blocking stimuli to the brain centers that are responsible for maintaining wakefulness. Unlike many other hypnotics, nitrazepam apparently does not cause a generalized depression of brain activities, so the patient can be aroused and allowed to return to sleep again without difficulty. Effects of the drug are observed about 30 minutes after oral administration; and when it is used as a hypnotic, sleep lasts 6 to 8 hours. The drug is used for sleep disturbances, such as those due to depression or anxiety, insomnia in elderly patients and those who should avoid use of barbiturates, sleep disturbances due to organic causes, and myoclonic seizures (marked by spasms or twitching of muscles).

**PRECAUTIONS**—Nitrazepam should not be administered to patients with myasthenia gravis, patients with severe chronic obstructive respiratory disorders, children, women of childbearing potential, or nursing mothers. Caution should be used in giving the product to patients with impaired kidney or liver function, elderly or debilitated patients, or those with suicidal tendencies or a history of drug abuse. Paradoxical reactions, such as agitation, hyperactivity, excitement, or increased muscle spasticity, have been reported. Patients also may experience rebound insomnia after use of nitrazepam has been discontinued. The most common side effects reported include fatigue, dizziness, drowsiness, mental confusion, and loss of coordination with staggering and falling, with a greater incidence of such adverse effects occurring among elderly or debilitated patients. Patients should be advised that mental and physical abilities may be impaired by the use of nitrazepam, making operation of motor vehicles or machinery potentially hazardous. Patients also should be advised that nitrazepam may interact with alcohol, producing an additive effect, as well as other drugs that affect the central nervous system, such as barbiturates, phenothiazines, and morphine derivatives.

**DOSAGE AND ADMINISTRATION**—Nitrazepam is supplied in 2.5, 5, and 10 mg tablets and 10 mg suppositories. The usual initial dose for adults is 5 to 10 mg before retiring, followed by gradual increases as necessary up to a maximum daily dose of 20 mg. The recommended dosage for elderly patients is 2.5 to 5 mg per day. Although nitrazepam is generally not recommended for children, the suggested dosage when ordered by a physician is 2.5 to 5 mg per day. The tablets may be chewed, swallowed whole, or dissolved in liquid.

**SOURCES**—Produits Roche, S.A., 52, bvd du Parc, 92521 Neuilly-sur-Seine Cedex, France; Laboratorio Palenzona y Palenzona & Cia., Urbanizacion La Trinidad, Caracas 1.081, Venezuela; Vita Farmaceutici s.p.a., Via Boucheron 14, 10122 Torino, Italy; A/S Apothekernes Laboratorium for Specialpræparater, Skøyen, Oslo 2, Norway.

## **Nomifensine Maleate**—Alival, Anametrin, Hostalival, Merital, Merival, Psichronizer

**ACTIONS AND USES**—Nomifensine maleate is a central nervous system stimulant and mood-elevating drug used in the treatment of depression, particularly in patients whose depression is accompanied by feelings of anxiety. The product also has been used in the treatment of parkinsonism and in patients who show some signs of retardation. The exact manner in which nomifensine maleate functions as a psychic energizer is not fully understood, and the product is not related to any of the other known antidepressant medications. Studies indicate the drug is very well tolerated; it produces fewer and milder side effects and is less likely to cause adverse effects on the heart than other antidepressants. It causes little or no sedation and does not appear to diminish psychomotor performance.

**PRECAUTIONS**—The safety of nomifensine maleate in pregnancy has not been established, and the drug therefore should not be given to pregnant women. The product is transmitted in breast milk ir quantities, but the effect on offspring has not been established. Because of insufficient clinical experience, the drug is not recommended for children. The drug should be used with caution in patients with heart disease or impaired liver or kidney function, in patients with Parkinson's disease, and in patients also being treated for schizophrenia. Nomifensine maleate may interact with alcohol and other drugs, particularly drugs prescribed for emotional or mental disorders, including tranquilizers. Side effects observed include a fever of unknown origin in certain patients, insomnia, headache, dryness of the mouth, constipation, diarrhea, difficulty in urination, and a skin rash.

**DOSAGE AND ADMINISTRATION**—Nomifensine maleate is supplied in 25 and 50 mg capsules. The usual recommended dosage is initially 25 or 50 mg taken two or three times daily, followed by gradually increasing doses up to a maximum of 200 mg per day if necessary to achieve the required response. Some severely depressed patients have been able to tolerate up to 300 mg of nomifensine maleate daily. For older patients who may be sensitive to psychotropic drugs, lower initial and maintenance doses are recommended. Because of the stimulant effect, the last dose of the day should be given no later than early evening.

**SOURCES**—Hoechst UK Ltd., Pharmaceutical Division, Hoechst House, Salisbury Rd., Houslow, Middx TW4 6JH, England; Quimica Hoechst de Mexico, S.A., Tecoyotitla No. 412, Mexico 20, D.F., Mexico; Hoechst Australia Ltd., 606 St. Kilda Road, Melbourne, Vic. 3000, Australia.

## **Norethandrolone**—Nilevar, Solevar

**ACTIONS AND USES**—Norethandrolone is an anabolic steroid used for protein building in patients recovering from severe illness, major surgery, burns, or serious injury. It also is used in preparing debilitated patients for surgery and for the management of malnutrition and mineral loss in patients who are bedridden or who have experienced protein tissue loss or osteoporosis, a bone defect, due to a corticosteroid hormone abnormality. Norethandrolone has been employed in the treatment of osteoporosis associated with postmenopausal and other aging problems. In younger men, norethandrolone has been used with testosterone enanthate to increase normal spermatozoa production as a part of a therapy for infertility. Uses of anabolic steroids to improve athletic performance, as body builders, and to increase the height of children have been challenged by some authorities, who note that side effects in such applications may outweigh the claimed benefits.

**PRECAUTIONS**—Norethandrolone should not be given to pregnant women because of the risk of masculinization of the fetus. It also should not be administered to premature or newborn infants. Caution should be used in giving the drug to young children because of the possibility of causing serious disturbances of growth and normal sexual development. Prolonged or excessive use of anabolic steroids in growing children can result in premature closing of the bone epiphyses, so that long bones of the body fail to reach normal adult length. Physicians using such products are advised to monitor bone growth at the wrists every three to six months during therapy. Anabolic steroids also may produce amenorrhea or other menstrual problems. Norethandrolone should not be given to patients who are hypersensitive to anabolic steroids, or to patients with cancer of the breast or prostate, or enlargement of the prostate. Anabolic steroids can cause a wide range of sexual development aberrations, ranging from precocious puberty in boys to testicular atrophy and impotence in adult males, clitoral enlargement with male balding patterns in females, and either increased or decreased libido in both sexes. The changes generally are not reversible by discontinuing therapy nor prevented by the administration of female sex hormones. Women with certain types of breast cancer may develop hypercalcemia, with depletion of other minerals. The drug also may alter blood cholesterol levels, blood coagulation time, and results of glucose tolerance and other laboratory tests. Jaundice may develop occasionally, and liver tumors have occurred in patients on long-term anabolic steroid therapy. While recommended as an aid in the recovery from injuries and burns, norethandrolone should not be given during the acute phases of these conditions.

**DOSAGE AND ADMINISTRATION**—Norethandrolone is supplied as 10 mg tablets. The dosage varies according to individual patient needs, response, and symptoms of adverse reactions. The usual adult dosage is 10 to 30 mg daily. For children, the dosage is calculated at a rate of 500 mcg per kg of body weight per day. Therapy should be intermittent, with continuous treatment periods limited to 90 days followed by a drug-free period of at least 30 days. Anabolic steroid therapy requires a balanced diet with adequate protein intake in order to be effective.

**SOURCES**—Laboratoires Searle, 7, boulevard Romaine-Rolland, 92128 Montrouge, France; G.D. Searle and Co. of Canada, Ltd., 400 Iroquois Shore Rd., Oakville, Ontario L6H 1M5, Canada.

## Obidoxime Chloride—Toxogonin

**ACTIONS AND USES**—Obidoxime chloride is an antidote for poisoning by organophosphorus compounds, such as the pesticides used in agriculture. Organic phosphorus pesticides, including parathion and malathion, produce their toxic effects by inhibiting cholinesterase, an enzyme that destroys molecules of the nerve impulse transmitter substance acetylcholine. By inhibiting the enzyme activity, excessive amounts of acetylcholine accumulate and flood parts of the nervous system, particularly the smooth and skeletal muscles, heart, and glands, with stimulation. So-called military nerve gases utilize the same principle. Obidoxime chloride reactivates the body's cholinesterase activity, thereby reducing the surplus of acetylcholine. Obidoxime chloride is reported to have greater potency and rapidity of reactivating cholinesterase than pralidoxime, a similar drug.

**PRECAUTIONS**—Obidoxime chloride may have somewhat greater side effects than pralidoxime, and it is believed that large doses may affect brain functions. Side effects include pain at the site of injection, increased blood pressure and heart rate, a temporary prickling sensation but decreased sensitivity to pain, and a feeling of warmth in the facial area.

**DOSAGE AND ADMINISTRATION**—Obidoxime chloride is supplied in injection ampules containing 250 mg per ml. The drug is administered by intramuscular or slow intravenous injection. The usual adult dose of obidoxime is 250 mg. The drug is administered concurrently with intravenous injections of atropine in initial amounts of 2 to 5 mg for adults and 500 mcg to 3 mg for children. Atropine administered should be continued for 24 to 48 hours. Total amounts of atropine during the period may be 40 to 100 mg.

**SOURCES**—E. Merck Atiebolag, Post adress: Sturegaten 8, 114 35, Stockholm, Sweden; E. Merck, Frankfurter Strasse 250, 6100 Darmstadt 1, West Germany.

## Opipramol—Ensidon, Insidon, Nisidona

**ACTIONS AND USES**—Opipramol is a psychotropic drug that is used primarily as an antidepressant, although it has also been applied as a tranquilizer. It is similar to amitriptyline, which also is an antidepressant drug with tranquilizing properties. The patient receiving opipramol experiences at first a mild sedative effect, followed by relief of anxiety and tension, after which there is an elevation of mood. The product has been used in the treatment of anxiety and depression associated with functional disorders, such as the emotional problems that develop in some menopausal patients. Opipramol is also employed in the management of psychosomatic disorders and emotional problems of childhood and old age.

**PRECAUTIONS**—Opipramol should not be given to patients who are using monoamine oxidase inhibitors or who have taken such drugs within the previous two weeks. For patients who have previously been treated with monoamine oxidase inhibitors for symptoms of depression, caution should be used in introducing opipramol in small doses with gradual increments to a maintenance dose. Opipramol should not be given to patients with impaired liver function or to those with coronary artery insufficiency or a recent myocardial infarction. The drug should not be given to women of childbearing potential or to nursing mothers. Caution is recommended in administration of opipramol to patients who are young, elderly, or debilitated. Opipramol is not recommended for patients with severe depression, hyperthyroidism, a history of epilepsy, blood disorders, or acute glaucoma. Opipramol may interact with alcohol, methyldopa, central nervous system depressants, or guanethidine-type antihypertensive drugs. Side effects include drowsiness, dizziness, dry mouth, and occasionally changes in blood count. Patients should be advised that use of opipramol may impair physical or mental abilities, making it hazardous to operate motor vehicles or machinery.

**DOSAGE AND ADMINISTRATION**—Opipramol is supplied in 50 mg sugar-coated tablets. The usual recommended dosage for adults is 150 to 300 mg daily in divided doses. The recommended dosage for children is 50 to 150 mg daily in divided doses. It is suggested that dosages for elderly and debilitated patients be started at 50 to 100 mg per day and adjusted according to response. Patients with sleep disturbance problems may take a larger share of a divided dose before retiring.

**SOURCES**—Ciba Geigy Pharma A/S, Strømsv. 49-53, Postboks 124, 2011 Strømmen, Norway; Geigy Pharmaceuticals, 70 Northumberland Road, Dublin 4, Ireland.

## Ornidazole—Tiberal

**ACTIONS AND USES**—Ornidazole is an antiinfective drug used in the treatment of amebic dysentery and various other diseases caused by bacteria and protozoa. It is effective in the treatment of trichomoniasis in both women and men and reportedly does not affect the normal bacterial flora of the vagina. In the treatment of vaginal trichomoniasis, a success rate of 98.5 percent has been claimed for ornidazole. In the treatment of bacterial infections, ornidazole is reported to be as effective as metronidazole and somewhat more effective against certain strains of microorganisms. In addition to its use in bacterial infections, amebiasis, and trichomoniasis, ornidazole has been employed in the treatment of Crohn's disease (an intestinal disorder) and giardiasis (a disease caused by a type of protozoa that attaches itself to the inner walls of human intestinal tracts, producing symptoms of cramps, diarrhea, nausea, and malabsorption).

**PRECAUTIONS**—Ornidazole should not be given to women who may be pregnant or to nursing mothers. It also should not be administered to patients with a central nervous system disease or to persons with blood disorders. Although ornidazole reportedly does not interact with alcohol to produce the disulfiram-like reactions of metronidazole, patients should be advised that because of the chemical relationship an alcohol interaction may be possible in some individuals. Among the side effects reported are gastrointestinal distress, nausea, vomiting, loss of appetite, unpleasant taste, headache, and skin rash. Some patients have experienced dizziness, loss of coordination, drowsiness, or insomnia.

**DOSAGE AND ADMINISTRATION**—Ornidazole is supplied in 500 mg tablets and also in injection ampules containing 500 mg of the drug. The usual recommended dosage for amebiasis and giardiasis is 500 mg taken twice a day, once in the morning and again before retiring. The dosage for children between the ages of 6 and 12 is 375 mg in the morning and 375 mg at bedtime. For children between 1 and 6 years of age, the dosage is 250 mg in the morning and 250 mg at bedtime. The medication should be taken for a period of 5 to 10 days. In the treatment of trichomoniasis, the recommended dosage is 1.0 or 1.5 g taken daily by mouth or 1.0 g by mouth and 500 mg vaginally each day. The sexual partners should receive concurrent treatment to avoid reinfection.

**SOURCES**—Productos Roche, S.A. de C.V., Av. de la Universidad No. 902, Mexico 12, D.F., Mexico; Produits Roche, S.A., 52, bvd du Parc, 92521 Neuilly-sur-Seine Cedex, France.

## Ornipressin—Por 8

**ACTIONS AND USES**—Ornipressin is a vasoconstrictor, or drug used to constrict blood vessels and thereby to reduce or stop bleeding. It is used primarily in surgical procedures in which bleeding may be a problem, such as plastic surgery including hair transplants and skin grafts, gynecological procedures including vaginal repair or vaginal hysterectomy, and surgery of the head and neck including tonsillectomy and eye and ear operations. Ornipressin is derived from a hormone, vasopressin, that is normally secreted by nerve endings in the pituitary gland. Ornipressin is more potent as a vasoconstrictor than vasopressin but has only weak diuretic properties. Ornipressin acts by causing a contraction of the smooth muscle cells of the blood vessels in the area where it is administered.

**PRECAUTIONS**—Ornipressin should not be administered to patients with heart disease. The drug also should not be given to women who may be pregnant. Caution should be used in giving ornipressin to patients with high blood pressure. Although the product is administered locally near the site of the surgical procedure, some of the ornipressin may be absorbed into the general blood circulation, resulting in vasoconstrictive effects throughout the body. The patient may experience some pallor because of the effect of the drug on capillaries in the face or other body regions. The side effects are temporary, as the vasoconstrictive action of the drug usually lasts about one hour after injection.

**DOSAGE AND ADMINISTRATION**—Ornipressin is supplied in 1 ml ampules containing 5 units of the drug, which must be diluted in a saline solution or a solution of local anesthetic. It is recommended that solutions for surgical procedures about the head and neck be diluted to 20 ml for each ampule; for abdominal or gynecological surgery an ampule may be diluted in 50 to 60 ml of solution. The solution is administered by regional infiltration at the site of the surgery.

**SOURCES**—Sandoz Produkte (Schweiz) AG, Missionsstrasse 60, 4012 Basel, Switzerland; Sandoz Australia Pty. Ltd., 54 Waterloo Rd., North Ryde N.S.W. 2113, Australia.

## Oxprenolol Hydrochloride—Apsolox, Oxanol, Slow Trasicor, Trasacor, Trasicor, Trasidex, Trasitensina

**ACTIONS AND USES**—Oxprenolol is a beta-blocker used in the treatment of anxiety, hypertension, and a variety of heart disorders, including myocardial infarction, angina pectoris, heart arrhythmias, and some forms of tachycardia or abnormally rapid heartbeat. The drug has also been used in the treatment of parkinsonism, enlarged heart associated with thyroid disorder, abnormal heartbeats due to anesthetics, and heart arrhythmias due to digitalis overdosage. As a beta-blocker, oxprenolol exerts an inhibitory effect on nerve receptors of the beta pathways of the autonomic system, causing a slowing of the heart rate, reducing the oxygen requirements of the heart muscle, and lowering the blood pressure. In angina pectoris, oxprenolol improves the ability of the heart to function without pain during exercise or some degree of physical exertion.

**PRECAUTIONS**—Oxprenolol should be used with extreme caution in pregnancy and lactation because of the risk of the drug effect on the fetus or infant. In pregnancy, oxprenolol can produce an abnormally slow heartbeat in the fetus that will continue after birth. The drug should not be given to patients afflicted with bradycardia (abnormally slow heartbeat), nor to patients with certain other heart disorders, including atrioventricular block of the second or third degree or heart failure that resists digitalis therapy. The drug also should not be administered to patients suffering from bronchospasm or a condition predisposing to the disorder. Oxprenolol may interact adversely with certain drugs, such as verapamil and other calcium-channel-blocking heart drugs. Oxprenolol also may interact adversely with certain types of anesthesia. The drug should be used with caution in diabetic patients or patients who are fasting, because of the tendency of beta-blockers to produce symptoms of severe hypoglycemia. Patients should be advised to avoid allowing their supply of beta-blocker drug to become exhausted; and when withdrawal is necessary, it should be done slowly, over a period of 7 to 14 days. An abrupt discontinuation of the drug can result in severe exacerbation of heart disorders.

**DOSAGE AND ADMINISTRATION**—Oxprenolol hydrochloride is supplied in 20, 40, 80, and 160 mg tablets and 2 mg injection ampules. For hypertension, the usual recommended initial dose is 80 mg of oxprenolol hydrochloride twice daily, followed by gradual increases as necessary to achieve satisfactory blood pressure control. When used with a diuretic, a maximum daily dose of oxprenolol of 320 mg is recommended, but larger doses may be required if a diuretic is not prescribed. The usual recommended adult dose for treatment of angina pectoris is 40 to 160 mg three times daily, with a maximum daily dose of 480 mg. For heart arrhythmias, the recommended initial dose is 20 to 40 mg three times daily, followed by gradual increases in dosage to achieve a satisfactory response. The injection ampules usually are employed for intramuscular or intravenous emergency treatment of severe heart rhythm disorders. Dosages for children have been calculated at 1 mg per kg of body weight, when required for control of abnormal heart rhythms.

**SOURCES**—Ciba-Geigy Mexicana, S.A. de C.V., Calz. de Tlalpan No. 1779, Mexico 21, D.F., Mexico; Ciba Laboratories, Horsham, West Sussex RH12 4 AB, England.

## Oxyfedrine Hydrochloride—Ildamen, Modacor

**ACTIONS AND USES**—Oxyfedrine hydrochloride is a vasodilator believed to act partly as a beta-blocker and partly as a stimulator of heart muscle contractions while also causing dilation of the arteries in the peripheral areas of the body. In addition to its use in cases of angina pectoris, oxyfedrine is employed in the management of patients who have suffered a myocardial infarction and those afflicted with coronary artery insufficiency. Oxyfedrine has been compared with propranolol in its beneficial effects in heart disease patients.

**PRECAUTIONS**—Adverse effects reported include visual aberrations, including changes in color vision and visual fields, and abnormal sensations such as numbness or increased sensitivity.

**DOSAGE AND ADMINISTRATION**—Oxyfedrine hydrochloride is supplied in 8 and 16 mg tablets and 2 ml injection ampules containing 4 mg of the drug. The usual recommended dosage is 16 mg by mouth taken three times a day, before or after meals, or 4 mg by intravenous injection one to three times a day. The injections should be administered over a period of between 30 seconds and 1 minute. The tablets may be taken with water or a flavored fluid.

**SOURCES**—Laboratoires Houde-I.S.H., 15, rue Olivier-Metra, 75980 Paris Cedex 20, France; Laboratorios Sanfer, S.A., Calz. de Tlalpan No. 550, Mexico 13, D.F., Mexico; Laboratorios Vargas, S.A., Las Piedras A Puente Restaurador, Apartado 2.461, Caracas, Venezuela.

## Oxypertine Hydrochloride—Equipertine, Equipertine Forte, Forit, Integrin, Opertil

**ACTIONS AND USES**—Oxypertine hydrochloride is a tranquilizer used in the management of a variety of mental disorders ranging from anxiety to schizophrenia. It has been employed in the treatment of insomnia, hypochondriasis, acute agitation, behavioral disorders, delirium, mania, hyperactivity, and chronic schizophrenia. In the treatment of schizophrenia, oxypertine was found in clinical tests to be equivalent to chlorpromazine, a commonly prescribed tranquilizer. Oxypertine also was found to be more effective than certain other psychotropic drugs in treating depressed schizophrenic patients but less effective in paranoid schizophrenics. In addition to its antidepressant action, oxypertine has been found to have a sedative effect useful for calming patients awaiting surgery. Oxypertine is believed to act by blocking nerve impulses associated with the neural transmitter chemical dopamine in the brain.

**PRECAUTIONS**—Oxypertine hydrochloride is not recommended for use in pregnancy unless the physician considers that potential benefits may outweigh the risks. The drug should not be given with, or within three weeks of the use of, monoamine oxidase inhibitors; laboratory animal studies indicate that oxypertine causes the release of small amounts of neural transmitter substances produced naturally by the body but which would interact with the monoamine oxidase inhibitor. Patients should be advised that oxypertine, like other tranquilizers, may impair physical and mental abilities, thereby making it potentially hazardous to operate motor vehicles or machinery. The drug can also interact with alcohol, anesthetics, narcotic analgesics, and other psychotropic drugs that tend to depress the central nervous system, producing an additive effect. High doses of oxypertine may produce involuntary muscle activity, ranging from tremors and restlessness to rigid muscle contractions. However, the involuntary muscle activity may be less severe than similar effects produced by other tranquilizers. Other side effects include nausea, vomiting, sedation, and dizziness.

**DOSAGE AND ADMINISTRATION**—Oxypertine hydrochloride is supplied in 10 mg capsules and 20 and 40 mg tablets. The usual recommended dosage is 80 to 120 mg per day initially for psychoses, with gradual increases as necessary up to a maximum of 300 mg daily. The drug should be administered in divided doses. For anxiety, the recommended dosage is 10 mg taken after meals, three to four times daily. The drug is not recommended for children.

**SOURCES**—Laboratoires Winthrop, 92-98 bvd Victor-Hugo, 92115 Clichy, France; Sterling Research Laboratories, Sterling-Winthrop House, 2-5 Warrington Place, Dublin 2, Ireland; Sterling Research Laboratories, St. Mark's Hill, Surbiton-upon-Thames, Surrey KT6 4PH, England.

**Paroxypropione**—Frenantol, Frenantole, Frenantole-Amobarbitol, Frenormon Forte, Possipione

**ACTIONS AND USES**—Paroxypropione is used to block the activity of the portion of the pituitary gland that secretes the gonadotropic hormones. The hormones stimulate the functions of the male testes and female ovaries and are involved in a variety of human reproductive processes such as controlling menstruation, maintaining pregnancy, the production of breast milk, and the descent of testicles into the scrotum. Paroxypropione is administered in the regulation of menstrual cycles and in the treatment of premenstrual syndrome, menorrhagia (abnormally long or heavy menstrual periods), metrorrhagia (nonmenstrual bleeding from the uterus), breast abnormalities including mastitis, menopausal disorders, and ovarian fibromas and polycystic disease. Paroxypropione is reported to exert its action on only the pituitary-gonadal hormonal axis without influencing activity of the adrenal sex hormones.

**PRECAUTIONS**—Some paroxypropione products are formulated with barbiturates, adding a sedative effect. Paroxypropione-barbiturate combinations can result in drowsiness, making it hazardous for the patient using the product to operate motor vehicles or machinery. The combination products also may interact with alcohol, increasing the depressant effect of both the alcohol and the barbiturate. There is a lack of information in the medical literature regarding adverse effects from the use of paroxypropione alone.

**DOSAGE AND ADMINISTRATION**—Paroxypropione is supplied in 100 and 500 mg tablets and in combination tablets containing 250 mg of paroxypropione and 25 mg of amobarbital. The usual recommended dosage is 1 to 3 g per day as necessary to achieve an adequate response.

**SOURCES**—Anglo-French Laboratories, 582 rue Orly, Dorval, Quebec H9P 1E9, Canada; Recordati Industria Chimica e Farmaceutica s.p.a., Via Civitali 1, 20148 Milano, Italy; Laboratoires Laroche Navarron, 20, rue Jean-Jaures, 92800 Puteaux, France.

## Penfluridol—Semap

**ACTIONS AND USES**—Penfluridol is an antipsychotic drug, or major tranquilizer, used in the management of schizophrenia. It is regarded as a potent tranquilizer with prolonged duration and is generally effective when given orally only once a week. Clinical studies show penfluridol reduces hallucinations and episodes of delirium and autistic behavior. It is intended for the treatment of chronic schizophrenia, and authorities recommend that penfluridol be used in combination with another antipsychotic drug when the patient shows signs of acute schizophrenia with psychomotor agitation. It has actions similar to those of chlorpromazine and pimozide, which inhibit the functions of dopamine nerve transmitter molecules in the brain. But autonomic nervous system side effects reportedly are fewer with penfluridol than with some other dopamine inhibitors.

**PRECAUTIONS**—Because of the prolonged duration of action of penfluridol, any adverse effects also may be expected to persist over a longer time period. Penfluridol produces less sedation than chlorpromazine but a greater incidence of abnormal muscle activity, particularly grimacing, grunting, sucking movements, and tongue protrusion. The purposeless activity may extend to the arms and legs. The patient may complain of dry mouth, nasal congestion, insomnia, and ejaculation difficulty. Side effects may also include skin rashes, abnormally high or low body temperature, convulsions, and postural hypotension, characterized by an abrupt drop in blood pressure when arising from a sitting or reclining position. Penfluridol should not be given to women of childbearing potential. The drug reportedly produces some effects involving the sex hormones, including frigidity, impotence, amenorrhea, an excessive flow of breast milk associated with abnormally high levels of prolactin hormone in the blood, and gynecomastia (enlarged and sometimes functioning mammary glands in male patients).

**DOSAGE AND ADMINISTRATION**—Penfluridol is suppled in 20 mg tablets. The usual recommended dosage is 20 to 60 mg per week, with a recommended maximum of 120 mg per week for the more difficult cases. Caution should be observed in administration of large doses to elderly or debilitated patients, who are likely to be more sensitive to the effects of the drug.

**SOURCES**—Janssen Farmaceutica, S.A. de C.V., Blvd. A. Ruiz Cortines No. 3453, Mexico 20, D.F., Mexico; Janssen-Le Brun, 5, rue de Lubeck, 75116 Paris, France.

## Penicillin V Benzathine (Benzathine Phenoxymethylpenicillin—Benoral, Cilicaine V, Falcopen-V, Kelacilline, LPV, Minervacil, Monocillin, Oracilline, Ospen, Penorline, Pen-Vee, Phenocillin, PVF, Stabicilline

**ACTIONS AND USES**—Penicillin V benzathine is an antibiotic used for mild to moderately severe infections caused by penicillin V-sensitive microorganisms, including streptococcal pharyngitis, staphylococcal infection without bacteremia, and pneumococcal infection. It has been recommended for the prevention of bacteremia (bacteria in the bloodstream) following tooth extraction. It has also been used before dental procedures to prevent bacterial endocarditis in patients with congenital or rheumatic heart lesions, for the prevention of bacterial infections following rheumatic fever or chorea, and before surgery or use of exploratory instruments involving the upper respiratory tract. Penicillin V benzathine has the actions and uses of phenoxymethylpenicillin and its potassium and calcium salts, which are commonly used antibiotics. Penicillin V benzathine is regarded as bactericidal in its action, which is directed toward preventing bacteria from building their cell walls.

**PRECAUTIONS**—Penicillin V benzathine should not be administered to patients who are known to be hypersensitive to penicillins. Adverse reactions to penicillin are most likely to occur in individuals with a history of sensitivity to multiple allergens. Physicians should be informed of any previous hypersensitivity reactions to penicillins, cephalosporins, or other allergens. Although the incidence of reactions to oral penicillins is much lower than to injections of the antibiotic, all degrees of hypersensitivity, including fatal anaphylactic shock, have been reported in the medical literature. The most common reactions to oral penicillin include nausea, vomiting, epigastric distress, diarrhea, and black hairy tongue. Less common reactions are skin eruptions, chills, fever, edema, and anaphylaxis. Oral penicillins should not be relied on for the treatment of infections accompanied by nausea, vomiting, gastric dilatation, cardiospasm, or intestinal hypermotility. Oral penicillin also should be avoided as an infection-preventive agent in instrumentation or surgery involving the genitourinary tract, lower intestinal tract surgery, sigmoidoscopy, childbirth, active treatment of syphilis, subacute bacterial endocarditis, diphtheria, gas gangrene, or other severe infections due to penicillin-susceptible organisms. The prolonged use of antibiotics may help promote the overgrowth of fungi or other nonsusceptible disease organisms.

**DOSAGE AND ADMINISTRATION**—Penicillin V benzathine is supplied in flavored oral suspensions of 90, 125, 180, 250, and 300 mg of the antibiotic. A 5 ml (one teaspoonful) 90 mg dose provides approximately 150,000 units of antibiotic. The drug also is available in 125, 250 and 500 mg capsules and in 250 and 300 mg tablets. The dose administered varies according to the sensitivity of the microorganisms, the severity of the infection, and the response of the patient. For streptococcal infections, without associated bacteremia, of the upper respiratory tract and for scarlet fever and mild erysipelas, the recommended dosage is 300,000 to 500,000 units, or 180 to 300 mg, three times a day for ten days. The recommended dosage for pneumococcal infections of the respiratory tract and for otitis media is 400,000 to 500,000 units, or 250 to 300 mg, every six hours until the patient's temperature has returned to normal for at least two days. The same dosage is recommended for Vincent's angina (fusospirochetosis of the throat). For routine prophylaxis against streptococcal infections in patients with a history of rheumatic fever or congenital heart disease, the usual recommended dosage is 200,000 units, or 180 mg, once or twice daily, with the dosage increased to 500,000 units, or 300 mg, every six hours for two days before minor surgery such as tonsillectomy or tooth extraction, and with the dosage continued for two days following the procedure. For children under the age of 12, dosages are calculated on the basis of body weight; for infants and small children, suggested daily dosages are 25,000 to 90,000 units in three to six divided doses.

**SOURCES**—Frosst Division, Merck Frosst Canada, Inc., P.O. Box 1005, Pointe Claire-Dorval, Quebec, H9R 4P8, Canada; Wyeth Ltd.,

P.O. Box 370, Downsview, Ontario M3M 3A8, Canada; Sigma ( Ltd., 1408 Centre Rd., Clayton Vic. 3168, Australia; F. H. Fauldi & Co. Ltd., 48 Beans Rd., Thebarton SA 5031, Australia.

**Pentoxifylline (Oxpentifylline)**—Elorgan, Tarontal, Terental, Torental, Trental

**ACTIONS AND USES**—Pentoxifylline is a vasodilator used primarily to dilate the blood vessels in peripheral areas of the body such as the legs and hands. The drug also is used in the treatment of cerebral vascular disorders in patients with cerebral arteriosclerosis, migraine and other types of headaches, faulty memory, inability to concentrate, susceptibility to motion sickness, vertigo, and hearing and visual difficulties due to insufficient blood flow to the brain. Peripheral disorders due to occlusion of blood vessels for which pentoxifylline is administered include intermittent claudication; night cramps; chilblains; Raynaud's disease; and rest pain, a condition marked by a burning sensation that develops in the foot after reclining but which is relieved by sitting or standing. Pentoxifylline acts by relaxing the walls of the smaller branches of the peripheral arteries so that the flow of freshly oxygenated red corpuscles to oxygen-starved tissue cells is increased. In some blood vessels of older individuals, the accumulation of plaque narrows the bore of the vessels to a size that is less than the diameter of the red blood cells that need to flow through them. A vasodilator is required to increase the caliber of the blood vessels.

**PRECAUTIONS**—Pentoxifylline should not be given to patients who may be hypersensitive to the drug or its metabolites. Caution should be used in giving the drug to diabetic patients using either insulin or oral hypoglycemic medications, because pentoxifylline may increase the hypoglycemic effect, requiring a lower dosage of the diabetic therapy. Caution also should be exercised in giving the drug to patients taking antihypertensive medications, because pentoxifylline also can increase the effects of the hypertension medication, requiring a reduced dosage of the agent. The hypotensive effect also may aggravate the condition of patients with abnormally low blood pressure and could affect those with coronary artery disease by reducing the perfusion of blood to heart tissues. For the same reason, pentoxifylline should not be given to a patient recovering from myocardial infarction. Among side effects reported are nausea, gastric distress, dizziness, and flushing. The side effects usually are temporary. A rare adverse effect is a skin rash.

**DOSAGE AND ADMINISTRATION**—Pentoxifylline is supplied in 100 and 400 mg sugar-coated tablets and in injection ampules containing 20 mg per ml. The usual initial dosage is 200 mg three times a day by mouth or the intravenous injection of 100 mg in 250 to 500 ml of appropriate fluid, given by slow infusion over a period of 90 to 180 minutes. Pentoxifylline can also be administered by intraarterial infusion of 100 to 300 mg in 20 to 50 ml of sodium chloride solution over a period of 10 to 30 minutes. The usual maintenance dosage is 100 mg three times a day.

**SOURCES**—Hoechst-Remedia, S.A., Urbanizacion La Trinidad, Calle Los Vegas, Apartado 80.222, Caracas 108, Venezuela; Hoechst Aktiengesellschaft, Bruningstrasse 45, Postfach: 800320, 6230 Frankfurt (Main) 80, West Germany.

## Perhexiline Maleate—Corzepin, Daprin, Pexid

**ACTIONS AND USES**—Perhexiline maleate is used in the control of moderate to severe attacks of angina pectoris due to coronary artery disease, particularly in patients who have failed to respond to other remedies or who are unable to tolerate alternative drugs for this purpose. Perhexiline maleate also has been used in the treatment of certain heart arrhythmias. The drug has no effect on the heart in a resting state, but it has been found to reduce rapid heartbeats due to physical exertion and to produce a mild diuretic effect.

**PRECAUTIONS**—Because of the high rate of side effects experienced by patients using perhexiline maleate, it is recommended that the product be used only when alternative therapies have proved unsatisfactory. The safety of perhexiline maleate in pregnant women, nursing mothers, and children has not been established, and use by patients in these groups is not recommended. The drug should not be administered to persons with impaired liver or kidney function, to patients who are known to be hypersensitive to the product, or to patients who have recently recovered from myocardial infarction. Patients receiving the drug may experience a significant weight loss, nerve dysfunction that can affect sensory and motor nerves in all four extremities, and hypoglycemia (low blood sugar). Because of the association between perhexiline use and hypoglycemia, caution is advised in administering the drug to diabetic patients. Some inflammation and bleeding at the posterior of the eye, near the optic nerve, have occurred in patients using perhexiline, with temporary and permanent impairment of vision. Patients using perhexiline should use caution when driving motor vehicles or operating machinery. In addition to the adverse effects just noted, some patients may experience nausea, vomiting, loss of appetite, dizziness, headache, weakness, tremors, faintness, and abnormalities in walking. The half-life of perhexiline, normally 2 to 6 days, may extend to 30 days in some patients, and this should be taken into account when perhexiline is discontinued and another drug substituted for it.

**DOSAGE AND ADMINISTRATION**—Perhexiline maleate is supplied in 100 mg tablets scored with a bisecting line. The usual initial dosage is 100 to 200 mg per day in divided doses, followed by gradual increases or decreases in daily dosage until the minimum effective and well-tolerated level is established. It is generally not recommended that the dosage exceed 300 mg per day.

**SOURCES**—Merrell Pharmaceuticals Ltd., Meadowbank, Bath Road, Hounslow TW5 9QY, England; Richardson-Merrell Pty Ltd., 9 Help Street, Chatswood, N.S.W. 2067, Australia.

## **Periciazine (Pericyazine)**—Aolept, Apamin, Nemactil, Neulactil, Neuleptil

**ACTIONS AND USES**—Periciazine is a tranquilizer used in the treatment of certain behavioral and character disorders, for the control of residual hostility, impulsiveness, and aggressiveness. It has been employed in acute and chronic schizophrenia, severe anxiety and tension conditions, and in the control of outbursts of violent behavior. Authorities report that periciazine has moderate sedative effects with fewer side effects involving functions of the motor nerves than chlorpromazine and certain other major tranquilizers. Periciazine has been found to be particularly effective in treating children with behavioral disorders and as a maintenance drug for outpatients. Periciazine generally is prescribed for use in conjunction with other psychotropic drugs.

**PRECAUTIONS**—The safety of periciazine in pregnant women and nursing mothers has not been established, and the drug therefore is not recommended for use by patients in these groups. The drug should not be used in cases of circulatory collapse, acute intoxication caused by central nervous system depressants, altered states of consciousness, impaired liver function, a medical history of blood disorders, or a known sensitivity to phenothiazine drugs, such as chlorpromazine. If periciazine is used in conjunction with other psychotropic drugs, the dosages should be adjusted by reducing the other compounds as necessary. Adverse reactions reported include initial temporary drowsiness, a drop in blood pressure on standing, rapid heartbeat, faintness, gastrointestinal distress, and excessive salivation and sweating. Some side effects, including occasional signs of parkinsonism such as restlessness and tremors, are often due to high dosage. Children and elderly patients may require dosage adjustments to reduce side effects. There is a risk of tardive dyskinesia, characterized by involuntary movements of tongue, mouth, face, and jaw, in some patients after long-term therapy or after the drug has been discontinued. The risk appears to be greatest among elderly female patients on high-dose therapy.

**DOSAGE AND ADMINISTRATION**—Periciazine is supplied in 2.5, 5, 10, 20, and 25 mg tablets and capsules and in oral drops and syrups. Oral drops provide 10 mg per ml, and the syrups contain 2.5 and 10 mg per ml. The usual initial adult dosage is 5 to 20 mg in the morning and 10 to 40 mg in the evening. In moderate to severe cases, the total daily dose may be increased to 75 mg. For most elderly patients the initial daily dose may be 5 mg, with gradual increases to a maximum daily dose of 30 mg. For young children, the daily dose should not exceed 0.5 mg per year of age, with increases in older children to 1 to 3 mg per year of age.

**SOURCES**—Rhône-Poulenc Pharma Inc., 8580 Esplanade, Montreal, Quebec H2P 2R9, Canada; May & Baker Limited, Dagenham, Essex RM10 7XS, England.

## **Pimozide**—Opiran, Orap

**ACTIONS AND USES**—Pimozide is an antipsychotic, or major tranquilizer, drug used in the treatment of schizophrenia, particularly in patients with withdrawn apathetic manifestations. It is similar to the widely used antipsychotic drug chlorpromazine, but is less sedating. Pimozide has been recommended for chronic schizophrenic patients undergoing therapy to make them more communicative and sociable, as initial therapy for outpatients and new and readmitted patients, as well as for patients handicapped by sedative or other effects of different antipsychotic drugs. Pimozide has been used in the treatment of anxiety, anorexia nervosa, behavioral disorders, Gilles de la Tourette's syndrome, hypochondriacal delusions, and some cases of mania. It also has been used to induce a partial remission in a case of malignant melanoma. Pimozide is believed to act by blocking activity of a nerve impulse transmitter, dopamine, in the brain. That action, however, can produce in some, but not all, patients symptoms of parkinsonism, which is due in part to dopamine activity failure.

**PRECAUTIONS**—Depression, epilepsy, and preexisting symptoms of Parkinson's disease may be aggravated by the use of pimozide. As the safety of the drug in pregnancy has not been established, pimozide is not recommended for women of childbearing potential. The drug also is not recommended for nursing mothers. Pimozide should not be given to patients who may be allergic to phenothiazine drugs related to pimozide, to comatose patients, nor to those in danger of circulatory collapse. Pimozide has an antiemetic effect and thus may suppress nausea and vomiting, which could be symptoms of another underlying disorder. It is not recommended for use in manic phases of manic-depressive psychoses or for the control of aggressiveness, agitation, or hyperactivity. Both the patient and the physician should be aware that pimozide may impair mental and physical abilities, making it hazardous to operate motor vehicles or machinery—even though pimozide lacks the sedative properties of other antipsychotic drugs. Pimozide is not recommended for children under the age of 12 years. The drug may interact with alcohol, barbiturates, anesthetics, and other substances that tend to depress central nervous system functions, producing an additive effect. Elderly and debilitated individuals are likely to be unduly sensitive to the effects of antipsychotic drugs. Adverse effects include parkinsonlike abnormalities of neuromuscular actions, marked by tremors, rigidity, restlessness, or decreased reflexes.

**DOSAGE AND ADMINISTRATION**—Pimozide is supplied as 1, 2, 4, and 10 mg tablets and as drops containing 2.5 mg of pimozide per ml of solution. The usual recommended dosage is 2 to 4 mg once daily, with weekly increments of 2 to 4 mg until a satisfactory response is achieved or side effects are observed. The usual range of dosage is 2 to 12 mg per day, with a maximum of 30 mg daily in severe cases.

**SOURCES**—McNeil Laboratories (Canada) Ltd., 600 Main Street West, Stouffville, Ontario L0H 1L0, Canada; Laboratoires Cassenne, 3, square Desaix, 75015 Paris, France; Janssen-Le Brun, 5, rue Lubeck, 75116 Paris, France; Janssen Farmaceutica, S.A. de C.V., Blvd. A. Ruiz Cortines No. 3453, Mexico 20, D.F., Mexico.

## Pinaverium Bromide—Dicetel

**ACTIONS AND USES**—Pinaverium bromide is a nervous system agent that controls smooth muscle spasms of the gastrointestinal tract by reversing the action and relaxing the smooth muscle fibers. The antispasmodic activity occurs at several levels of the digestive tract—the esophagus, the stomach, the pyloric valve between the stomach and the small intestine, the small intestine, and the large intestine. The drug also exerts a measurable effect on pain in the gastrointestinal tract, but it does not slow the transit time of a meal passing through the tract. Pinaverium bromide is used in the treatment of spasms of the esophagus, in gastrointestinal spasms related to peptic ulcers and colitis, and in faulty filling and emptying of the gallbladder.

**PRECAUTIONS**—Pinaverium bromide should not be given to patients with certain obstructive disorders of the gastrointestinal tract, obstructive disorders of the urinary tract associated with an enlarged prostate, poor intestinal muscle tone, and certain complicated cases of ulcerative colitis and hiatus hernia. The safety of pinaverium bromide during pregnancy has not been established, and the drug should not be administered to pregnant patients unless the benefits outweigh the risks. Caution should be observed in giving the product to patients with glaucoma or who are at risk of glaucoma, patients who suffer from chronic constipation, and elderly patients afflicted with enlargement of the prostate. Side effects observed include a burning sensation in the abdomen, dryness of the mouth, diarrhea, constipation or exacerbation of constipation, vomiting, headache, palpitations, dizziness, an unpleasant taste, and skin allergy.

**DOSAGE AND ADMINISTRATION**—Pinaverium bromide is supplied in capsules containing 50 mg each of the drug. The usual dose is one capsule taken three times daily, with one-half glass of water, during meals.

**SOURCE**—Herdt & Charton (1971) Inc., 9393 Louis-H. Lafontaine, Montreal, Quebec H1J 1Y8, Canada.

## Pipemidic Acid—Deblaston, Dolcol, Pipedac, Pipedase, Pipemid, Pipram, Urotractin

**ACTIONS AND USES**—Pipemidic acid is an antibiotic used in the treatment of pyelonephritis, pyelitis, cystitis, urethritis, prostatitis, and related infections of the genitourinary tract. Pipemidic acid also is used in the treatment of otitis media, or bacterial infections of the middle ear. The drug is taken orally and is transferred in high concentrations from the digestive tract to the liver, intestinal tract, kidneys, and urinary bladder, where it interferes with the production of DNA molecules in the nuclei of bacteria. This activity, in turn, prevents the bacteria from multiplying. There also is evidence that pipemidic acid is bactericidal. Because it shows no cross-resistance to other antibiotics, pipemidic acid can be used in the treatment of infectious strains of bacteria that are resistant to other antibiotics, particularly nalidixic and piromidic acids.

**PRECAUTIONS**—The safety of pipemidic acid for children has not been established. The drug also should not be given to pregnant women, women suspected of being pregnant, or nursing mothers. Others who should avoid use of pipemidic acid are patients who may be hypersensitive to the product and patients with severely impaired kidney function. Adverse effects may include skin eruptions, loss of appetite, nausea, vomiting, gastric discomfort, diarrhea, constipation, dizziness, headache, fatigue, thirst, and inflammation of the mouth. Patients using pipemidic acid should be monitored for signs of changes in blood chemistry and renal dysfunction. The drug should be used only under the direction of a physician.

**DOSAGE AND ADMINISTRATION**—Pipemidic acid is supplied in 200, 250, and 400 mg tablets and capsules. The recommended dosage for pyelonephritis, pyelitis, cystitis, urethritis, prostatitis, and related urinary tract infections is 500 mg to 2 g daily taken in three or four divided doses. For the treatment of otitis media, the recommended adult dosage is 1.5 to 2 g daily taken in three or four divided doses. The doses should be adjusted according to the age and condition of the patient.

**SOURCES**—Laboratoire Roger Bellon, B.P. 105-159, av. du Roule, 92201 Neuilly-sur-Seine Cedex, France; Mediolanum Farmaceutici s.r.l., Stabilimento e Direzione Amministrativa, Via S.G. Cottolengo 31, 20143 Milano, Italy; Dainippon Pharmaceutical Co., Ltd., 25, Doshomachi 3-chome, Higashi-ku, Osaka, Japan.

## Pipotiazine Palmitate—Piportil L4

**ACTIONS AND USES**—Pipotiazine palmitate is a tranquilizer used in the maintenance treatment of nonagitated schizophrenic and other chronically psychotic patients. Pipotiazine is related chemically to chlorpromazine and certain other major tranquilizers, but it reportedly has less of a sedating effect. Clinical studies indicate pipotiazine palmitate treatment results in significant reduction or elimination of hallucinations and delusions; it acts also on emotional withdrawal, uncooperativeness, and other residual symptoms that interfere with a return to normal social integration. Improvements usually appear within two or three days of injection, and effects may last from three to six weeks. In most cases, adequate control is maintained with one injection every four weeks.

**PRECAUTIONS**—Pipotiazine palmitate should not be administered in the presence of circulatory collapse, altered states of consciousness or coma, particularly when these conditions are due to intoxication with central nervous system depressants, such as narcotics, alcohol, or certain sedatives. It should not be given to severely depressed patients or patients with blood disorders, liver or kidney impairment, severe heart disease, or a known sensitivity to phenothiazine-type drugs. The drug is not recommended for psychoneurotic patients, elderly persons with symptoms of confusion or agitation, or patients receiving large doses of sedative-hypnotic drugs. Because of potentially severe and unpredictable reactions, pipotiazine palmitate should be administered under the supervision of a physician experienced in the use of psychotropic drugs and with facilities available to cope with emergencies. The drug is not recommended for children, and its safety in pregnancy has not been established. Caution should be exercised in administering pipotiazine palmitate to patients with a history of convulsive disorders or epileptic seizures. The drug can impair the ability of patients to operate a motor vehicle or machinery or to perform other hazardous tasks. The drug also can increase the effects of alcohol or other depressant drugs.

**DOSAGE AND ADMINISTRATION**—Pipotiazine palmitate is supplied in 1 ml ampules providing 25 mg per ml, and 2 ml ampules containing 50 mg per ml, for intramuscular injection. The usual initial dose is 50 to 100 mg, followed as necessary by gradual increments of 25 mg every two or three weeks until a satisfactory response is achieved. Most patients are controlled on a 100 mg dose every four weeks; others may require as little as 25 mg or as much as 250 mg every four weeks. Lower initial doses are recommended for patients over the age of 50 years.

**SOURCES**—Rhodia Mexicana, S.A. de C.V., Jose Ma. Rico No. 611, Mexico 12, D.F., Mexico; Rhône-Poulenc Pharma Inc., 8580 Esplanade, Montreal, Quebec H2P 2R9, Canada.

## Piracetam—Breinox, Cerebrospan, Dinagen, Gabacet, Neutrofin-Hobson, Nootrop, Nootropil, Nootropyl, Normabrain, Norzetam, Pirroxil, Stimucortex

**ACTIONS AND USES**—Piracetam is a cerebral stimulant used in the treatment of disorders associated with a deficiency of oxygen in the brain tissues. The drug has been used in the treatment of disorders associated with stroke, alcoholism, vertigo, senile dementia, involutional melancholia, sickle-cell anemia, and childhood behavioral problems. Animal and human experiments indicate piracetam can be employed with choline to improve the retention of memorized information. The drug is also used in the treatment of brain disorders associated with injuries and surgical procedures in which the flow of freshly oxygenated blood to the brain may be impaired; epileptic seizures; encephalopathies due to toxic effects of chemicals or other poisons; psychomotor agitation; fatigue; confusion; problems of psychological adaptation; and difficulties in attention, concentration, and coordination.

**PRECAUTIONS**—Piracetam may interact with certain drugs, such as amphetamines and psychotropic drugs, to increase their effects. Adverse effects include insomnia, psychomotor agitation, particularly at the start of piracetam therapy, nausea, gastrointestinal distress, and headaches.

**DOSAGE AND ADMINISTRATION**—Piracetam is supplied in 400 mg capsules, 800 mg tablets, and injection vials containing 1 g per 5 ml. The usual recommended oral dosage is 800 mg taken two or three times a day for a period of four to six weeks. The suggested intravenous or intramuscular dosage is 3 g per day. The recommended dosage for children is 400 mg, or one capsule, three times daily.

**SOURCES**—Laboratorios Hormona, S.A., Blvd. M. Avila Camacho No. 470, Naucalpan, Edo. de Mexico; Laboratori UCB s.p.a., Via S. Clemente 8, 10143 Torino, Italy; Dysfa, C.A., Avda. Principal de Los Ruices, Edif. Farma, Ofic. 112, Apartado 8.257, Caracas 101, Venezuela; Laboratoires Carrion, 30, rue Henri-Regnault, 92400 Courbevoie, France.

## Pirglutargine (Arginine Pidolate, Arginine Pyroglutamate)—Adiuvant

**ACTIONS AND USES**—Pirglutargine is an amino-acid-based agent that is used in the treatment of mental retardation because of a belief by some researchers that it enhances cerebral functions. The drug is also used in the treatment of senility. The value of the product in stimulating mental functions is based on still controversial studies, mainly with animals, showing that mental performance is increased by administration of glutamates over a protracted period and that learning ability is reduced by administration of drugs that destroy glutamates. A significant proportion of the protein in brain tissue is glutamic acid or glutamates.

**PRECAUTIONS**—No serious adverse effects from the use of pirglutargine have been reported. Arginine and glutamic acid are common amino acids contained in natural foods consumed by most individuals each week.

**DOSAGE AND ADMINISTRATION**—Pirglutargine is supplied in 500 mg capsules and vials containing 500 mg per 5 ml. The usual recommended dose is 500 mg to 1,000 mg of pirglutargine per day.

**SOURCE**—Manetti L. & Roberts H. s.p.a., Via Antonio da Noli 4, 50127 Firenze, Italy.

## Pivalexin (Pivcephalexin Hydrochloride)—Sigmacef

**ACTIONS AND USES**—Pivalexin is a cephalosporin antibiotic that is taken by mouth for use in the treatment of respiratory and urinary tract infections. It is used against a wide range of bacteria and is effective against some strains that are resistant to penicillin. Pivalexin is less potent than some other cephalosporins and is recommended for mild infections, particularly those involving the urinary tract. Pivalexin produces its effects by inhibiting efforts of the bacteria to build cell walls.

**PRECAUTIONS**—Pivalexin should not be given to patients who may be allergic to cephalosporin-type drugs. Caution should be used in administering pivalexin to individuals who may be sensitive to penicillin or who have a history of allergies. Care also is recommended in giving the drug to patients with impaired kidney function. Side effects include abdominal discomfort, nausea, vomiting, diarrhea, and skin rash.

**DOSAGE AND ADMINISTRATION**—Pivalexin is supplied in 250 and 500 mg tablets and in 20 g packets of granules. The usual recommended dosage is 2 to 3 g per day in three to four divided doses. For children, the recommended dosage is 100 mg per day per kg of body weight given in three to four divided doses.

**SOURCE**—Sigma Tau s.p.a., Via Pontina Km. 30,400, 00040 Pomezia (Roma), Italy.

**Pizotyline Maleate (Pizotifen Malate)**—Mosegor, Sandolitec B Plus, Sandolitec Forte, Sandomigran, Sandomigrin, Sanmigran, Sanomigran

**ACTIONS AND USES**—Pizotyline maleate is a drug with antihistamine properties that is used primarily in the treatment of migraine headaches. The product is also used as an antidepressant; a remedy for pruritus; an appetite stimulator; and as a therapy for Cushing's disease, a disorder caused by hypersecretion of the adrenal cortex and characterized by weakness, fatigue, and loss of protein tissue while gaining fat. The action of pizotyline maleate is due in part to its ability to inhibit the functions of serotonin, a central nervous system nerve impulse transmitter, smooth muscle stimulator, and vasoconstrictor. Pizotyline has been used in the treatment of carcinoid syndrome symptoms, including diarrhea and facial flushing, a condition associated with overproduction of serotonin. It also has been used to relieve the painful neck and face symptoms of carotodynia.

**PRECAUTIONS**—Pizotyline maleate should not be given to patients known to be sensitive to pizotyline nor patients with an ulcer or obstruction in the pyloroduodenal area (between the stomach and small intestine). Because pizotyline is related chemically to tricyclic antidepressant drugs, it should not be administered to patients also using monoamine oxidase inhibitors. The drug should be administered with caution to patients with diabetes, heart disease, or impaired liver or kidney function. Caution should also be exercised in giving the drug to patients with acute glaucoma or an enlarged prostate. Some patients may develop a tolerance to pizotyline, requiring increased doses to achieve a therapeutic response. The drug should be administered to pregnant patients only when the benefits may outweigh the risks. Pizotyline may cause drowsiness and decreased alertness in the patient, making operation of motor vehicles or machinery dangerous. The product also may interact with alcohol and a number of other drugs, particularly hypnotics, sedatives, and psychotropic medications. The most common side effects include weight gain, increased appetite, and drowsiness. Less frequent complaints are impotence, nausea, headache, dry mouth, muscle pain, edema, and confusion.

**DOSAGE AND ADMINISTRATION**—Pizotyline maleate is supplied in 500 and 750 mcg and 1 mg tablets. The usual recommended dosage is 1.5 mg daily, taken as 500 mcg in the morning and 1.0 mg at bedtime. In severe cases, the intake has been gradually raised to from 3.0 to 6.0 mg daily. The drug is not recommended for children. In some areas pizotyline is combined with B complex vitamins for use as an appetite stimulant.

**SOURCES**—Wander Pharmaceuticals, 98 The Centre, Feltham, Middlesex TW13 4EP, England; Sandoz A.B., Box 122, 183 22 Taby, Sweden; Sandoz de Mexico, S.A. de C.V., Amores No. 1322, Mexico 12, D.F., Mexico; Sandoz s.p.a., Via C. Arconati 1, 20135 Milano, Italy.

## **Polyphloroglucinol Phosphate**—Dealyd

**ACTIONS AND USES**—Polyphloroglucinol phosphate is an agent used in the treatment of certain skin disorders, particularly oozing eczema and burns. The product inhibits the action of hyaluronidase and phosphatases, which would otherwise break down the "cement," or hyaluronic acid, that binds tissue cells together. Hyaluronidase is produced by a variety of bacteria, enabling the organisms to spread rapidly through the tissues of an infected person. It also is present in snake and spider venom and is used in some pharmaceutical preparations to help medications spread rapidly through tissues. By blocking the destruction of the tissue cement of the body, polyphloroglucinol helps prevent the entry and spread of infection through damaged skin surfaces. The drug is mixed with polyethylene glycols and other moisture-preserving substances for skin application.

**PRECAUTIONS**—Polyphloroglucinol phosphate should not be used internally, and it should not be used on large areas of the skin, nor in concentrations greater than 5 percent. There have been no reports in the medical literature of serious adverse effects from the use of polyphloroglucinol phosphate when used externally in recommended dosages.

**DOSAGE AND ADMINISTRATION**—Polyphloroglucinol phosphate is supplied in 50 g tubes of 1 percent cream for external application. The cream is applied in a thin layer over the affected skin area. Because the preparation also contains polyethylene glycols, care should be exercised in limiting the application of the product to the specific skin area requiring treatment and limiting its use to the period needed to achieve a satisfactory response. While generally safe for skin applications, polyethylene glycols can cause contact dermatitis.

**SOURCE**—AB Mekos, Norrbroplatsen 2, Postoffice Box 944, 251 09, Helsingborg, Sweden.

**Prenylamine Lactate**—Angormin, Angorsan, Bismetin, Carditin, Crepasin, Epocol, Eucardion, Herzcon, Hostaginan, Incoran, Lactamine, NP 30, Nyuple, Onlemin, Piboril, Reocorin, Sedolatan, Segontin, Synadrin, Wasangor

**ACTIONS AND USES**—Prenylamine lactate is a calcium antagonist used prophylactically in the treatment of angina pectoris. Calcium channel blockers appear to have a generally beneficial effect by dilating the peripheral vessels to ease the work load on the heart. They also function as potent dilators of the heart's own coronary arteries, thereby improving the blood flow to heart muscle, by increasing the distribution of whatever coronary artery blood flow is available. The action of calcium blockers involves the inhibition of the flow of calcium ions across the cell membranes of the smooth muscle cells of the artery.

**PRECAUTIONS**—Prenylamine lactate should not be given to patients with severe kidney or liver impairment or certain heart disorders, including uncompensated heart failure and defects in the conduction of heart contraction signals. Adverse effects reported include nausea, vomiting, diarrhea, and an abnormally rapid heartbeat complicated by deficient blood levels of potassium. An excessive heart rate (tachycardia) can also be a sign of overdosage. Some patients may experience central nervous system effects, such as dizziness, tremor, and loss of coordination. Prenylamine lactate tends to interact with antihypertensive drugs, beta-blockers, and medications that depress heart function; so concurrent administration of calcium blockers with such agents should be avoided.

**DOSAGE AND ADMINISTRATION**—Prenylamine lactate is supplied in 60 mg tablets. The usual recommended dosage is one 60 mg tablet taken three times daily. The dosage may be increased to 300 mg daily if the patient response is unsatisfactory at the lower dosage. However, it is recommended that the intake then be reduced gradually to the lowest effective maintenance dosage.

**SOURCES**—Hoechst UK Ltd., Pharmaceutical Division, Hoechst House, Salisbury Road, Hounslow, Middx TW4 6JH, England; Isola-Ibi, Instituto Bioterapico Internazionale, Viale Pio VII 50, 16148 Genova Quarto, Italy; Norske Hoechst A/S, Økernv. 145, Postboks 177, Økern, Oslo 5, Norway.

## **Proglumide (Xylamida, Xylamide)**—Buscalide, Milid, Milpiride, Nulsa, Xyde, Xyde Compuesto

**ACTIONS AND USES**—Proglumide inhibits gastric secretion and is therefore used in the treatment of stomach and duodenal ulcers and gastritis. The drug also has been used in the treatment of hiatus hernia, reflux esophagitis, pyrosis (heartburn), and gastric disorders due to stress, food and drink, and medications such as salicylates that may irritate the lining of the digestive tract. Proglumide is believed to act by interfering with the function of gastrin, a hormone that stimulates the release of gastric juices into the stomach.

**PRECAUTIONS**—Except for minor complaints of nausea or other types of gastric distress, few significant side effects have been reported as a result of administration of proglumide. However, some patients may show hypersensitivity or other adverse effects to other substances included in various formulations of proglumide, including sodium salts (used as excipients in injection ampules) or sedating or tranquilizing drugs.

**DOSAGE AND ADMINISTRATION**—Proglumide is supplied in 200, 250, 300, 400, 700, and 800 mg doses for oral administration or intramuscular or intravenous injection. The usual recommended dosage is 800 to 1,200 mg daily in divided doses before meals when taken as tablets or an equivalent amount by injection.

**SOURCES**—Laboratoires Beytout, 10-12, rue Guynemer, 94160 Saint-Mande, France; Rotta Farmaecutici s.p.a., Via Valosa di Sopra

3, 20050 San Fruttuoso Monza (M1), Italy; Laboratorios Promeco de Mexico, S.A. de C.V., Insurgentes Sur No. 1457-8o. piso, Mexico 19, D.F., Mexico; Laboratorios Lepetit de Mexico, S.A. de C.V., Paseo de las Palmas No. 555, 3er. piso, Mexico 10, D.F., Mexico; Productos Gedeon Richter (America), S.A., Miguel de Quevedo No. 247, Mexico 21, D.F., Mexico.

## **Propiram Fumarate**—Algeril

**ACTIONS AND USES**—Propiram fumarate is an analgesic used to relieve moderate to severe pain. When administered orally or by injection, propiram fumarate is about one-tenth as potent as an intramuscular injection of morphine of the same dose size. Propiram is slightly more effective than codeine on a basis of equal doses. The drug is similar to the opiate analgesics in actions, although it differs chemically from opium-derived drugs.

**PRECAUTIONS**—Adverse effects of propiram fumarate are similar to those of morphine, but the risk of dependence is less. Side effects include drowsiness, sweating, nausea, vomiting, dizziness, and flushing, although the adverse effects are less common with propiram than with morphine. The euphoric effects of propiram fumarate are less than those of propoxyphene, a close chemical cousin of methadone, but the dependence risk is greater with propiram. Because of its opiate properties, propiram fumarate should be used with the same precautions required for morphine and related narcotics.

**DOSAGE AND ADMINISTRATION**—Propiram fumarate is supplied in 25 mg tablets and 50 mg suppositories. The usual recommended dosage is 75 to 150 mg taken orally each day in three divided doses or one suppository used at intervals of approximately eight hours.

**SOURCE**—Bayropharm Italian s.p.a., Via dei Cignoli 9, 20151 Milano, Italy.

**Proscillaridin—Caradrin, Proscillan, Sandoscill, Stellarid, Sucblorin, Talucard, Talusin, Tradenal, Wirnesin**

**ACTIONS AND USES**—Proscillaridin is a heart tonic similar to digitalis used by patients who are unable to tolerate digitalis for treatment of cardiac insufficiency or senile heart. Proscillaridin has a positive influence on heart contractions, equivalent to that of digoxin, one of the commonly used forms of digitalis. It is derived from a species of squill, or sea onion, whereas the digitalis drugs are derived from species of foxglove plants. Proscillaridin has a rapid onset of action, is easily controlled, and is rapidly inactivated. The effect of the heart drug also is rapid, with full response being observed on the first day of treatment.

**PRECAUTIONS**—Adverse reactions include mainly digestive disorders, with nausea, vomiting, and diarrhea at the beginning of the treatment. Caution should be exercised in administering the drug to patients with digitalis intoxication and certain heart disorders, including heart block, sinus arrest, infarct, and abnormally slow heartbeat. The product also should be used with caution in pregnant women and nursing mothers.

**DOSAGE AND ADMINISTRATION**—Proscillaridin is supplied in 0.25 and 0.50 mg tablets and capsules. The usual initial procedure for severe cardiac insufficiency is a saturation dose of 1.5 to 2.5 mg daily, followed by a maintenance dosage of 1.0 to 2.0 mg per day in two or three divided doses. The usual initial dose for moderate cardiac insufficiency is 1.5 mg per day initially, followed by a maintenance dose of 1.0 mg. For mild cardiac insufficiency, the saturation and maintenance doses recommended are 1.0 mg and 0.75 to 1.0 mg daily. Patients previously treated with digitoxin usually receive an initial dose of 0.5 mg per day, with increases to 0.75 mg on the 9th day and 1.0 mg on the 15th day. Patients previously treated with digoxin or lanatoside C, another digitalis-derived drug, usually are given 1.0 mg daily as both the initial and maintenance dose. The drug is not recommended for children.

**SOURCES**—Knoll A.G., 44 Dartmouth Square, Dublin, Ireland; Boehringer Biochemia Robin s.p.a., Via S. Uguzzone 5, 20126 Milano, Italy; Zambeletti dr. L., Via Zambeletti, 20021 Baranzate (Ml.), Italy.

**Pyrazinamide (Pyrazinoic Acid)**—Aldinamide, Braccopiral, Eprazin, Piraldina, Pyrazine, Tebrazid, Unipyranamide, Zinamide

**ACTIONS AND USES**—Pyrazinamide is used in the treatment of tuberculosis. It is used mainly for short-term therapy and in conjunction with other antituberculosis drugs. It is believed that pyrazinamide adds to the potency of the other antituberculosis drugs when they are used together. It has been employed as a retreatment drug and after a regular course of treatment with alternative medications has failed. Pyrazinamide is related chemically to nicotinamide, one of the members of the vitamin B complex.

**PRECAUTIONS**—Pyrazinamide should not be given to patients who have experienced permanent liver damage; liver damage is a common side effect. The drug also routinely causes high blood levels of uric acid and therefore should be used with caution in patients with a history of kidney disease or gout. The drug usually is administered to patients who have been hospitalized. It is recommended that liver tests be made before and during treatment with pyrazinamide. The drug is given to children only when the possible benefits outweigh the risks. Adverse effects reported include nausea, vomiting, loss of appetite, joint pains, fever, difficulty in urinating, and skin disorders.

**DOSAGE AND ADMINISTRATION**—Pyrazinamide usually is supplied in 500 mg tablets. The usual recommended dosage is calculated at 20 to 35 mg per kg of body weight, with a maximum of six tablets daily, or 3 g in divided doses. Pyrazinamide should be administered with at least one other effective antituberculosis drug.

**SOURCES**—Bracco de Mexico, S.A. de C.V., Calzada de las Armas No. 110, Tlalnepantla, Edo. de Mexico; Cahill May Roberts Ltd., P.O. Box 1090, Chapelizod, Dublin 20, Ireland.

**Pyridinol Carbamate**—Alofran, Anginin, Angiovital, Angioxine, Aterofal, Aterosan, Cicloven, Colesterinex, Efil, Eluen, Encefadil, Enitrax, Iridol, Movecil, Orbol, Ravenil, Vasagin, Vasapril, Vasocil, Vasoverin, Veranterol

**ACTIONS AND USES**—Pyridinol carbamate is an antiatherosclerotic drug used to protect the walls of arteries from the formation of atheroma, or the fatty degeneration of artery walls that is associated with aging. Pyridinol carbamate also has antiinflammatory properties. Studies indicate the product removes fluids and fatty substances from atheromatous lesions on artery walls and enhances the regeneration of smooth muscle cells in the areas affected by the lesions. Fibrous substances in the atheromatous lesions are absorbed, according to the study reports. Other therapeutic effects associated with pyridinol carbamate include prevention of thrombosis and prevention and cure of hemorrhage. The drug has been used in the treatment of angina pectoris, certain cases of myocardial infarction and cerebral thrombosis, episodes of heart arrhythmia, fibrillation and flutter, venous thrombosis, and peripheral vascular disorders such as arteriosclerosis obliterans, chronic arterial occlusion, and Buerger's disease. As an antihemorrhagic drug, pyridinol carbamate has been used in kidney bleeding, hemorrhagic cystitis and nephritis, purpura, and diabetic retinopathy. Still another reported use is in the treatment of aortitis, an inflammatory disease of the aorta, the main artery leading from the heart; one form of the disorder, called pulseless disease, is marked by the loss of a pulse in the arms of the patient and also in the carotid arteries of the neck.

**PRECAUTIONS**—Caution should be used in the administration of pyridinol to patients with impaired liver function. Periodic liver function tests should be made on all patients using the product. Adverse effects include mainly gastrointestinal distress, nausea, vomiting, loss of appetite, and diarrhea. Some neurological side effects reported are headache and dizziness. The product may aggravate symptoms of stomach or duodenal ulcers in some patients.

**DOSAGE AND ADMINISTRATION**—Pyridinol carbamate is supplied in 250 and 500 mg tablets and capsules. The usual recommended dosage is 1 g (four 250 mg tablets) per day in two to four divided doses after meals. The dosage should be adjusted according to the age of the patient and the severity of the condition.

**SOURCES**—Banyu Pharmaceutical Co. Ltd., 7,2-chome, Nihonbashi-Honcho, Chuo-ku, Tokyo, Japan; Laboratorios Cosmos S.A., Final Avda. Romulo Gallego, Edificio Torre K.L.M. (4.° piso), Apartado 62.419, Chacao, Venezuela; Laboratoires Roussel, 97, rue de Vaugirard, 75279 Paris Cedex 06, France; Ist. Sieroterapico Mil. S. Belfanti (Ente Morale aggregato all' Universita di Milano), Via Darwin 20, 20143 Milano, Italy.

## Ranitidine Hydrochloride—Zantac

**ACTIONS AND USES**—Ranitidine hydrochloride is used to treat stomach and duodenal ulcers by reducing gastric acid production. The drug also blocks stimulation of gastric acid secretion by histamine, pentagastrin, and other substances that can affect cells in the stomach lining to release gastric acid through their influence on nervous system receptors. The action of ranitidine is similar to that of cimetidine, a commonly used antiulcer drug, but ranitidine is reported to be from four to nine times more potent. Ranitidine also inhibits the production of the enzyme pepsin, but secretion of gastric mucus, which normally forms a protective layer over the stomach lining, is not affected. Ranitidine also does not alter the secretion of bicarbonate or enzymes from the pancreas, which empties into the intestinal tract at the duodenum. Ranitidine also is used in the treatment of reflux esophagitis (a common cause of heartburn), in the Zollinger-Ellison syndrome (a condition of peptic ulcers associated with excessive gastric acidity and gastrin tumors of the pancreas or duodenum), in the treatment of severe liver disease resulting in coma, and for certain nonspecific types of gastric distress. Peak concentrations of ranitidine in the blood are observed within two or three hours after oral administration; the blood levels of ranitidine are not affected by food in the stomach or antacids at the time the drug is taken. It is important that ranitidine be used only when ulcers are confirmed as benign peptic ulcers and, in the case of gastric distress, that the condition can be treated by reducing gastric acid output in the stomach. Ranitidine can mask the symptoms of stomach cancer and in some cases even create the mistaken appearance of healing the lesion.

**PRECAUTIONS**—Ranitidine should be administered only in single short courses of treatment lasting four to six weeks, but may be repeated in patients with infrequent recurrences. The treatment course has occasionally been extended to as much as three months in patients with particularly resistant cases of peptic ulcers. In patients with severe renal impairment, blood levels of ranitidine tend to become increased and prolonged, requiring adjustment of the dosage. The safety of ranitidine in pregnancy has not been established for humans, although animal studies have failed to show evidence of impaired fertility or fetal damage. Ranitidine also is secreted in breast milk, but the clinical significance of this effect has not been fully evaluated. Although experience with the drug in children as young as 8 years of age has been limited, ranitidine has been given to children without serious adverse effects. Side effects observed in persons using ranitidine have included tiredness, headache, dizziness, diarrhea, mental confusion, and temporary skin rashes. However, the same side effects have also occurred in patients using cimetidine and with a greater frequency.

**DOSAGE AND ADMINISTRATION**—Ranitidine hydrochloride is supplied in 150 mg tablets and in 5 ml injection ampules containing 10 mg per ml. The usual recommended dosage is 150 mg taken twice a day initially, once in the morning and again before retiring. The oral dosage for peptic ulcers can be increased to a maximum of 900 mg daily, in divided doses, if necessary. The recommended dosage for children is a maximum of 150 mg taken twice daily. The therapy for reflux esophagitis is 150 mg taken twice daily for up to eight weeks. The injection dosage is 50 mg given intravenously by slow injection every six to eight hours. The recommended rate by intravenous infusion is 25 mg per hour for two hours, repeated if necessary after six to eight hours.

**SOURCES**—Glaxo Laboratories, 1025 The Queensway, Toronto, Ontario M8Z 5S6, Canada; Glaxo Laboratories, Ltd., Greenford, Mddx, UB6 OHE, England.

**Raubasine (Ajmalicine)**—Circolene, Defluina, Duoserpina, Hydrosarpan, Isoarteril, Lamuran, Raubalgina, Rauban, Raubasil, Raucitol, Sarpan, Vasoreflex

**ACTIONS AND USES**—Raubasine is a multipurpose drug obtained as an alkaloid from the rose periwinkle plant. It is used as a tranquilizer, as an antihypertensive medication, and as a blood vessel dilator. Specific applications include treatment of cerebral ischemia, or blood deficiency of the brain; intermittent claudication, or reduced blood flow to the extremities; diabetic blood vessel disorders; Raynaud's disease; night cramps; cold feet and hands; essential and secondary hypertension; migraine headache; headache due to head injuries; preeclampsia and eclampsia; acrocyanosis, characterized by bluish coloration of the hands and feet due to poor circulation; coronary artery insufficiency; Buerger's disease; and ulcers associated with poor circulation in the extremities. Raubasine is related chemically to reserpine, a tranquilizing drug obtained from the *Rauwolfia*, or snakeroot, plant.

**PRECAUTIONS**—Raubasine produces side effects similar to those of reserpine, which include nasal congestion, dry mouth, depression, drowsiness, sleep disturbances, gastrointestinal distress and diarrhea, dizziness, breathing difficulties, and skin rash. The drug should be avoided by patients with an active stomach or duodenal ulcer or ulcerative colitis and by individuals with a history of mental depression. It should be used with caution in patients with epilepsy, gallbladder disorders, bronchial asthma, or heart disease. Caution should be used in giving raubasine to patients with blood disorders, including hemorrhagic syndromes.

**DOSAGE AND ADMINISTRATION**—Raubasine is supplied in 1 and 5 mg tablets and in formulations with other drugs. The product also is available in injection vials containing 10 mg per 3 ml. The usual dosage is 1 or 2 mg three times a day before meals on a continuous basis or 5 mg two or three times a day before meals on an intermittent basis of alternate weeks. Dosages can be adjusted during the early weeks of treatment to achieve a satisfactory response.

**SOURCES**—Organon Mexicana, S.A., Calz. de Camarones No.

134, Mexico 16, D.F., Mexico; Les Laboratoires Servier, 45400 Gidy, France; Sigma Tau s.p.a., Via Pontina Km. 30,400, 00040 Pomezia (Roma), Italy.

## **Razoxane**—Razoxin

**ACTIONS AND USES**—Razoxane is an anticancer drug that is used in the treatment of both solid tumors and leukemias. It is administered with radiation therapy in the treatment of cancers of the bone, cartilage, and soft tissues. Razoxane is used alone or with other anticancer drugs in the treatment of cancers involving the lymph nodes and other lymphatic tissues. The product also is used alone or with other anticancer drugs in the treatment of leukemias. Studies indicate the drug increases the effect of radiation therapy on cancer treatment. Alone, razoxane acts by inhibiting the division of cancer cells in the early stages of the cell reproductive process. It has been used in cases in which alternative forms of cancer therapy have failed to control the disease.

**PRECAUTIONS**—Because of its action on tissue cell division, razoxane is not recommended for pregnant women or nursing mothers. On the basis of laboratory animal studies, razoxane is not recommended for use in treating nonmalignant skin disorders such as psoriasis. Side effects include an abnormal increase in white blood cells and an abnormal decrease in blood platelets, particularly in patients who have received extensive chemotherapy before starting razoxane treatment. Physicians are advised to monitor white blood cell and platelet counts in patients receiving razoxane therapy. Nausea, vomiting, diarrhea, skin disorders, and hair loss are among other side effects reported. Overdosage symptoms are similar to those of side effects.

**DOSAGE AND ADMINISTRATION**—Razoxane is supplied in 125 mg tablets. The usual dosage for soft tissue, bone, or cartilage tumors is one tablet (125 mg) twice daily for three days before the start of radiation treatments and continued through radiation therapy. On days of radiation therapy, the patient should take one tablet from one to three hours before exposure to radiation and a second tablet at the end of the day. The maintenance dosage after remission has been obtained is one tablet twice daily. For lymphatic system tumors, the precise dosage is based on body size, but it may be in the range of 125 mg twice daily for three to five days of the week, or two doses of six tablets (750 mg per dose), taken eight hours apart, once a week. Leukemia dosages also are based on body size and range from 150 to 500 mg per square meter of body surface daily for three to five days, with the therapy repeated at intervals of two to four weeks. It is recommended that allopurinol, an antigout medication, be administered with the razoxane in the treatment of leukemia to prevent an accumulation of uric acid deposits in the patient's tissues.

**SOURCES**—ICI (Ireland) Ltd., 5-9 South Frederick Street, Dublin 2, Ireland; Imperial Chemical Industries Limited, Pharmaceuticals Division, Alderley Park, Macclesfield, Cheshire SK10 4TF, England.

## **Rimiterol Hydrobromide**—Asmaten, Pulmadil

**ACTIONS AND USES**—Rimiterol hydrobromide is used in the treatment of bronchial asthma and chronic bronchitis. Rimiterol is believed to provide relief from symptoms of bronchial asthma and bronchospasm occurring in bronchitis and other respiratory disorders by acting directly on autonomic nerve receptors in smooth muscle tissue of the bronchial tree. In clinical studies, rimiterol was found to produce fewer circulatory system side effects than isoprenaline, another drug commonly used in the treatment of respiratory disorders.

**PRECAUTIONS**—Rimiterol is not recommended for pregnant women, nursing mothers, or children under the age of 12 years. It should not be used by persons who are hypersensitive to sympathomimetic amines, adrenalinelike substances that stimulate the heart, nervous system, and other body organs. The drug also should not be given to hyperthyroid patients or persons sensitive to aerosol sprays. The product should be used with caution by patients suffering from heart disease, diabetes, hypertension, or impaired liver or kidney function. Rimiterol may interact with certain other drugs, particularly agents with psychotropic effects. Side effects may include blood pressure changes with dizziness and faintness, anxiety, rapid heartbeat, tremor, headache, and changes in body chemistry, particularly changes in hormonal activity and carbohydrate metabolism.

**DOSAGE AND ADMINISTRATION**—Rimiterol hydrobromide is supplied in metered-dose vials with disposable plastic mouthpieces. A vial may deliver 300 or 400 doses of 200 or 250 micrograms per metered dose of the drug. The usual recommended dose is one or two inhalations, with at least one minute between inhalations. The procedure should not be repeated in less than 30 minutes. The patient should not inhale more than 4,000 mcg of the drug in eight treatments during a 24-hour period. Overdosage may produce palpitations, tremor, rapid heartbeat, excitement, restlessness, insomnia, anxiety, or other symptoms of hypertactivity.

**SOURCES**—Riker Laboratories, Morley Street, Loughborough, Leics LE11 1EP, England; Riker Laboratories Australia Pty Ltd., 9-15 Chilvers Road, Thornleigh, N.S.W. 2120, Australia.

## Spiramycin—Foromacidin, Provamicina, Rovamicina, Rovamycin, Rovamycine, Selectomycin, Sequamycin

**ACTIONS AND USES**—Spiramycin is an antibiotic that is active against certain strains of bacteria, including *Staphylococcus*, *Streptococcus*, pneumococcus, and enterococcus. It is effective against strains of *Staphylococcus aureus* that are resistant to erythromycin, a commonly prescribed antibiotic. Spiramycin is used in a wide range of respiratory tract infections, including tonsillitis, pharyngitis, bronchitis, and otitis (ear infections). The product also is reported to be effective against pneumonopathy (a generalized lung disease) and infections caused by *Mycoplasma pneumoniae* and *Toxoplasm-agondii*. Spiramycin is believed to act against bacteria by crossing the membrane of the bacterial cell wall and interfering with the organism's production of protein molecules. The bacterium, thus, is unable to grow and reproduce.

**PRECAUTIONS**—The drug is not recommended for pregnant women during the first trimester. Spiramycin also is not recommended for meningitis because it does not diffuse into the spinal fluid in adequate amounts to be effective. Cross-resistance to spiramycin from previous use of other antibiotics is possible. Side effects include nausea, vomiting, diarrhea, abdominal pain, and skin disorders.

**DOSAGE AND ADMINISTRATION**—Spiramycin is supplied in 250 and

500 mg capsules and 500 mg tablets. The recommended adult dosage is 2 or 3 g daily taken in three or four divided doses. For extremely severe conditions, the dosage has been increased to as much as 5 g per day. The recommended dosage for children is 50 to 100 mg per kg of body weight per day in three or four divided doses.

**SOURCES**—Rhône-Poulenc Pharma Inc., 8580 Esplanade, Montreal, Quebec H2P 2R9, Canada; Rhodia Mexicana S.A. de C.V., Jose Ma. Rico No. 611, Mexico 12, D.F., Mexico.

**Sulfadimethoxine (Sulphadimethoxine)**—Bensulfa, Chemiosalfa, Crozinal, Deltin, Diasulfa, Diazinol, Dimetossilina, Dimetoxan, Fultamid, Ipersulfa, Jatsulph, Lensulpha, Lentrap, Levisul, Madribon, Micromega, Neosulfamyd, Oxazina, Pansulph, Redifal, Risulpir, Ritarsulfa, Sulfabon, Sulfadomus, Sulfaduran, Sulfastop, Sulfathox, Sulfomikron, Sulfoplan, Sulf-Reten, Tempodiazina

**ACTIONS AND USES**—Sulfadimethoxine is a long-acting sulfonamide, with a metabolic half-life that has been reported as long as 40 hours in some patients; blood concentrations after a single dose are about 50 percent of the original value 24 hours after reaching peak levels. The product is used in the treatment of urinary tract infections and bronchitis.

**PRECAUTIONS**—Because sulfadimethoxine is a long-acting drug with a relatively long half-life, several days are required for complete elimination of the drug and its metabolites in the event that adverse side effects develop in a patient. The product is contraindicated in cases of pregnancy, liver or kidney diseases, or blood disorders. Caution should be observed in administration of sulfadimethoxine to nursing mothers. Side effects may include nausea, vomiting, blood disorders, skin rashes, and erythema multiforme.

**DOSAGE AND ADMINISTRATION**—Sulfadimethoxine is supplied in 0.2 g/ml drops and 500 mg tablets. For adults, the usual initial dose is 1 to 2 g, followed by a daily dose of 0.5 to 1 g. For children, the initial dose is calculated at 30 mg/kg of body weight, followed by daily doses of 15 mg/kg of body weight.

**SOURCE**—Rivopharm Pharmaceutical Laboratories, Rivopharm SA, 6911 Manno, Lugano, Switzerland.

## Sulfadimidine (Sulphadimidine, Sulphamethazine)—Deladine, Diazil, Nutradimidine, S-Dimidine, Sulphamezathine

**ACTIONS AND USES**—Sulfadimidine is a form of sulfonamide that has been used for a variety of bacterial infections, including histoplasmosis, meningococcal meningitis, and urinary tract infections. Sulfadimidine is rapidly absorbed from the intestinal tract, and about 70 percent becomes bound to plasma albumin. Approximately half of the dose may be excreted in the urine within 48 hours, more than two-thirds of it appearing as an acetyl derivative. The antibacterial action of sulfadimidine is similar to that of other sulfonamides that interfere with the synthesis of nucleic acids in a wide variety of bacteria.

**PRECAUTIONS**—Use of sulfadimidine is contraindicated in patients with liver or kidney diseases, in pregnancy, in recently born infants, and in individuals with blood disorders. Nausea, vomiting, and skin and blood disorders are among side effects reported. Adequate fluid intake is advised to reduce the small risk of crystalluria. Studies indicate that solubility of sulfadimidine and its acetyl derivative in urine is directly related to the pH of the urine. Symptoms of the Stevens-Johnson erythema multiforme syndrome have been reported in some patients treated with sulfadimidine.

**DOSAGE AND ADMINISTRATION**—Sulfadimidine is supplied in 500 mg tablets and suspensions of 500 mg/5 ml, as well as a fruit-flavored mixture for children. An injection form, for intramuscular injection, provides 1 g of sulfadimidine sodium in a 3 ml ampule. The usual recommended adult dosage for urinary tract infections is an initial dose of 2 g, followed by 500 mg to 1 g every six to eight hours. For other infections by susceptible organisms, the usual adult dosage is 3 g initially, followed by 1 to 1.5 g every four to six hours. Dosages for infants and children range from one-sixth the adult dose for infants to two-thirds the adult dose for children 13 to 15 years of age.

**SOURCE**—Rivopharm Pharmaceutical Laboratories, Rivopharm SA, 6911 Manno, Lugano, Switzerland.

## Sulfamethoxypyridazine (Acetyl Sulfamethoxypyridazine)—Aseptilex, Asey-Sulfa, Durasul, Eusulfa, Exazol, Ketiak, Kiron, Lederkyn, Longisul, Metazina, Microcid, Midicel, Midikel, Minikel, Sulfadepot, Sulfadin, Sulfaintensa, Sulfalex, Sulfamizina, Sulfamyd, Sulfatar, Sulfa-Ulta, Sulforetent, Sulfo-Rit, Sultirene, Unisulfa

**ACTIONS AND USES**—Sulfamethoxypyridazine is a long-acting sulfonamide used in the treatment of urinary tract infections. The metabolic half-life of the product ranges between 36 and 64 hours, depending upon the individual patient. The drug usually is supplied in the acetyl form which is hydrolyzed in the gastrointestinal tract to sulfamethoxypyridazine. The drug and its metabolites are excreted slowly and may be detected in urine samples up to a week after use of the medication has been discontinued.

**PRECAUTIONS**—Like other long-acting sulfonamides, sulfamethoxypyridazine requires several days for complete elimination from the body in the event that adverse side effects develop. The Stevens-Johnson syndrome of severe erythema multiforme has been associated with the use of sulfamethoxypyridazine, and some cases of serious skin disorders have followed use of the product. Other side effects have included nausea, vomiting, and blood disorders. The drug is contraindicated in pregnancy and in patients with liver, kidney, or blood diseases.

**DOSAGE AND ADMINISTRATION**—Sulfamethoxypyridazine usually is supplied in 500 mg scored tablets. The usual recommended dosage for urinary tract infections is 1 to 2 g initially, followed by 500 mg daily. Adequate fluid intake should be maintained during treatment and for several days after therapy has ceased.

**SOURCE**—Rivopharm Pharmaceutical Laboratories, Rivopharm SA, 6911 Manno, Lugano, Switzerland.

**Sulfametopyrazine (Sulphalene)**—Kelfizina, Kelfizine W, Longum, Policydal

**ACTIONS AND USES**—Sulfametopyrazine is a long-acting sulfonamide used in the treatment of chronic bronchitis and urinary tract infections. The drug has also been employed in the treatment of falciparum malaria. Sulfametopyrazine is easily absorbed from the gastrointestinal tract and is slowly metabolized and excreted. The half-life of the drug has been reported to range from about 45 hours in small children to approximately 72 hours in older children and adults. In one clinical study, sulfametopyrazine was found to be as effective as ampicillin in the therapy of urinary tract infections.

**PRECAUTIONS**—Because of its long-acting properties, several days may be required for complete elimination of sulfametopyrazine from the body in the event adverse effects develop. Side effects may include the Stevens-Johnson syndrome of severe erythema multiforme, nausea, vomiting, and various skin or blood disorders. The drug is contraindicated in pregnancy and in patients with liver, kidney, or blood diseases.

**DOSAGE AND ADMINISTRATION**—Sulfametopyrazine is supplied in 500 mg tablets and in a suspension of 500 mg/5 ml. The usual recommended adult regimen is 2 g taken as a single dose once a week. For children, the dose is 30 mg/kg of body weight once a week.

**SOURCE**—Farmitalia Carlo Erba Ltd, Kingmaker House, Station Rd., Barnet, Herts EN5 1NU, England.

**Talampicillin (Talampicillin Hydrochloride, Talampicillin Napsylate)**—Penbritin-T, Talampicillina Midy, Talpen, Yamacillin

**ACTIONS AND USES**—Talampicillin is an antibiotic used in the treatment of bacterial infections of the respiratory and urogenital systems. It has been used to treat acute and chronic bronchitis, pneumonia, ear, nose, and throat infections, and gynecological infections, including gonorrhea. Talampicillin has also been used to treat infections of the skin and soft tissues of the body. Talampicillin is related chemically to ampicillin and is converted to ampicillin by the body's chemistry. Various studies indicate that talampicillin's side effects include a greater incidence of gastric distress but less diarrhea, as compared with ampicillin. Talampicillin is administered as either the hydrochloride or napsylate form, although some proprietary brands contain both.

**PRECAUTIONS**—Talampicillin should not be given to patients who have shown sensitivity to penicillin or penicillinlike antibiotics. Caution should be exercised in administering the drug to patients with severe kidney or liver impairment. Caution also should be used in patients with chronic lymphatic leukemia or the skin rash associated with mononucleosis. A red skin rash is one of the more common side effects and is particularly frequent in patients with infectious mononucleosis.

**DOSAGE AND ADMINISTRATION**—Talampicillin is supplied in 250 and 500 mg tablets of the hydrochloride form and as syrups providing the equivalent of 125, 250, or 500 mg of talampicillin hydrochloride per 5 ml dose. The syrups are supplied as talampicillin napsylate, which is slightly less potent than the hydrochloride form, so that 1.33 g of the napsylate form is equal to 1 g of the hydrochloride. Thus, a 332 mg dose of talampicillin napsylate is equivalent to a 250 mg dose of talampicillin hydrochloride. The usual recommended adult dosage is 750 mg as three 250 mg tablets or 15 ml of syrup each day in three divided doses. For the treatment of gonorrhea, a single dose of 1,500 to 2,000 mg is required. Children's doses are calculated at 3 to 7 mg per kg of body weight, three times a day, for those under the age of 2 years. For older children, the usual dosage is 5 ml of syrup (125 mg equivalent) three times a day. Dosages for both adults and children can be doubled in the treatment of severe infections.

**SOURCES**—Beecham Research Laboratories, Great West Road, Brentford, Middlesex TW8 9BD, England; MIDY s.p.a., Via Piranesi 38, 20137 Milano, Italy.

## Teniposide—Vehem-Sandoz, Vumon

**ACTIONS AND USES**—Teniposide is an anticancer drug used in the treatment of lymphomas, or tumors of the lymphatic system, as well as solid tumors of the brain and the bladder. The lymphatic growths treated with teniposide include Hodgkin's disease and lymphosarcomas. Teniposide is related chemically to etoposide, another anticancer drug, and both act by interfering with the ability of cancer cells to undergo mitosis, a stage necessary for their proliferation. Like etoposide, teniposide is derived from a resin, podophyllotoxin, produced from the roots and rhizome of *Podophyllum*, also known as mayapple or American mandrake. The resin itself is sometimes used as a purgative.

**PRECAUTIONS**—Teniposide should not be administered to women with childbearing potential, to patients with blood disorders, or in the presence of bacterial infections that are not being treated with appropriate drugs. Adverse effects may include gastric distress, with nausea, vomiting, or diarrhea, the temporary loss of hair, and reduced blood counts of platelets and white cells. Caution should be used in administering teniposide to patients with impaired kidney or liver function or neurological or cardiovascular disorders. Hypotension, or abnormally low blood pressure, may result during intravenous injection of teniposide if the perfusion is too rapid. Some local inflammatory reaction may occur at the site of the injection. Like other chemotherapeutic agents used for cancer, teniposide may suppress the patient's natural immune response, resulting in increased susceptibility to infectious diseases. Because teniposide acts by interfering with reproduction of tissue cells, it may affect the development of spermatozoa or ova in the gonads of the patient being treated.

**DOSAGE AND ADMINISTRATION**—Teniposide is supplied in injection ampules containing 50 mg per 5 ml ampule. Dosage is based on the body surface area of the patient and is calculated at 30 mg per square meter of body surface daily for 5 days by intravenous infusion as an initial course of treatment. Doses of 40 to 50 mg per square meter of body surface have been used in the treatment of malignant lymphomas and higher doses for brain tumors. The drug usually is administered in 5-day courses with intervals of 5 to 15 days between treatment courses, the cycles being repeated four or five times if needed to obtain remission.

**SOURCES**—Bristol Laboratorier AB, Box 4100, 171 04 Solna, Sweden; Laboratoires Sandoz S.A.R.L., 14 bvd. Richelieu, 92500 Rueil-Malmaison, France.

## Terodiline Hydrochloride—Bicor

**ACTIONS AND USES**—Terodiline hydrochloride is used in the treatment of angina pectoris. The drug has also been employed as a bronchodilator to relieve symptoms of obstructive pulmonary disease. Studies indicate the drug acts by lowering the pulmonary capillary vein pressure while increasing the force of the left ventricular contractions of the heart. It has been used in heart disease both with and without infarct complications.

**PRECAUTIONS**—Side effects reported include dryness of the mouth, urinary retention, nausea, excitation, and tremors. In many cases, the side effects are dose-related. The safety of terodiline in pregnant women and nursing mothers has not been established.

**DOSAGE AND ADMINISTRATION**—Terodiline is supplied in 25 mg tablets. The usual initial dosage is one-half tablet twice a day, followed by a gradual increase in dosage to one-half tablet three times a day or one full tablet twice daily, depending upon the amount needed to achieve optimum patient response.

**SOURCE**—Kabi Vitrum Sverige AB, Box 30064, 104 25 Stockholm, Sweden.

## Tetrabenazine—Nitoman

**ACTIONS AND USES**—Tetrabenazine is used in the treatment of involuntary muscle movements associated with central nervous system conditions, such as Huntington's chorea, senile chorea, tardive and buccolingual dyskinesia (characterized by involuntary movements of the muscles of the mouth and jaws), hemiballismus (marked by a constant writhing contraction and relaxation of the hands and fingers), and other muscle tone abnormalities. The drug also has been used as a tranquilizer. Tetrabenazine is believed to act by depleting the body's neurotransmitter chemicals in the central nervous system and preventing their storage at synapses, thereby reducing the level of automatic transmission of nerve impulses responsible for the involuntary body movements.

**PRECAUTIONS**—Tetrabenazine should not be given to patients being treated for parkinsonism or depression, because the drug may exacerbate these conditions. It should also not be given to persons with a known sensitivity to tetrabenazine or to individuals sensitive to the artificial food coloring tartrazine used to tint the tablets. The drug should also not be given within 24 hours before or in combination with levodopa or reserpine products, because tetrabenazine can block the action of these nervous system medications. The effects of tetrabenazine in pregnancy and breast milk are not known, and therefore the drug is not recommended for pregnant women or nursing mothers. Tetrabenazine may interact with alcohol, levodopa, reserpine, monoamine oxidase inhibitors, antihypertensive drugs, and central nervous system depressants. Animal studies indicate that tetrabenazine may also interact with certain antidepressant drugs which may antagonize the activity of tetrabenazine. In other laboratory animal studies an association between tetrabenazine and mammary gland enlargement was observed at doses several times larger than the recommended dose for adult humans. The most serious side effect reported was a swallowing difficulty with choking attacks. More common side effects include a drowsiness in some patients that could make driving motor vehicles or operating machinery dangerous, parkinsonian symptoms, depression, loss of appetite, nausea, excessive salivation, blood pressure changes, abnormally slow heart rhythm, and akathisia, a condition marked by an inability to sit down because of anxiety and restlessness.

**DOSAGE AND ADMINISTRATION**—Tetrabenazine is supplied in 25 mg tablets scored with a break bar, or line for dividing tablets into 12.5 mg units. The usual recommended adult dosage is one 25 mg tablet twice daily initially, followed by 25 mg increases on every third or fourth days until a satisfactory response is achieved or a maximum daily dose of 200 mg is reached. For elderly patients, it is recommended that dosage increases be made at a slower rate. For children, the recommended dosage is one-half tablet, or 12.5 mg, twice daily, with 12.5 mg increases every three or four days until a therapeutic effect is achieved. The maximum limit for children is calculated at 3 mg per kg of body weight per day. For both children and adults, it is recommended that treatment be discontinued or dosages reduced if adverse effects appear.

**SOURCES**—Roche Products Ltd., P.O. Box 8, Welwyn Garden

City, Hertfordshire AL7 3 AY, England; Cahill May Roberts Ltd., P.O. Box 1090, Chapelizod, Dublin 20, Ireland.

**Thiamphenicol (Racephenicol, Tiamfenicol)**—Descocin, Dexawin, Fluimucil, Glitisol, Hydrazin, Igralin, Macphenicol, Neomyson, Propacin, Raceophenidol, Rigelon, Rincrol, Thiamcol, Thiocymetin, Thionicol, Thiophenicol, Urfamycin, Urfamycine, Urophenyl, Vicemycetin

**ACTIONS AND USES**—Thiamphenicol is an antibiotic used in the treatment of a variety of infections. The drug has been used in the treatment of acute bronchitis, acute and chronic sinusitis, pneumonia, typhoid fever, bacterial enterocolitis, bacillary dysentery, infections of the liver and gallbladder, urinary tract infections including pyelitis, pyelonephritis, and cystitis. Thiamphenicol also is used in the treatment of prostatitis, epididymitis, and urethritis due to gonorrhea or other infectious agents, infections of the uterus, and complications of abortion. In surgery, thiamphenicol is employed as a broad-spectrum antibiotic with capacity to destroy a wide range of infectious agents. The drug is rapidly absorbed, whether given by mouth or injection, with significant blood levels of the antibiotic within 30 minutes after administration. Thiamphenicol may produce a temporary depression of blood formation in the bone marrow, but it is less likely than chloramphenicol to cause anemia or other blood disorders.

**PRECAUTIONS**—If use of thiamphenicol requires more than 15 days of treatment, it is necessary to order periodic studies of the patient's blood samples to ensure against the development of blood disorders. Thiamphenicol should not be administered to patients with a known sensitivity to antibiotics or to individuals with kidney impairment. The drug should also not be given to a woman during the first trimester of pregnancy. Because thiamphenicol crosses the placenta and enters breast milk, it should be administered with caution to all pregnant women and nursing mothers. Side effects reported include nausea, vomiting, flatulence, fever, and allergies, particularly skin disorders. The medication should be discontinued in the event of any severe adverse effect.

**DOSAGE AND ADMINISTRATION**—Thiamphenicol is supplied in 250 mg capsules, a suspension providing 125 mg per 5 ml (teaspoonful), and in 500 mg ampules for injection. The average adult dose is six capsules, or 1.5 g, daily. For children, the dose is calculated at 30 mg per kg of body weight.

**SOURCE**—Bracco de Mexico, S.A. de C.V., Calzada de las Armas No. 100, Tlalnepantla, Edo. de Mexico; Inpharzam S.A., 6814 Cadempino, P.O. Box 6812, Switzerland.

## Thiopropazate Hydrochloride—Dartal, Dartalan

**ACTIONS AND USES**—Thiopropazate hydrochloride is a tranquilizer with actions similar to those of chlorpromazine, a prototype neuroleptic drug widely used in the treatment of psychotic patients. Thiopropazate is used for a variety of psychotic states and also has been found useful in treating autonomic nervous system dysfunctions, such as hemiballismus and tardive dyskinesia, in which patients experience involuntary skeletal muscle movements. The product has been used in the treatment of pain in cases of inoperable cancer and other terminal illnesses, Huntington's chorea, acute and chronic schizophrenia, anxiety tension states, obsessive-compulsive behavior, involutional psychoses, neurotic conditions during withdrawal from alcohol or sedative drugs, anxiety, tension, agitation and aggressive states, particularly in elderly patients.

**PRECAUTIONS**—The safety of thiopropazate hydrochloride in pregnancy has not been established and should not be given to pregnant patients unless the potential benefits outweigh the risks. The drug should not be administered to patients in a coma nor to patients with impaired liver function or bone marrow depression. The product may increase the effect of antihypertensive drugs, general anesthetics, alcohol, barbiturates, or alcohol. The drug may also interact with anticonvulsant medications administered to epileptics, and such drug dosages should be modified while also using low initial doses of thiopropazate and monitoring plasma levels and patient responses. Caution should be used in patients with heart or liver disorders, blood diseases, or respiratory conditions, particularly severe asthma or emphysema. Patients on long-term therapy should be evaluated periodically to determine the need to discontinue therapy or reduce the dosage. Adverse effects include parkinsonian symptoms, loss of muscle tone, akathisia (a condition of extreme restlessness), blurred vision, dry mouth, low blood pressure, constipation, nasal congestion, and skin rash. Caution should be used in administering thiopropazate to patients also taking barbiturates or other central nervous system depressants, and patients using thiopropazate should be advised that the drug may affect their ability to operate motor vehicles or machinery safely.

**DOSAGE AND ADMINISTRATION**—Thiopropazate hydrochloride is supplied in 5 mg tablets. For the management of adults with psychotic conditions, the usual dosage is 10 mg three times a day at the start, with adjustments upward or downward as needed to achieve a satisfactory response. The maximum total daily dose is 100 mg. For elderly patients and for the treatment of nausea and vomiting, a dosage of 5 mg three times daily is suggested.

**SOURCES**—G.D. Searle and Co. of Canada, Limited, 400 Iroquois Shore Rd., Oakville, Ontario 16H 1M5, Canada; Searle Laboratories, 8 West Street, North Sydney, N.S.W. 2060, Australia.

## **Thioproperazine Mesylate**—Majeptil, Mayeptil

**ACTIONS AND USES**—Thioproperazine mesylate is a tranquilizer used in the treatment of psychotic overactivity, including manic phases of manic-depressive psychosis and acute and chronic schizophrenia. The drug also has action as an antiemetic. The product differs from other major tranquilizers in that it has relatively little sedative action, possesses virtually no antiserotonin, antihistaminic, or hypotensive action, and is one of the most active antiemetic agents known. Thioproperazine affects both the central nervous system and the autonomic nervous system. It is used in the treatment of acute and chronic schizophrenia patients who fail to respond to other tranquilizers.

**PRECAUTIONS**—Thioproperazine mesylate should not be administered to patients in a coma or depressive state, particularly when the condition has been induced by a central nervous system depressant. The drug should not be used in patients with spastic diseases, blood disorders, or Parkinson's disease; in patients known to be sensitive to phenothiazine drugs; in children under 3 years of age; nor in senile patients with parkinsonian symptoms. The safety of thioproperazine in pregnancy has not been established, and the drug is not recommended for use in the first trimester. The drug should be used cautiously in patients with a history of seizures, in patients with impaired kidney or liver function, in asthmatic and epileptic patients, and in mentally retarded individuals, who may be unusually sensitive to the agent. Adverse reactions include tremors or other involuntary muscular movements, anxiety or apathy, drowsiness or insomnia, mood changes, and hormonal disturbances including menstrual disorders. Autonomic effects of profuse sweating, watery eyes, excessive salivation, and urinating difficulties have been reported. The potent antiemetic action of thioproperazine may obscure symptoms of nausea and vomiting associated with some types of organic disorders. Neuromuscular symptoms usually are dose-related and generally subside when the dose is reduced.

**DOSAGE AND ADMINISTRATION**—Thioproperazine mesylate is supplied in 1, 5, and 10 mg tablets and in 1 ml ampules containing 10 mg each of the drug. The usual route of administration is oral, and the recommended initial dosage is 5 mg per day in a single dose or in divided doses. The dosage is gradually increased by 5 mg every two or three days until an effective level, usually 30 to 40 mg per day, is reached. For children under 10 years of age, a similiar procedure is followed except that initial dosage is 1 to 3 mg per day. Intramuscular injections of the drug are used chiefly to initiate certain treatments and may begin with doses of 1 to 3 mg two to three times a day, gradually increased if necessary. For symptoms of acute mania, a single intramuscular dose of 5 mg has been used.

**SOURCES**—Rhône-Poulenc Pharma Inc., 8580 Esplanade, Montreal, Quebec H2P 2R9, Canada; May & Baker Limited, Dagenham, Essex RM10 7XS, England.

**Tiemonium Iodide (Tiemonium Methylsulfate)**—Bort, Colchimax, Nefurox Compuesto, Tiemozyl, Visceralgin, Visceralgina, Visceralgine, Xyde Compuesto

**ACTIONS AND USES**—Tiemonium iodide is an antispasmodic drug used in the treatment of spasms of the gastrointestinal tract, the urinary tract, the respiratory system, the gallbladder and biliary tract, and the uterus. It is prescribed for the treatment of spasmodic dysmenorrhea, in the management of certain obstetric procedures, for chronic and acute asthma, and as an auxiliary medication in the management of stomach and duodenal ulcers. Tiemonium has activity similar to that of atropine in blocking the effects of acetylcholine, a nerve impulse transmitter, at neural pathways used to stimulate smooth muscle activity, particularly of the viscera. The blocking action occurs because tiemonium has an affinity for the same nerve-ending receptors needed by acetylcholine in order to stimulate smooth muscle contractions. By competing with acetylcholine, tiemonium reduces the stimulation of muscle contractions experienced as spasms. Tiemonium is used both as an iodide and as a methylsulfate compound; patients who are hypersensitive to iodine are given the methylsulfate form.

**PRECAUTIONS**—Tiemonium should not be administered to patients with glaucoma or an enlarged prostate gland, conditions that are aggravated by atropinelike drugs. Side effects include dry mouth, blurred vision, and urinary retention, which occur mainly in sensitive patients and at higher than therapeutic doses. Caution should be used in giving tiemonium to patients with impaired liver or kidney function, cardiac insufficiency, obstruction in the pyloric area between the stomach and duodenum, and blood disorders. Tiemonium is frequently prepared in combination with amebicides for use in treating dysentery, with analgesics to relieve pain, or with sedatives. Such preparations may produce additional side effects related to the other drug or drugs used in the combinations.

**DOSAGE AND ADMINISTRATION**—Tiemonium iodide and tiemonium methylsulfate are supplied in 30, 40, and 50 mg tablets, in 20 mg suppositories, in drops containing 10 or 20 mg per ml, and in injection ampules containing 5 mg per ml. The usual recommended dosage for most spasmodic disorders is 50 to 100 mg by mouth three times daily, one 20 mg suppository in the morning and in the evening, and 5 to 10 mg by intramuscular or intravenous injection as needed to control the symptoms.

**SOURCES**—Provita S.A., La Route-Neuve, 1920 Martigny, Switzerland; Laboratories de l'Ozothine, 18/22, rue d'Arras, 92003 Nanterre Cedex, France; Productos Gedeon Richter (America) S.A., Miguel Angel de Quevedo No. 247, Mexico 21, D.F., Mexico.

## Tofenacin Hydrochloride—Elamol, Tofacine

**ACTIONS AND USES**—Tofenacin hydrochloride is an antidepressant used primarily in the treatment of mild to moderate depression in older individuals. Tofenacin has also been used in the treatment of the parkinsonian syndrome (parkinsonism). The drug is a derivative of orphenadrine, a drug used to reduce skeletal muscle spasms by acting on the brain centers that control motor nerve functions. Because of its action on motor nerves, the product is utilized in the treatment of parkinsonian types of disorders, including muscle spasms due to the use of drugs. The ability of a psychotropic drug to have both antidepressant and antiparkinsonism effects is believed to be due to a lack of specific influence on the nervous system. Tofenacin drugs are found to be most effective in treating depression in patients over the age of 50 years.

**PRECAUTIONS**—Tofenacin should not be administered to patients with glaucoma, an enlarged prostate, or those receiving monoamine oxidase inhibitors. Patients receiving a monoamine oxidase inhibitor should discontinue use of the drug for a period of 14 days before beginning tofenacin therapy. Tofenacin is not recommended for pregnant women, for patients receiving electroconvulsive therapy, or for persons with known suicidal tendencies. Caution is advised in administering tofenacin to persons with urination difficulties or patients being treated with other psychotropic drugs, such as tranquilizers or antidepressants. Side effects may include dry mouth, blurred vision, or tremors, which may be signs of overdosage or accommodation of the body to the dosage and which may disappear spontaneously or be controlled by adjusting the dosage. Other reported side effects include gastrointestinal disorders, drowsiness, agitation, dizziness, and skin rashes. The drug may affect the ability of the patient to concentrate, and the patient should not operate motor vehicles or machinery until it has been demonstrated that such activities will not be hazardous. Special care should be exercised in giving the product to patients with a history of epilepsy or seizures.

**DOSAGE AND ADMINISTRATION**—Tofenacin hydrochloride is supplied in 80 mg capsules. The usual dosage is up to 240 mg, or three capsules, daily in divided doses, as recommended by a physician for effective response. The drug is not recommended for children.

**SOURCE**—Brocades House, Pyrford Road, West Byfleet, Weybridge, Surrey KT14 6RA, England.

## **Tranexamic Acid (Cyclohexanecarboxylic Acid)**—Amcacid, Amchafibrin, Amstat, Anvitoff, Carxamin, Cyclokaptron, Cyklokapron, Emorhalt, Exacyl, Frenolyse, Hexapromin, Hexatron, Pridemon, Tranex, Tranexan, Transamin, Transmalon, Ugurol

**ACTIONS AND USES**—Tranexamic acid is a drug used to prevent and control hemorrhage by preventing the activity of substances in the blood that tend to dissolve blood clots as they form. Tranexamic acid has been used to control excessive bleeding in prostate and bladder surgery, nosebleeds, profuse menstruation, bleeding associated with dental extraction, certain types of brain hemorrhage, hemorrhage in partial excision of the uterine cervix, hemorrhage within the eyeball, and hereditary angioneurotic edema (a condition marked by abnormal accumulation of fluids in the skin, mucous membranes, and viscera). Tranexamic acid also has been used to treat bleeding associated with abortion and use of intrauterine contraceptive devices, aplastic anemia, leukemia, cancer, purpura (characterized by bleeding under the skin), and pulmonary tuberculosis. The product is reported to be effective in controlling hemorrhage in patients with hemophilias, including Christmas disease, during dental extraction. Tranexamic acid is believed to be ten times more potent but with fewer side effects than aminocaproic acid, another antihemorrhage drug with similar action in human blood chemistry.

**PRECAUTIONS**—Tranexamic acid may stabilize blood clots that have already formed, and it may result in kidney obstruction, particularly in hemophiliac patients. Among side effects observed have been complaints of diarrhea, headache, dizziness, heartburn, nausea, muscle pain and weakness, nasal congestion, watery eyes, increased urination urge, and skin rashes. Several cases of temporary loss of ejaculatory ability have been reported.

**DOSAGE AND ADMINISTRATION**—Tranexamic acid is supplied in 250 and 500 mg tablets and capsules and in injection ampules containing 50 or 100 mg per ml. A syrup containing 100 mg of tranexamic acid per ml is also available. The usual recommended dosage is 1,000 to 1,500 mg (two to three 500 mg tablets, or equivalent) every 8 to 12 hours for most bleeding problems. For dental extractions in hemophilic patients and for traumatic hyphema (bleeding within the eyeball), dosage is calculated on a basis of 25 mg per kg of body weight, given every eight hours. For general management of fibrinolysis (excessive activity by natural substances that interfere with blood clotting), dosage is based on a ratio of 15 mg per kg of body weight and is administered by slow intravenous injection every six to eight hours. The general rule for children is 25 mg of tranexamic acid per kg of body weight for each dose.

**SOURCES**—Kabi Vitrum Limited, Bilton House, Uxbridge Road, Ealing, London W5 2TH, England; Kabi Vitrum Canada, Inc., Suite 204, 3300 Côte Vertu, St. Laurent, Quebec H4R 2B7, Canada; Kabi AB, Nesbruv 33, Postboks 22, 1362 Billingstad, Norway; Laboratoire Choay, 46, av. Theophile-Gautier, 75782 Paris Cedex 16, France; H. Kern & Co., S.A., Avenida Principal de los Cortijos de Lourdes, Edif. Kern, Apartado 1.567, Caracas, Venezuela.

## Treosulfan (Dihydroxybusulfan)—Treosulfan Leo

**ACTIONS AND USES**—Treosulfan is an anticancer drug that is used alone or in conjunction with other therapies in the treatment of cancer of the ovary. Treosulfan is an alkylating agent, which is extremely reactive with many chemical compounds existing in living tissue. Alkylating agents produce their anticancer effect by reacting with the DNA molecules that form the chromosomes in the nuclei of tissue cells, rendering them incapable of reproducing and spreading. While destroying cancer cells, alkylating agents also can damage some normal tissue cells, particularly the gametes, or egg cells, in the ovary. The patient is thus made infertile during therapy. This is often reversible if the therapy is not prolonged, but it also may become permanent.

**PRECAUTIONS**—Treosulfan should not be used during pregnancy. The drug tends to have a depressant effect on bone marrow activity, and blood counts of thrombocytes and white cells will be reduced during therapy. The blood counts generally return to normal within four weeks after use of the drug has been discontinued. Side effects of alkylating agents, including treosulfan, may include nausea, vomiting, and some degree of alopecia, or hair loss. These effects also are generally reversible and end after use of the drug has been discontinued. Patients are advised to swallow the treosulfan capsules without biting into them; chewing the capsules can result in a side effect of stomatitis, or inflammation of the mouth. Some patients have reported skin eruptions after starting treosulfan therapy.

**DOSAGE AND ADMINISTRATION**—Treosulfan is supplied in 250 mg capsules and also as a powder for reconstitution for injection. The usual recommended oral dosage is 1 g, or four capsules, daily in four divided doses for one month, followed by one month without treatment. The cycle is repeated, with adjustments made according to blood cell counts and the concurrent use of radiation therapy or other anticancer drugs. When radiation is used with treosulfan, the drug dosage generally is reduced by 50 percent. The usual dosage by intravenous injection is 5 to 15 g every one to three weeks. A maintenance dose of 500 mg daily as continuous therapy is sometimes used, blood count permitting.

**SOURCES**—Leo Laboratories Limited, Longwick Road, Princes Risborough, Aylesbury, Bucks, HP17 9RR, England; Pennwalt of Canada Ltd., Pharmaceutical Division, 393 Midwest Road, Scarborough, Ontario M1P 3A6, Canada.

## Trilostane—Modrenal

**ACTIONS AND USES**—Trilostane is a hormone suppressant drug used in the treatment of disorders such as Cushing's syndrome and primary aldosteronism caused by overproduction of certain hormones by the adrenal gland cortex. Cushing's syndrome is marked by loss of protein tissue and accumulation of fat pads, weakness and fatigue, thinning of bones, thinning of skin resulting in "stretch marks," and sex hormone changes associated with impotence in men and amenorrhea in women. Primary aldosteronism is characterized by changes in the body's mineral balance; excessive thirst and excessive urination; hypertension; and episodes of weakness, tingling sensations, and paralysis. Trilostane acts by inhibiting the enzyme system reponsible for the adrenal cortex hyperactivity.

**PRECAUTIONS**—Trilostane should not be given to women with childbearing potential; it may also interfere with the activity of oral contraceptives. Caution should be used in giving the drug to patients with impaired kidney or liver function. Blood samples of patients using trilostane should be analyzed periodically for signs of abnormal mineral balance or corticosteroid levels. Trilostane may interact with certain diuretics to alter potassium levels in the blood. The only reported side effects—flushing, nausea, vomiting, runny nose, and edema of the palate—were associated with initial doses that were several times the recommended amount.

**DOSAGE AND ADMINISTRATION**—Trilostane is supplied in 60 mg capsules for oral administration. The recommended initial dosage is 60 mg taken four times a day for at least three days, after which the dosage is adjusted according to the patient's response and results of laboratory tests. The usual range after adjustment is 120 to 480 mg per day in divided doses. The recommended maximum dose per day is 960 mg.

**SOURCE**—Sterling Research Laboratories, St. Mark's Hill, Surbiton-Upon-Thames, Surrey KT6 4PH, England.

**Tripotassium Dicitrato Bismuthate**—De-Nol, Duosol, Peptol, Ulcerine, Ulcerone

**ACTIONS AND USES**—Tripotassium dicitrato bismuthate is a drug that combines potassium, bismuth, and citrate in one compound for the treatment of stomach and duodenal ulcers. It is believed the drug interacts with the gastric juices of the stomach, which cause the bismuth to precipitate. The bismuth in turn forms a chelate, or chemical complex, with amino acids and related substances present in the stomach, which is deposited as a protective coating over the lining of the stomach. A similar action occurs in the duodenum, the first segment of the intestine beyond the stomach. It is reported that the bismuth chelate coating provides longer-lasting healing action for ulcers of the stomach and duodenum than many of the alternative therapies. The product does not have antacid activity and the protective layer is not affected by gastric juices of the stomach or intestinal enzymes. The bismuth chelate layer is gradually broken down and excreted, mainly with feces which may be blackened by the bismuth.

**PRECAUTIONS**—Tripotassium dicitrato bismuthate should not be given to patients with impaired kidney function. It also is not recommended for use in pregnancy. Although bismuth may be transmitted through breast milk, the risk of adverse effects to an infant is reported to be very small. Caution should be used in avoiding overdosage of bismuth compounds because of evidence that bismuth can be absorbed by the central nervous system, leading to brain dysfunction. Caution is also recommended in giving the drug to patients with symptoms of acute gastritis. The drug also can interact with certain other medications, such as antibiotics, as well as with amino acids in foods, to form chemical complexes that deactivate it, thereby diminishing the effectiveness of tripotassium dicitrato bismuthate as an ulcer-healing agent. The main adverse effect of tripotassium dicitrato bismuthate seems to be the discoloration by bismuth deposits in feces and on the tongue, teeth fillings, and dentures. Occasional complaints of nausea and vomiting have been reported.

**DOSAGE AND ADMINISTRATION**—Tripotassium dicitrato bismuthate is supplied in 120 mg tablets and as a liquid containing 120 mg per 5 ml dose, approximately equal to one teaspoonful. The usual dosage is 120 mg in either the tablet or elixir form taken 30 minutes before each of the three main meals of the day and a fourth 120 mg dose two hours after the last main meal of the day. No liquids should be consumed for 30 minutes before or after each dose. However, it is recommended that the 5 ml liquid dose be diluted with 15 ml of water before it is ingested. For maximum therapeutic effect, it is recommended that the drug be taken regularly as indicated for 28 days, without missing a dose. For maximum effectiveness, it is recommended that the patient avoid drinking milk or carbonated beverages, including beer, during treatment. The patient also should avoid using antacids or consuming foods that neutralize acids. The use of tobacco and alcoholic beverages is permitted in moderation.

**SOURCES**—Brocades Great Britain Ltd., Brocades House, Pyrford Road, West Byfleet, Weybridge, Surrey KT14 6RA, England; Cooper S.A., 1701 Fribourg-Moncor, Switzerland.

## **Troxerutin (Vitamin $P_4$)**—Factor P-Zyma, Paroven, Pherarutin, Pur-Rutin 20%, Relvène, Rufen P4, Rutilémone, Varemoid, Venamitil, Venorutin, Venoruton

**ACTIONS AND USES**—Troxerutin is an oral medication used in the treatment of hemorrhoids, varicose veins, and other disorders of the venous system. It has been used in the treatment of heavy, painful, and swollen legs; edema of the ankles; lower limb circulatory disorders of pregnancy; night cramps; superficial thrombophlebitis; restless legs; diabetic retinopathy; Raynaud's disease; paresthesias (burning or tingling sensations); and ulcers and dermatitis associated with insufficient venous blood flow. Troxerutin is believed to act on the capillaries, where it reduces fragility and permeability of the small vessels, improving the distribution of oxygen to the surrounding tissues and increasing the return of extracellular body fluids through the lymphatic vessels of the body. The product, which is related chemically to the rutin flavonoid found in buckwheat, is used either alone or in addition to surgery or other therapies for disorders of the veins.

**PRECAUTIONS**—Troxerutin is not recommended for children. It is also not recommended for pregnant patients in the first trimester. Side effects include mainly gastrointestinal complaints, headaches, and flushing.

**DOSAGE AND ADMINISTRATION**—Troxerutin is supplied in tablets, capsules, and a gel and in ampules for injection. The tablets contain 100 mg and the capsules 250 or 300 mg of the product. The gel is supplied in 100 g tubes containing 2 g of the drug, and the injectable form is supplied in 5 ml ampules containing 500 mg of troxerutin. The usual recommended initial oral dosage is two tablets or one capsule three times daily for three to four weeks, followed by a maintenance dosage of two tablets twice daily, or one or two capsules a day, as needed to achieve a satisfactory response. It is recommended that the oral doses be taken with meals. The gel is used for local application (as an ointment) as needed. The injectable form is administered by the intramuscular route at a rate of one ampule per day for 15 days.

**SOURCES**—Ofimex, S.A., Laboratorios, Calzada de Tlalpan No. 4369, Mexico 22, D.F., Mexico; Zyma (UK) Limited, Macclesfield, Cheshire SK10 2LY, England.

## Ubidecarenone (Coenzyme $Q_{10}$, Ubiquinone$_{10}$)—Neuquinon

**ACTIONS AND USES**—Ubidecarenone is a cardiovascular drug used in the treatment of mild to moderate congestive heart failure with edema, pulmonary congestion, or liver disorders. The drug acts by improving the metabolic functions of heart muscle tissue, protecting the muscle against disorders due to oxygen deficiency. The oxygen deficiency may be the result of drugs, surgery, or other causes. Ubidecarenone improves depressed heart output of blood, particularly in elderly patients affected by hypertension or oxygen deficiency associated with arteriosclerosis. The drug is reported to inhibit adverse effects of isoproterenol, a potent heart stimulant drug, and high doses of aldosterone, an adrenal hormone that causes sodium retention. Ubidecarenone also is used to prevent the toxic effects of certain anticancer drugs in heart tissue. In animal studies, the product has been found to correct suppression of the immune response, a condition associated with aging, and is used experimentally to prevent some of the degenerative processes that occur in the brain of aging individuals.

**PRECAUTIONS**—Adverse effects reported in patients using ubidecarenone include gastrointestinal discomfort, loss of appetite, nausea, diarrhea, and skin rashes. Because the product also occurs naturally in the mitochondria of living tissue cells, side effects may be due to overdosage rather than reactions to the substance itself.

**DOSAGE AND ADMINISTRATION**—Ubidecarenone is supplied in 5 and 10 mg tablets, 5 mg capsules, and granules that contain 10 mg of ubidecarenone per g of product. The usual recommended dosage is 10 mg of the drug, taken as tablets, capsules, or granules, three times a day after meals.

**SOURCE**—Eisai Co., Ltd., 6-10, 4-chome, Koishikawa, Bunkyo-ku, Tokyo, Japan.

## Ursodeoxycholic Acid (UDCA, Ursodesoxycholic Acid)—
Destolit, Deursil, Ursacol, Urso, Ursochol

**ACTIONS AND USES**—Ursodeoxycholic acid is a cholagogic drug, or one that stimulates the flow of bile into the intestine. It is used to dissolve cholesterol gallstones in patients with a functioning gallbladder. The technique is employed when surgery is not recommended, symptoms are mild, the stones are small, and the gallbladder is not impaired. Ursodeoxycholic acid is a close chemical relative of chenodeoxycholic acid, a naturally occurring bile acid that also is used to dissolve gallstones. It acts by altering the ratio of cholesterol to bile salts, causing gradual dissolution of gallstones formed in cholesterol-saturated bile. Ursodeoxycholic acid has also been used in the treatment of liver disorders, excessive fat levels in the blood, and steatorrhea, a condition characterized by fatty stools.

**PRECAUTIONS**—Ursodeoxycholic acid should not be used in patients with nonfunctioning gallbladders, with inflammatory diseases of the intestinal tract, or with impaired liver function. Reported side effects include occasional diarrhea, mainly as a result of overdosage. Diarrhea and other adverse effects, such as liver changes, occur less frequently with ursodeoxycholic acid than with chenodeoxycholic acid. Use of the product in pregnancy is not recommended; some authorities recommend that nonhormonal contraceptives be used by women of childbearing age or that treatment be discontinued if pregnancy develops during therapy. Oral contraceptives and other sources of estrogen tend to increase cholesterol elimination in bile. Patients are advised to avoid such drugs and also cholesterol-lowering medications when using ursodeoxycholic acid. Patients are also advised to follow a diet of reduced calories and low cholesterol during gallstone dissolution treatment.

**DOSAGE AND ADMINISTRATION**—Ursodeoxycholic acid is supplied in 50, 100, 150, and 300 mg tablets and capsules. The daily dosage is calculated on a basis of 8 to 10 mg per kg of body weight, or approximately 450 to 700 mg per day for a 150-pound person. The daily dosage should be divided into two parts, taken after meals, one-half of the dosage always taken after the evening meal.

**SOURCES**—Lepetit Pharmaceuticals Limited, Meadowbank, Bath Road, Hounslow, Middlesex TW5 9QY, England; Guiliani s.p.a., Via Palagi 2, 20129 Milano, Italy; Zambon Farmaceutici s.p.a., Lab. Rc. Direz. Gen. Amm., prop. e vend. Italia Estero, Via Lillo del Duca 12, 20091 Bresso (M1), Italy; Inpharzam, 6814 Cadempino, P.O. Box 6812, Switzerland; Tokyo Tanabe Co., Ltd., 7-3, Nihonbashi-Honcho 2-chome, Chuo-ku, Tokyo, Japan.

## Valerian (Baldrianwurzel, Valer, Valerianae Radix)—Baldrisedon, Cardiosedin Kutz, Lupassin, Neurinase, Neurotrofina Valerianata, Neurotrofina Valerobromata, Pasifluidina, Pasiphal, Recvalysat, Valdispert, Valeriana Dispert, Valerianato Pierlot, Valero Camomilla Rossi, Valetal, Veriane Buriat

**ACTIONS AND USES**—Valerian is a sedative prepared from the roots and other underground parts of the garden heliotrope plant, *Valeriana officinalis*. It is used as a sedative and carminative (agent to reduce flatulence), primarily in the treatment of hysteria, rapid heartbeat, heart arrhythmias, anxiety, nervous manifestations of menopause, "nervous stomach," and insomnia. Valerian has been used as a medicinal herb since ancient times, as the plant's name suggests, *Valeriana* being derived from the Latin *valere*, meaning "to be well," and *officinalis*, a term originally applied to medicines prepared in monasteries. During the Middle Ages, valerian was known as "all-heal" and was used as an herbal remedy for many disorders. In some countries, valerian is prepared in formulations that also contain other herbals, such as chamomile, or barbiturates.

**PRECAUTIONS**—Valerian should not be given to patients with impaired kidney function. The drug may interact with alcohol, barbiturates, certain antihistamines, muscle relaxants, natural or synthetic narcotics, or psychotropic drugs, increasing the effects of the drugs. Caution should be used in administering the drug to patients with impaired liver function, to elderly or debilitated individuals, or to those hypersensitive to the product. Side effects may include skin rash, fatigue, asthenia, and drowsiness. In formulations containing other ingredients, side effects may be due to the additional substances.

**DOSAGE AND ADMINISTRATION**—Valerian is prepared as extracts, tinctures, and infusions, and usually combined with bromides or other ingredients in tablets, elixirs, or syrups containing varying amounts of valerian. Most tablets contain 35, 45, or 50 mg of valerian, and the recommended dosage is one to three tablets three times a day.

**SOURCES**—Quimica Y Farmacia, S.A., Apdo. Postal 951, Monterey, N.L., Mexico; Laboratoires Millot-Solac, 16, avenue George V, 75008, Paris, France; Laboratoires Genevrier S.A., 45, rue Madeleine-Michelis, B.P. 149, 92202 Neuilly-Sur-Seine, France; Laboratorios Ergos, S.A., 2.a Transversal 8, Urb. Buena Vista, Petare, Apartado del Este 60.590, Caracas, Venezuela.

## **Valethamate Bromide**—Epidosan, Epidosin, Frenant, Murel, Narest, Resitan

**ACTIONS AND USES**—Valethamate bromide is used in the treatment of stomach and duodenal ulcers and to relieve symptoms of gastrointestinal tract spasms. The product is believed to act by impeding the transmission of nerve impulses that normally stimulate the flow of gastric juices in the stomach. Valethamate bromide is not recommended as a drug to be used alone but rather as an adjunct to antacids or other peptic ulcer therapies. Because of its chemical relationship to belladonna alkaloids, used in reducing the tone and motility of smooth muscles, valethamate also has antispasmodic activity.

**PRECAUTIONS**—Valethamate bromide may cause increased heart rate, difficulty in urination, and reduced production of saliva, sweat, tears, and nasal and bronchial secretions. It also tends to decrease stomach and intestinal secretions and gastrointestinal motility. In some patients, the drug may be a cause of postural hypotension, in which the blood pressure falls rapidly when arising from a sitting or reclining position, producing sensations of faintness or dizziness. Caution should be used in administering the drug to patients with glaucoma or other forms of visual impairment because of the atropinelike effects of valethamate. Patients should be advised that blurred vision and photophobia may occur as temporary effects of drugs of this type.

**DOSAGE AND ADMINISTRATION**—Valethamate bromide is supplied in 10 mg tablets and in vials containing 8 mg per ml of solution for injection. The usual dosage is 10 to 20 mg by mouth three or four times daily or 20 mg at four- to six-hour intervals by intravenous or intramuscular injection, up to a maximum of 60 mg daily.

**SOURCE**—Farmades s.p.a., Farmaceutici Degussa & Schering, Via di Tor Cervara 282, 00155 Roma, Italy.

## **Valnoctamide (Valmethamide)**—Axiquel, Nirvanil

**ACTIONS AND USES**—Valnoctamide is a tranquilizer used to treat all forms of anxiety and tension, particularly those producing functional or organic symptoms. The drug also is used in the treatment of insomnia. The activity of the anxiolytic product is not fully understood.

**PRECAUTIONS**—Valnoctamide should not be administered during the first three months of pregnancy. The use of alcoholic beverages during valnoctamide treatment is not recommended. The drug should be used with caution in patients also receiving barbiturates or opium-based medications because of the risk of increasing their effects. The most common side effect is drowsiness during the first few days of treatment with valnoctamide.

**DOSAGE AND ADMINISTRATION**—Valnoctamide is supplied in 200 mg tablets or capsules. The usual recommended dosage is 400 to 800 mg per day in divided doses.

**SOURCES**—Midy s.p.a., Via Piranesi 38, 20137 Milano, Italy; Laboratoires Clin Midy. 20, rue des Fosse Saint-Jacques, 75240 Paris Cedex 05, France.

## Viloxazine Hydrochloride—Vicilan, Vivalan, Vivarint

**ACTIONS AND USES**—Viloxazine hydrochloride is an antidepressant used to treat cases of depression marked by apathy and withdrawal. It is also used to treat mixed states of anxiety and depression and in depression when sedation is not required. Viloxazine has less sedative effect and fewer side effects, such as dry mouth, constipation, urinary difficulty, visual disturbances, and rapid heartbeat, than antidepressants of the amitriptyline type of tricyclic drugs. Viloxazine is believed to act by inactivating substances in the central nervous system that may account for the symptoms of depression.

**PRECAUTIONS**—The safety of viloxazine in pregnancy has not been established, and it is therefore not recommended for use in pregnant patients unless the benefits outweigh the risks. The drug is also not recommended for children under the age of 14 years. While viloxazine seems to produce fewer side effects involving the heart than many other commonly prescribed antidepressants, the product should not be given patients who have recently recovered from myocardial infarction. Also, the drug should be used with caution in patients with heart block, congestive heart failure, angina pectoris, or other heart disorders. Patients who have known suicidal tendencies should be monitored closely. There also is a risk that a highly sensitive patient may suddenly change from depressed to manic under the influence of an antidepressant. Symptoms of anxiety, agitation, insomnia, confusion, dizziness, tremors, drowsiness, and hypertension may be exacerbated by the drug. Viloxazine should be administered with caution to patients with epilepsy, peptic ulcer, or impaired liver or kidney function. Viloxazine should not be given within two weeks of the use of monoamine oxidase inhibitors by the same patient. Viloxazine may diminish the effects of certain antihypertensive drugs and can interact with a variety of substances, including alcohol, phenytoin, and levodopa. Nausea, vomiting, and headaches are side effects that may occur with the start of viloxazine therapy and during withdrawal from the therapy. Patients should be monitored closely during the first two weeks of treatment because effects may occur slowly. Patients should be advised that viloxazine may impair alertness and make operation of motor vehicles or machinery hazardous.

**DOSAGE AND ADMINISTRATION**—Viloxazine hydrochloride is supplied in 50 and 100 mg tablets. The usual adult dosage is 150 to 300 mg per day in divided doses. The last dose should not be taken later than 6 P.M. For elderly patients, the dosage should begin with 100 mg per day, followed by gradual increases as necessary to reach an optimum response. The maximum total daily dose for all patients is 400 mg.

**SOURCES**—Icpharma, Reporto Farmaceutici della Imperial Chemical Industries (Italia) s.p.a., Viale Isonzo 25, 20135 Milano, Italy; Imperial Chemical Industries Ltd., Pharmaceuticals Division, Alderley Park, Macclesfield, Cheshire SK10, 4TF, England.

**Vincamine**—Aethroma, Anasclerol, Artensen, Arteriovinca, Asnai, Atervit, Ausomina, Centractiva, Cerebramina, Cerebroxine, Cetal, Cetal Retard, Cetovinca, Devincan, Equipur, Esberidin, Gibivi, Horusvin, Novicet, Oxicebral, Oxygeron, Perphal, Perval, Pervincamin, Pervincamina, Pervincamine, Pervone, Sostenil, Tefavinca, Teproside, Tonifor, Tripervan, Vadicate, Vascologene, Vasonett, Venoxigen Retard, Vinca, Vincabioma, Vincabrain, Vincacen, Vincadar, Vincadil, Vincafolina, Vincafor Retard, Vincagalup, Vincagil, Vincahexal, Vincalex, Vincamed, Vincamidol, Vincane, Vincapan, Vincapront, Vincasaunier, Vincavix, Vincimax, Vinodrel

**ACTIONS AND USES**—Vincamine is an alkaloid obtained from *Vinca minor*, or periwinkle, a plant that is the source of several medicinal substances. The drug is used to increase the blood circulation in the brain and to improve the brain's utilization of oxygen. It has also been used as a blood vessel dilator and as a therapeutic agent for high blood pressure. Vincamine preparations have been used for the treatment of a variety of disorders associated with a blood circulation deficiency of the brain areas, including vertigo, memory defects, inability to concentrate, mood changes, depression, sleep difficulties, certain effects of brain injuries, Meniere's syndrome, hearing difficulties, and disorders associated with the blood supply to the eyes.

**PRECAUTIONS**—Most reports of adverse effects have involved symptoms of gastrointestinal distress at the beginning of the vincamine therapy regimen, but the symptoms cease spontaneously when use of the product is discontinued.

**DOSAGE AND ADMINISTRATION**—Vincamine can be administered by intramuscular injection, by intravenous infusion, or by mouth in 30 mg capsules. The usual recommended dose is one 30 mg capsule every 12 hours.

**SOURCE**—Armstrong Laboratorios De Mexico, S.A. de C.V., Av. Division del Norte 3311, Mexico 21, D.F., Mexico.

## Vindesine Sulfate—Eldisine

**ACTIONS AND USES**—Vindesine is an anticancer drug that is used in the treatment of acute lymphocytic leukemia in childhood that is resistant to other anticancer drugs. Vindesine is also used in an adult form of chronic myeloid leukemia characterized by a proliferation of new cancer cells in the bone marrow and is used in malignant melanoma. Acute lymphocytic leukemia tends to occur predominately in preschool-age children, while chronic myeloid leukemia is a form of the disease found chiefly in persons over 50 years of age. A malignant melanoma is a usually cancerous tumor that develops from dark pigment cells of the skin. Vindesine is a vinca alkaloid obtained from the periwinkle plant. In laboratory tests, vindesine was found to be three to ten times more potent than vincristine or vinblastine, two other vinca alkaloids which also act against cancer cells by interfering with the ability of tissue cells to multiply. Vindesine has been used to treat cancer patients who relapsed while being administered other anticancer drugs.

**PRECAUTIONS**—Vindesine should not be administered to patients with serious bacterial infections nor to patients who have experienced a deficiency of blood platelets or white cells as a result of the use of other anticancer drugs. Vindesine should also not be given to patients experiencing symptoms of neuropathy, which may range from constipation and abdominal pain to loss of feeling in a body part, diminished reflexes, or muscular weakness. The drug should not be given to pregnant women, and it is not recommended for nursing mothers. Studies with laboratory animals indicate that vindesine has the potential for causing birth defects, and it also blocks sperm production in males. The drug should be administered only in a hospital under the supervision of a qualified physician experienced in the use of cancer chemotherapy. Blood count changes are common, and the white cell count usually is the limiting factor in determining dosages. The effect is reversible, and recovery can be expected within two weeks after the last dose. Symptoms of neuropathy have been reported in a significant proportion of patients receiving vindesine. Alopecia (hair loss), also reversible, occurs in a majority of cases. Gastrointestinal side effects include nausea, vomiting, constipation, loss of appetite, abdominal pain, diarrhea, and inflammation of the mouth and tongue. Patients with brain involvement may experience epilepsylike convulsions after administration of vindesine.

**DOSAGE AND ADMINISTRATION**—Vindesine sulfate is supplied in vials of 5 mg powder to be reconstituted for intravenous injection. The powder is diluted to a concentration of 1 mg/ml and injected into the largest accessible vein. Leakage into surrounding tissues can cause severe irritation, requiring the injection of the enzyme hyaluronidase and the application of heat to disperse the drug and reduce the risk of inflammation. The usual dosage is 3 to 4 mg per square meter of body area for adults and 4 to 5 mg per square meter of body area for children. The average normal body surface area of an adult man is 1.8 square meters; for a child 4 feet 2 inches tall and weighing 63 pounds, the body surface area would be about 1.0 square meter. The drug is administered as a single injection repeated at weekly intervals after laboratory analysis of blood counts and examination of the patient for signs of toxicity, factors that will influence adjustments in dosage for future therapy. Experience indicates that use of small amounts of vindesine daily rather than in larger weekly doses increases the risk of adverse effects without adding significant therapeutic benefits.

**SOURCES**—Eli Lilly & Company Limited, Kingsclere Road, Basingstroke, Hants RG21 2XA, England; Eli Lilly (Australia) & Co., Wharf Road, West Ryde, N.S.W. 2114, Australia.

## Vinylbital (Butylvinal, Vinylbitone)—Bykonox, Optanox, Speda, Suppoptanox

**ACTIONS AND USES**—Vinylbital is a barbiturate sedative and hypnotic drug used in the treatment of insomnia, epilepsy, neuropsychiatric disorders, certain types of heart disease, fatigue, and to induce somnolence in patients being prepared preoperatively for a general anesthetic. The drug has been reported as particularly effective in older patients. Vinylbital induces sleep in 15 to 25 minutes after administration and has the advantage of rapid elimination from the body, so effects are not cumulative. Clinical studies also indicate the product does not alter normal sleep patterns of the patient.

**PRECAUTIONS**—Vinylbital should not be administered to patients afflicted with myasthenia gravis, arterial hypotension, liver impairment, porphyria, or a sensitivity to barbiturates. Caution should be used in giving the product to patients with kidney disorders and to those using coumarin anticoagulants, neuroleptics, tranquilizers, or antihistamine medications. Patients should be advised that vinylbital may also interact with alcohol to increase the effect of the central nervous system depressant. Side effects may include skin eruptions, loss of appetite, and weakness.

**DOSAGE AND ADMINISTRATION**—Vinylbital is supplied in tablets containing 100 and 150 mg and suppositories containing 200 mg of the drug. The usual recommended dose for insomnia is 100 to 300 mg about an hour before bedtime. The same dose is recommended for patients about to undergo surgery, an hour in advance of the start of the procedure. When used in the treatment of epilepsy, the usual dosage is 150 to 300 mg per day, depending upon the response of the patient. Children's doses should be given at levels of 50 to 100 mg for those between 8 and 15 years of age and 50 mg for those between 2 and 8. For children between the ages of 6 months and 2 years, the recommended dose is 25 mg.

**SOURCES**—Laboratoires Valpan, B.P. 8-77350 Le Mee-Sur-Seine, France; Byk-Gulden S.A. de C.V., Walter C. Buchanan No. 130, Naucalpan de Juarez, Edo. de Mexico, Mexico.

**Xanthinol Niacinate (Xanthinol Nicotinate)**—Angiomanin, Angiomin, Cafardil, Clofamin, Complamex, Complamin, Complamina, Complamine, Dacilen, Emodinamin, Pervium, Sadamin, Vasoprin, Vedrin, Xavin

**ACTIONS AND USES**—Xanthinol niacinate is used both as a blood vessel dilator and as an agent to lower the level of cholesterol in the blood. As a vasodilator, xanthinol niacinate is believed to act by reducing the resistance to normal blood flow in vessels that may be impaired by the development of arteriosclerosis. The drug has been used in the treatment of disorders associated with restricted blood flow to the brain (as in cerebral ischemia), to the coronary arteries, and to the extremities (as in intermittent claudication). In the treatment of hypercholesterolemia (excess blood cholesterol levels), xanthinol niacinate is believed to act in the liver and in the body's fat deposits to interfere with physiological processes resulting in the release of free fatty acids and other lipids (fatty substances) into the bloodstream. The drug has also been used to treat preeclampsia.

**PRECAUTIONS**—The safety of xanthinol niacinate in pregnant women and nursing mothers has not been established, and therefore it is not recommended for patients in these groups. Because of its vasodilator action, the drug may cause postural hypotension (a drop in blood pressure when arising suddenly from a sitting or reclining position). The drug should not be given to patients with a known hypersensitivity to xanthinol niacinate or related products nor to patients being treated for peptic ulcers, congestive heart failure, a recent myocardial infarction, severe hypotension, or impaired liver function. Adverse effects may include flushing and a sensation of warmth, heart palpitations, nausea, vomiting, heartburn, diarrhea, headache, muscle cramps, or blurred vision. Some patients may experience a skin rash, dry or itching skin, or changes in skin pigmentation.

**DOSAGE AND ADMINISTRATION**—Xanthinol niacinate is supplied in 150, 200, 300, and 500 mg tablets and capsules and in injection vials containing 150 mg per ml. The usual adult dosage is 900 to 1,800 mg per day, in divided doses, taken after meals. The recommended maximum daily dose is 3,000 mg. When used in the treatment of hypercholesterolemia, xanthinol niacinate is intended as an adjunct to other lipid-reducing therapies, including diet, weight control, and management of metabolic disorders such as diabetes mellitus.

**SOURCES**—Beecham-Wulfing GmbH & Co. KG, Stresemannallee 6, Postfach: 25, 4040 Neuss 1, West Germany; Italchimici s.p.a., Viale Tiziano 25, 00196 Roma, Italy; Humboldt, Especialidades Medicinales, C.A., Avenida Tamanaco, Calle Los Cariques, Edif. Datoma 2.° piso, E. Llanito, Petare, Apartado 68.767, Caracas 106, Venezuela.

## **Xipamide (Xipamida)**—Acturin, Aquafor, Aquaphor, Diurexan

**ACTIONS AND USES**—Xipamide is a thiazide type of diuretic that is more potent than other thiazides. It is used in the treatment of congestive heart failure, liver edema, kidney edema, peripheral edema due to circulatory disorders, edema of pregnancy, and all grades of hypertension. Thiazide-type diuretics act by preventing reabsorption of sodium as blood is being processed in the kidney tubules. By increasing the rate of excretion of sodium, greater amounts of water also are excreted, along with potassium, chloride, and bicarbonate electrolytes. The main diuretic effect usually begins within 2 hours of oral administration and continues for 12 hours. Antihypertensive effects last 24 hours.

**PRECAUTIONS**—Xipamide may induce hypokalemia, a condition marked by muscular weakness, cramps, numbness, and blood pressure changes, due to potassium depletion. The condition usually can be controlled by increasing potassium intake in foods or mineral supplement tablets. The drug should not be administered to patients with severe liver or kidney impairment nor to patients with severe deficiencies of electrolytes (body tissue chemicals needed for acid-base balance). Xipamide should be used with caution in patients with diabetes, an enlarged prostate, or heart patients taking cardiac glycoside medications. Side effects include mild gastrointestinal disturbances and dizziness. The drug, by increasing the excretion of fluids that hold uric acid crystals in solution, can exacerbate symptoms of gout. Xipamide should be avoided during the first trimester of pregnancy, although it may be used with caution in the second and third trimester if needed to treat edema. The drug is not recommended for children.

**DOSAGE AND ADMINISTRATION**—Xipamide is supplied in 20 and 40 mg tablets. The usual recommendation for hypertension is 20 mg daily as a single morning dose, with an increase to 40 mg per day if required to achieve a satisfactory response. For the treatment of edema, the usual initial dose is 40 mg daily, with later adjustments downward to 20 mg daily or upward to a maximum of 80 mg daily as required to achieve a proper patient response. When prolonged treatment is necessary, patient electrolytes should be monitored and potassium supplements given as needed.

**SOURCES**—Farmades s.p.a., Farmaceutici Degussa & Schering, Via di Tor Cervara 282, 00155 Roma, Italy; Laboratorios Vargas, S.A., Las Piedras a Puente Restaurador, Apartado 2.461, Venezuela.

## Yohimbine Hydrochloride (Aphrodine Hydrochloride, Corynine Hydrochloride, Quebrachine Hydrochloride)—Bakra, Nortis, Vikonon, Yohimbine Houdé

**ACTIONS AND USES**—Yohimbine is a vasodilator that acts as an alpha-blocking agent. It inhibits the effects of the hormone norepinephrine, which normally constricts blood vessels by aiding in the transmission of nerve impulses along the alpha receptor pathways of the autonomic nervous system. Yohimbine's dilating action affects mainly blood vessels serving the extremities. The drug is reported to produce its actions on arterial blood supplies to the skin, the kidneys, the intestinal tract, and the genitalia. Yohimbine is obtained from the bark of the yohimbé tree of central Africa and the quebracho tree of South America. It has been used for centuries as an aphrodisiac by the indigenous populations of those regions. Yohimbine is related chemically to reserpine, a psychotropic drug obtained from the *Rauwolfia* plant, but it lacks the sedative effect of reserpine. Because of its effects on the genitalia and its reputation as an aphrodisiac, yohimbine is used to treat psychic impotence and frigidity. It is also used to relieve constipation, but yohimbine has an antidiuretic action. Its ability to relieve the numbness, prickling, and tingling sensations of paresthesias has led to the use of yohimbine in treating paresthesias of the extremities of diabetic patients. Other properties claimed for yohimbine include the stimulation of breast milk production in nursing mothers.

**PRECAUTIONS**—Yohimbine is not recommended for patients with impaired kidney function because of its antidiuretic action. Its potent arterial dilation effect may result in cerebral artery disorders, including migraine headaches, tremors, dizziness, and excitation. The drug may also affect the heart, producing rapid heartbeat. Blood pressure changes and priapism have also been associated with the use of yohimbine by sensitive patients.

**DOSAGE AND ADMINISTRATION**—Yohimbine is supplied in tablets or granules providing doses of 1.5, 2, 2.5, and 5 mg of the drug. Yohimbine sometimes is combined with other drugs, such as methyl testosterone. The recommended dosage for treatment of constipation and related disorders is 12 mg per day, in two doses. For psychic impotence and frigidity, the recommended dosage is 15 to 20 mg per day in three divided doses. The drug should not be taken with meals. Although cases of overdosage with yohimbine are rare, the recommended maximum is 10 mg in a single dose.

**SOURCES**—Laboratoires Houdé-I.S.H., 15, rue Olivier-Métra, 75980 Paris Cedex 20, France; Zembeletti dr. L., via Zembeletti, 20021 Baranzate (M1), Italy.

## Zeranol (Zearalanol)—Frideron, Ralabol, Ralgro, Ralone

**ACTIONS AND USES**—Zeranol is an estrogenic agent, producing effects of the female sex hormone estrogen. It was derived from a nonsteroidal hormone used as a growth promoter in domestic animals and was found in studies to have benefits in female patients who have undergone hysterectomy and ovariectomy. Zeranol reportedly reduces the incidence of hot flushes and promotes the growth of vaginal lining cells without serious side effects. The drug is also used in the treatment of menopausal disorders and those associated with a deficiency of estrogen.

**PRECAUTIONS**—No significant side effects have been reported as a result of the use of zeranol.

**DOSAGE AND ADMINISTRATION**—Zeranol is supplied in 50, 75, and 100 mg tablets. The dosage used in the treatment of estrogen deficiency following hysterectomy and ovariectomy is 75 mg per day.

**SOURCE**—Sandoz s.p.a., Via C. Arconati 1, 20135 Milano, Italy.

## Zimelidine Hydrochloride—Zelmid

**ACTIONS AND USES**—Zimelidine hydrochloride is used in the treatment of depression, particularly in older patients. The drug produces its action by inhibiting the physiological processes involving serotonin, a nerve impulse transmitter. High levels of serotonin in the brain result in sedation, lethargy, and depressed mental functioning, while depletion of brain serotonin can cause insomnia. Zimelidine has less of a sedating effect than certain other antidepressants, such as amitriptyline. It also has fewer and milder side effects.

**PRECAUTIONS**—Zimelidine hydrochloride should not be given with monoamine oxidase inhibitors, which protect the breakdown of serotonin molecules and otherwise interact with zimelidine. Zimelidine should not be administered to pregnant women or nursing mothers. Caution should be exercised in giving zimelidine to patients also taking thyroid hormones, central nervous system depressants, and certain types of antihypertensive drugs. Caution should also be used in giving the drug to patients with epilepsy, liver impairment, blood disorders, hypothyroidism, glaucoma, urinary retention, heart block, recent myocardial infarction, or coronary artery insufficiency. Side effects include headache, gastrointestinal distress, and sweating. The drug is not recommended for children.

**DOSAGE AND ADMINISTRATION**—Zimelidine hydrochloride is supplied in 100 and 200 mg tablets. The usual recommended dosage is 200 mg per day in divided doses or as a single dose. The dosage is increased to 300 mg, in divided doses, if required. For elderly patients, a total daily intake of 100 mg is usually sufficient.

**SOURCE**—Astra Pharmaceuticals (Ireland) Ltd., 7 Lower Fitzwilliam Street, Dublin 2, Ireland.

## Zipeprol (Zipeprol Hydrochloride)—Respilene, Respirex, Talasa, Zitoxil

**ACTIONS AND USES**—Zipeprol is an antitussive with action that affects most of the respiratory tract. It is used in the treatment of acute and chronic cough, acute and chronic bronchitis, tracheobronchitis, chronic respiratory insufficiency, bronchial asthma, bronchiectasis marked by persistent coughing, the coughing due to pulmonary tuberculosis, and conditions that result in an increase in mucous viscosity. By diminishing the viscosity of bronchial secretions, the product increases the ability of the patient to expectorate. Zipeprol can be administered with other appropriate medications, such as antibiotics, antiinflammatory drugs, or aminophyllines. It is generally compatible with other drugs.

**PRECAUTIONS**—Side effects reported include nausea, vomiting, dizziness, and sleep disturbances.

**DOSAGE AND ADMINISTRATION**—Zipeprol is supplied in 75 mg sugar-coated tablets, 100 mg suppositories, and a syrup containing 500 mg zipeprol per 100 ml for adults. For children, the product is supplied in a syrup containing 300 mg zipeprol per 100 ml and in 50 mg suppositories. For adults, the usual recommended dosage is one or two teaspoonfuls (5 to 10 ml) of the syrup three times daily, two to four tablets daily, or two to three suppositories a day. For children the recommended dose of syrup ranges from 5 to 10 ml per day, in divided doses, for infants; to 20 to 40 ml per day, in divided doses, for school-age children. The suppository dosage for children is the same as for adults.

**SOURCE**—Laboratorios Columbia, S.A., Av. Insurgentes Sur No. 4120, Mexico 22, D.F., Mexico.

**Zolimidine**—Gastronilo, Mutil, Solimet, Solimidin, U.G.D.

**ACTIONS AND USES**—Zolimidine is a protective agent for the mucosal lining of the stomach and intestinal tract that is used in the treatment of stomach and duodenal ulcers and related disorders. It has been used in the treatment of gastritis, duodenitis, gastrointestinal disorders due to medications or toxic substances, and excesses in eating, drinking, or smoking. Zolimidine is believed to act systemically, without modifying the secretion or composition of gastric juices and without affecting the nervous pathways of the digestive tract or causing an anesthetic effect. Clinical studies report an 80 percent success in obtaining remissions of peptic ulcers and other gastrointestinal disorders through an increase in the quantity and quality of the mucosal lining of patients using the product.

**PRECAUTIONS**—At therapeutic dosages, few side effects have been reported, and they were mainly nausea and/or vomiting. However, patients who are hypersensitive to the medication should avoid its use.

**DOSAGE AND ADMINISTRATION**—Zolimidine is supplied in 200 mg capsules and 400 mg suppositories. The usual recommended dosage is 600 to 800 mg per day. The preferred oral dosage is four capsules per day, divided into a 1:2:1 ratio, taken before or after meals, with two capsules at the midday meal. Patients using suppositories take one or two a day, with a maximum of three per day if needed. Remissions usually are obtained within 30 to 45 days after the start of therapy.

**SOURCES**—Farmaceuticos Lakeside S.A., Diagonal 20 de Noviembre No. 294, Mexico 8, D.F., Mexico; Selvi & C. s.p.a., Via Gallarate 184, 20151 Milano, Italy.

# BIBLIOGRAPHY

## Computer Data Bases

Biosciences Information Service, 2100 Arch Street, Philadelphia, Pennsylvania 19103 (Dialog Files 5, 55; Orbit BIOSIS, BIOSIS7479, BIOSIS6973).

Chemical Abstracts Service, American Chemical Society, P.O. Box 3012, Columbus, Ohio 43210 (Dialog Files 2, 3, 4, 30, 31; Orbit CAS82, CAS77, CAS72, CAS67, CHEMDEX, CHEMDEX2 CHEMDEX3).

Excerpta Medica, P.O. Box 1126, 1000-BC Amsterdam, The Netherlands (Dialog Files 72, 73; Orbit DIOL).

International Pharmaceutical Abstracts, 4630 Montgomery Avenue, Washington, D.C. 20014 (Dialog File 74).

IRL Life Sciences Collection, Information Retrieval Limited, 1 Falconberg Court, London W1V 5FG, England, U.K.; Information Retrieval, Inc., 250 West 57th Street, New York, New York 10019 (Dialog File 76).

Medline, National Library of Medicine, 8600 Rockville Pike, Bethesda, Maryland 20209 (Dialog Files 152, 153, 154).

Pharmaceutical News Index, Data Courier, Inc., 620 South Fifth Street, Louisville, Kentucky 40202 (Dialog File 42).

(Orbit is an online computer service of SDC Information Services, 2500 Colorado Avenue, Santa Monica, California 90406. Dialog is an online computer service of Dialog Information Services, 3460 Hillview Avenue, Palo Alto, California 94304. Medline also may be directly accessible to certain qualified computer terminal operators.)

# Bibliography

## Books, Booklets

*AMA Drug Evaluations*. Chicago: American Medical Association, 1980.

Berkow, Robert, ed. *The Merck Manual*, 14th ed. Rahway, N.J.: Merck Sharp & Dohme Research Laboratories, 1982.

Bevan, John A. *Essentials of Pharmacology*. Hagerstown, Md.: Harper & Row, 1976.

Billups, Norman F., ed. *American Drug Index*. Philadelphia: J.B. Lippincott Company, 1982.

*British Approved Names*, British Pharmacopoeia Commission. London: Her Majesty's Stationery Office, 1981.

*British National Formulary*. London: British Medical Association and The Pharmaceutical Society of Great Britain, 1982.

*Datasheet Compendium, 1981–82*. London: Datapharm Publications Limited, 1981.

*Dictionnaire Vidal*. Paris: Cahiers de Bibliographie Therapeutique Francaise, 1982.

DiPalma, Josph R., ed. *Drill's Pharmacology in Medicine*. New York: 1971.

*European Pharmacopoeia*, 2nd ed. Moulins-Les-Metz: Maisonneuve, 1980.

Goldstein, Avram, Lewis Aronow, Sumner Kalman. *Principles of Drug Action*. New York: John Wiley & Sons, 1974.

Goodman, Louis S., Alfred Gilman. *The Pharmacological Basis of Therapeutics*. New York: The Macmillan Company, 1970.

Griffiths, Mary C., ed. *USAN and the USP Dictionary of Drug Names*. Rockville, Md.: United States Pharmacopeial Convention, Inc., 1980.

Hamilton, Helen K. *Professional Guide to Drugs*. Springhouse, Pa.: Intermed Communications, Inc., 1982.

Hedstrand, Anna-Greta, ed. *FASS (Farmacevtiska specialiteter i Sverige)*. Stockholm: Lakesmedelsinformation AB, 1982.

Holland, William C., Richard L. Klein, Arthur H. Briggs. *Introduction to Molecular Pharmacology*. New York: The Macmillan Company, 1964.

*International Nonproprietary Names (INN) for Pharmaceutical Substances*. Geneva: World Health Organization, 1976.

Karch, F.E. *Orphan Drugs*. New York: Marcel Dekker, 1982.

Krogh, Carmen M.E., ed. *Compendium of Pharmaceuticals and Specialties*. Ottawa: Canadian Pharmaceutical Association, 1982.

Lewis, Arthur J., ed. *Modern Drug Encyclopedia and Therapeutic Index*. New York: Yorke Medical Books, 1982.

Marini, Lucio. *L'Informatore Farmaceutico*. Milano: Organizzazione Editorale Medico-Farmaceutica S.R.L., 1981.

Martin, Jeff, Erika Maher. *Data Sheet Compendium, 1981–82*. Dublin: Federation of Irish Chemical Industries, 1981.

Meier, Hans. *Experimental Pharmacogenetics*. New York: Academic Press, 1963.

*Modern Pharmaceuticals of Japan VI, 1981*. Tokyo: Japan Pharmaceutical, Medical and Dental Supply Exporters' Association, 1980.

*Physician's Desk Reference, 1983*. Oradell, N.J.: Medical Economics Company, 1983.

*PMA Commission on Drugs for Rare Diseases, Annual Report*. Washington: Pharmaceutical Manufacturers Association, 1982.

Reynolds, James E.F. *Martindale, The Extra Pharmacopoeia*. London: The Pharmaceutical Press, 1982.

Rosenstein, Emilio. *Diccionario de Especialidades Farmaceuticas*. Mexico City: P.L.M., 1981.

Schmidt, R. Marilyn, Solomon Margolin. *Harper's Handbook of Therapeutic Pharmacology*. Philadelphia: Harper & Row, 1981.

*Significant Drugs of Limited Commercial* Value, Report of the Interagency Task Force to the Secretary of Health, Education, and Welfare. Washington. June 29, 1979.

Spilva, Austra de Lehr. *Guia de las Especialidades Farmaceuticas en Venezuela*. Madrid: Suc. de Rivadeneyra, S.F., 1981.

The Insight Team of *The Sunday Times* of London. *Suffer the Children: The Story of Thalidomide*. New York: The Viking Press, 1979.

Tørisen, Holger Moe. *Felleskatalog*. Oslo: Felleskatalogen, 1983.

Treleaven, Geoff K., Jack Thomas, eds. *Prescription Proprietaries Guide*. West Melbourne: Australasian Pharmaceutical Publishing Company Limited, 1982.

Udell, Gilman G. *Federal Food, Drug, and Cosmetic Act With Amendments*. Washington: U.S. Government Printing Office, 1976.

*United States Pharmacopeia*, 20th revision. Rockville, Md.: United States Pharmacopeial Convention, Inc., 1979.

Windholz, Martha, ed. *The Merck Index*, 9th ed. Rahway, N.J.: Merck & Co., Inc., 1976.

## Periodicals

Brody, Robert. 1981. Orphan drugs: Battleground between social responsibility and concern for the bottom line. *American Druggist*, July, 56–62.

## Bibliography


Finkel, M.J. 1982. The development of orphan products. *New England Journal of Medicine* 307(15):963–64.

Jick, Herschel, *et al.* 1970. Comprehensive drug surveillance. *Journal of the American Medical Association* 213:145–60.

Markowitz, J.S. 1981. Nurses, physicians, and pharmacists: Their knowledge of hazards of medications. *Nursing Research* 30(6):349–51.

Martindale, David. 1982. The drugs nobody will make. *Health* 14:40–42.

McMahon, F. Gilbert. 1983. How safe should drugs be? *Journal of the American Medical Association* 249(4):481–82.

Robert, L. 1982. Speeding new drug approval: Aid to patients or industry? Bioscience 32:839–42.

Schweiker, R.S. 1982. The drug application review process. *Vital Speeches of the Day* 46:646–48.

Sloan, Richard W. 1983. Drug interactions. *American Family Physician* 27(20)229–38.

Venning, Geoffrey, R. 1983. Identification of adverse reactions to new drugs. I: What have been the important adverse reactions since thalidomide? *British Medical Journal* 286:199–202.

Venning, Geoffrey R. 1983. Identification of adverse reactions to new drugs. II: How were 18 important adverse reactions discovered and with what delays? *British Medical Journal* 286:289–92.

Wallis, C. 1982. Adopting orphan drugs. *Time* 120:76.

Wardell, William M. 1978. The rate of development of new drugs in the United States, 1963 through 1975. *Clinical Pharmacology and Therapeutics* 24(2):133–45.

Wardell, William M. 1978. The drug lag revisited: Comparison by therapeutic area of patterns of drugs marketed in the United States and Great Britain from 1972 through 1976. *Clinical Pharmacology and Therapeutics* 24(5):499–524.

Wardell, William M. 1982. Will all new drugs become orphans? *Clinical Pharmacology and Therapeutics* 31(3):258–59.

Wardell, William M. 1982. New drug development by United States pharmaceutical firms with analyses of trends in the acquisition and origin of drug candidates, 1963–1979. *Clinical Pharmacology and Therapeutics* 32(4):407–17.

# INDEX OF DRUG NAMES

*This index is followed on page 275 by an Index of Drug Uses, which lists alphabetically the illnesses and ailments treated with the drugs discussed in the text.*

# INDEX OF DRUG USES

## Index of Drug Uses

# Acknowledgments

The author would like to acknowledge the contributions by the following individuals who helped make this book possible: Research Director Lois Anderson, Publishers Editorial Services, Inc.; Nicole Gilbert, European research; Patricia Park, Foundation for Innovation in Medicine; Dr. Steve Groft and Christopher Smith, U.S. Food and Drug Administration; Jeffrey Warren, Pharmaceutical Manufacturers Association; Congressmen Henry Waxman, California, and Hamilton Fish, Jr., and Theodore Weiss, New York.